IMAGES
of America

NOCONA

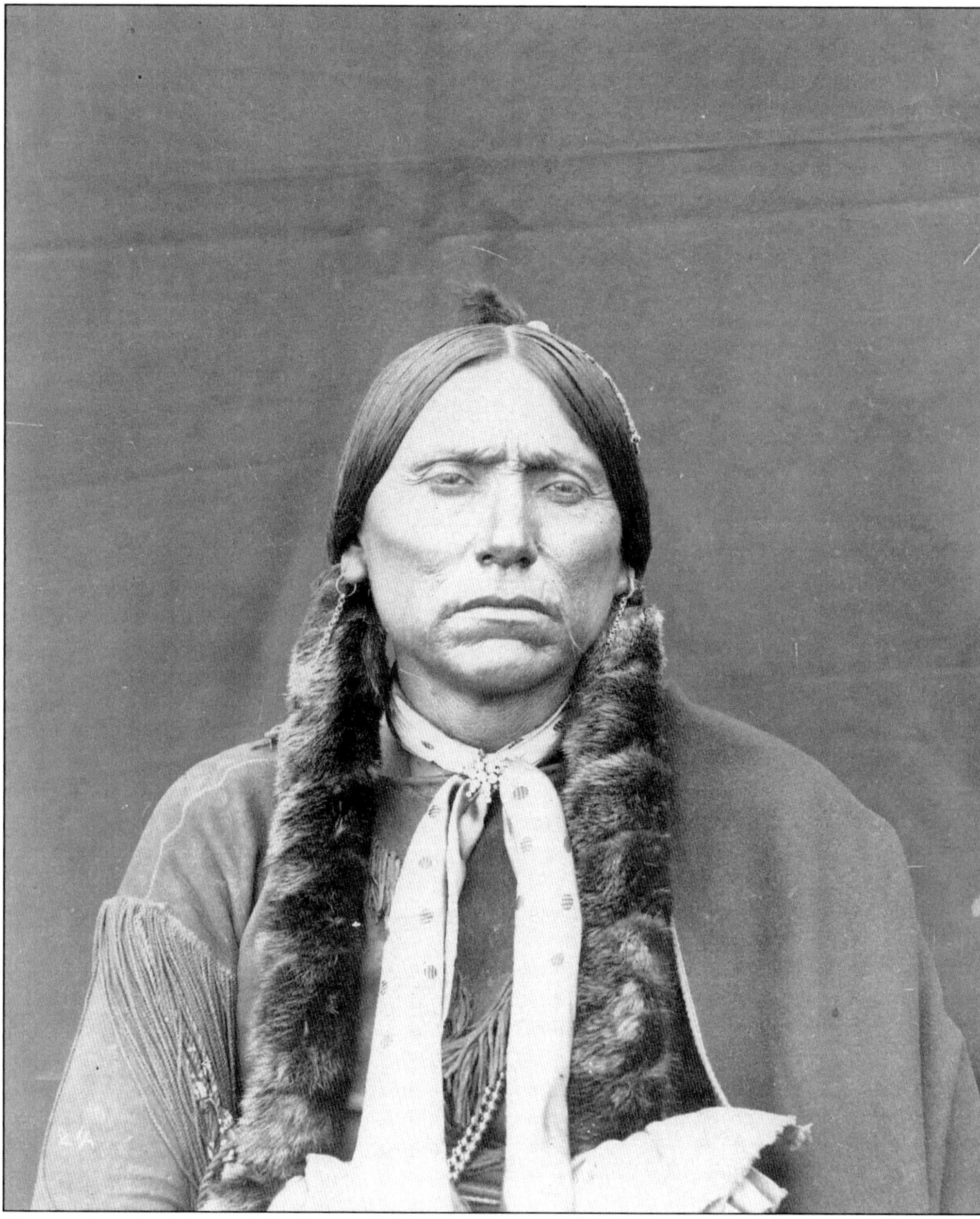

Comanche chief Quanah Parker was respected in both the white and Native American societies. His mother was Cynthia Ann Parker; the Comanche Indians had abducted her as a child. His father was Chief Peta Nocona, for whom Nocona, Texas, is named. During the Battle at Pease River, Cynthia Ann was recaptured and returned to white society. She grieved for her Native American family until her death. (Tales 'N' Trails Museum.)

On the Cover: The Justin Leather Goods Company was established in 1919 by Earl Justin, the son of H.J. Justin; G.W. Humphreys; and R.A. Moore. Their plan to use scrap leather from the H.J. Justin Boot Company to make small leather goods was quickly discarded when they realized scrap leather did not meet the standards of the Justin name. (Tales 'N' Trails Museum.)

IMAGES
of America

NOCONA

Shannon Gillette

ARCADIA
PUBLISHING

ISBN 978-0-7385-7997-9

Published by Arcadia Publishing
Charleston, South Carolina

Printed in the United States of America

Library of Congress Control Number: 2011920843

For all general information, please contact Arcadia Publishing:
Telephone 843-853-2070
Fax 843-853-0044
E-mail sales@arcadiapublishing.com
For customer service and orders:
Toll-Free 1-888-313-2665

Visit us on the Internet at www.arcadiapublishing.com

To Tony, whose constant love, encouragement,
and humor make my dreams come true.

Contents

ACKNOWLEDGMENTS

The generosity of the people of Nocona and Montague County made Tales 'N' Trails Museum a reality. Without their generous contributions, the photographic archives used for this project would not have been compiled. The majority of the images presented in this book are provided courtesy of the Tales 'N' Trails Museum (TNT). The board members of Tales 'N' Trails wholeheartedly supported every step of creating this book, and I greatly appreciate all of their help.

I would like to extend a special thanks to Nell Ann McBroom for going above and beyond the call of duty to ensure that this labor of love reached completion. Without her friendship, patience, and sense of direction, this project would have never come to life. Special thanks goes to Vicki Morton for all of the hours she spent proofreading. I owe Ella Williams a huge debt of gratitude for graciously giving up her office and desk for the duration of this process. Thank you, Tracy and Linda Mesler, your support has been unbelievable. There are few other people that I need to thank for their kindness and contributions, and they are Wanda Billings, Steve Bishop, Max Brown, Mel Chapman, Nancy and Jack Cunningham, Cecil Fenoglio, Dan Fenoglio, Bob Ferguson, Jeannine Fitts, Billie Grigsby, Gary Don King, Condell and Shirley Lowrie, Teddy McNabb, Sam and Robbie Mitchell, Wade Shelton, Tom Skinner, Rob Storey, Tom Uselton, Floyd Womack, and Wanda Wood. I would also like to thank each and every Tales 'N' Trails volunteer for the time and love they devote to the museum.

My greatest appreciation goes to Winnie Rodgers, my editor at Arcadia Publishing. Her gentle and much needed guidance was essential. I must also extend my undying gratitude to my wonderful husband and our eight beautiful children, who always think my adventures are worth the ride. Finally, thanks to my parents, who always said I could do whatever I chose to do and have believed in me every step of the way.

Introduction

Nocona's past is woven together from many different fabrics that tend to overlap in some areas, making it difficult to present in chronological order. Although the town was incorporated in 1890, its beginnings reach much further back in time. Nocona is located just a few miles from what once was a very large Taovoyas Indian village. This link to Native American culture shaped the lives of many who chose to make Nocona their home. The close proximity to the Red River has also played an important role in shaping Nocona's past. The Chisholm Trail crossed the river about 15 miles northwest of the present-day townsite of Nocona, making the cattle industry one of its largest economic sources. After the cattle trails faded from existence, ranching was still widespread, but it was combined with cotton and other crops, making agriculture a staple as well. The discovery of oil in the area around 1920 added yet another financial boost. While these factors may be common in many areas of North Texas, it is the addition of the leather industry that headquartered in Nocona for over 100 years that sets it apart.

The life and love of Comanche chief Peta Nocona inspired the town's name. On May 19, 1836, a group of Comanche braves raided the Fort Parker settlement. They abducted, among others, a young girl by the name of Cynthia Ann Parker. Over the next few years, most of the captives were returned or recaptured, but Cynthia Ann could not be located. As the years passed, Cynthia Ann adapted to the Comanche lifestyle. She fell in love with and married Chief Peta Nocona. She and Chief Nocona raised a family together consisting of three children, sons Quanah and Pecos and a daughter, Topsanna. Twenty-four years later, Texas Ranger captain Sul Ross and the Comanche battled at Pease River. After the bitter and bloody fight, Ross discovered that one of the young women of the village was not Native American, but light skinned and blue eyed. Upon further research, it was determined that this young woman was the missing Cynthia Ann Parker. She and her daughter, Topsanna, were reunited with the Parker family. Cynthia Ann never was able to readjust to the ways of white society. Not long after her return, her daughter became ill and died. Lost and grieving, Cynthia Ann quickly faded. It is often said that she died of a broken heart.

When Benjamin Southern Wathen was called on to survey the townsite for a fledgling settlement in Montague County, he recalled the story of Peta Nocona and Cynthia Ann Parker. He had heard the story many times from his friend John L. Davis. Davis had served with the Texas Rangers under Ross at the Battle of Pease River. Wathen thought Nocona would be an appropriate name for the new community. Wathen had just recently surveyed the townsite of Abilene. He noticed several similarities in the terrain between it and Nocona. He laid out the Nocona streets in much the same fashion as he did those in Abilene. Using the railroad tracks as the dividing line, Wathen named the streets. Those that were north of the tracks running east and west were named after shade and lumber trees, and streets running north and south were named after Texas counties. On the south side of the tracks, the streets running east and west were named after fruit-bearing trees, and the north and south running streets were named after Texas cities. The two exceptions to this rule were Main and Front Streets. Front Street was eventually renamed and is known as Willow Street today.

With the coming of the railroad in 1887, the town began to grow and prosper. Agriculture was the mainstay of the town's economy. Cattle and cotton were considered king. As the population grew, so did the needs of the residents. Churches and school were erected. Cotton gins were established, and livery stables and wagon yards were in operation. The little town was beginning to take shape. The first merchants set up shop on Front Street, facing the railroad to ensure easy access for freight and passengers. Some of the businesses that first lined Front Street were E.C. Blivens's grocery store, the Black and Maddox, H.J. Potts's dry goods stores, and the W.A. McCall Hardware and Furniture Store. Front Street also boasted two hotels and more than one saloon. The town continued to grow as more and more new businesses opened their doors. Front Street could not accommodate them all, and the overflow chose Clay Street as their new home. Clay Street soon became the principal thoroughfare in town, and it continues as such to this day.

One new business in particular is responsible for setting the course for Nocona more than any other—the H.J. Justin Boot Company. The relocation of H.J. Justin Boot Company from Spanish Fort in 1887 was the beginning of a long line of leather industrial traditions in Nocona. In 1919, Justin Leather Goods Company was established. The idea was to use the scrap leather from the boot-making operation for small leather good items such as purses and billfolds. The Justin name meant quality, and scrap material did not make the cut. Soon after the first run of merchandise made from scrap, Justin Leather Goods started buying leather for production. After H.J. Justin died in 1918, his sons decided to move the boot-making factory to Fort Worth. Their sister Enid Justin was against the idea and, when the boot company was moved, she chose to stay in Nocona. In 1925, she established her own boot-making operation, the Nocona Boot Company. Enid was an astute businesswoman, and her boot company was in continuous operation for almost 75 years. For many years, it was the largest source of employment in Nocona. Throughout the years, other important leather businesses were formed and operated in Nocona. The Nocona Leather Goods Company, later known as Nocona Athletic Goods, began manufacturing small leather good items. During the hard economic times of the Depression, they began to produce quality leather-based athletic goods such as helmets, footballs, and baseball gloves. The world-renowned Nokona baseball glove is still manufactured in Nocona today. With these large leather companies and others, such as F&E Leather Company and Motley Leather Goods, a large segment of Nocona's economy has been based in the leather industry since its beginning. The success of these companies is how Nocona became known as the "Leather Center of the Southwest."

The story of Nocona's rich and colorful past is told with images of yesteryear presented throughout this book. If there are any small gaps in time or missing elements, it is due to the lack of corresponding photographs and was not intended to diminish the importance of any event, organization, or establishment. As the snapshots into Nocona's past are examined, the small details of everyday life emerge. It is hoped that this photographic record will be enjoyed today and by future generations interested in keeping Nocona's past alive.

One

The Early Years

The Chisholm Trail played an integral role in the placement of Nocona. Red River Station, one of the largest crossing points along the famous cattle trail, was located just a few miles northwest of the present-day townsite of Nocona. The businesses that sprang up to meet the needs of the cowboys, such as blacksmiths, general stores, and saloons, eventually moved to Nocona after the demise of the Chisholm Trail.

In 1881, David Crockett Jordan and William Broaddus headquartered their ranches in the area. In 1887, Jordan donated a square mile of land to be used for a townsite and christened it Jordanville. This name was rejected when the application for a post office was denied; a town of that name was already registered in Texas. About the same time, the officials of the Missouri, Kansas, and Texas Railroad were trying to determine the path and designated stops of the railroad through Montague County. Montague, the county seat, was the leading contender for the coveted stop. The drought of the previous year left the businessmen of Montague unable to afford the money the railroad requested, widening the chances for other towns. Jordan and Broaddus began an aggressive campaign to win the prized designation. They traveled to St. Louis to meet with the railroad officials. Jordan and Broaddus offered several miles of right-of-way and a townsite location of their choice, winning the Missouri, Kansas, and Texas Railroad's approval.

The placement of the actual townsite was determined by the abundant water source discovered by local resident James Weiss when he dug his water well. Benjamin Southern Wathen was contacted to complete a survey of the land. Wathen's friend John L. Davis had served under Sul Ross at the Battle of Pease River. Having heard the tale of Peta Nocona's fierce battle and his love of Cynthia Ann Parker, Wathen decided that Nocona would an appropriate name for this new town. On June 7, 1887, the first passenger train came through Nocona. By 1890, Nocona was officially incorporated.

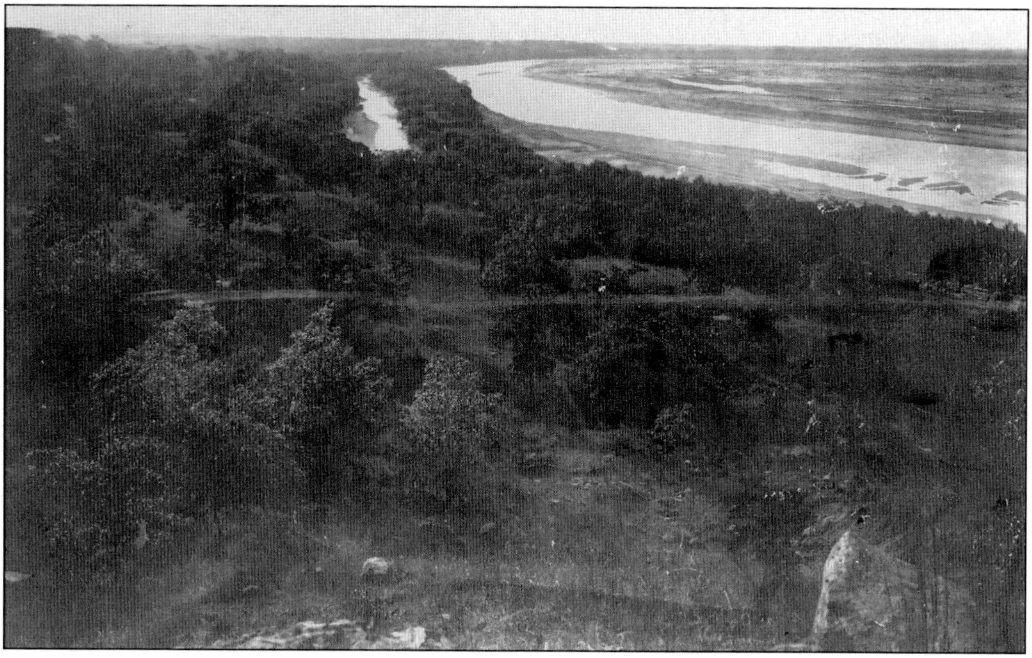

This bend in the Red River has provided a crossing point for centuries. It was used by buffalo and the Native Americans that hunted them. It also served as the gateway to the Chisholm Trail, leading from Texas into Indian Territory. The water it supplied was essential to early ranchers and farmers. (TNT.)

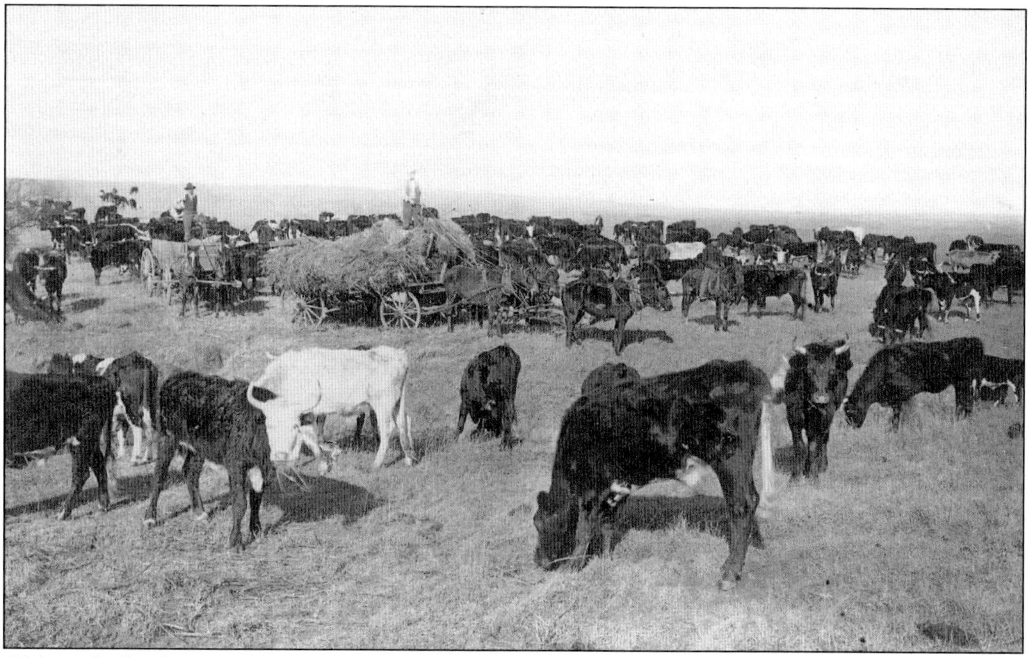

Although the famous Chisholm Trail was coming to an end by 1887, a few trail-wise cowboys returned to the area to establish their own cattle ranches. These ranches, like the one shown, encompassed several thousand acres of land in the Red River Valley. The cattle industry became the primary economic source in northern Montague County. (TNT.)

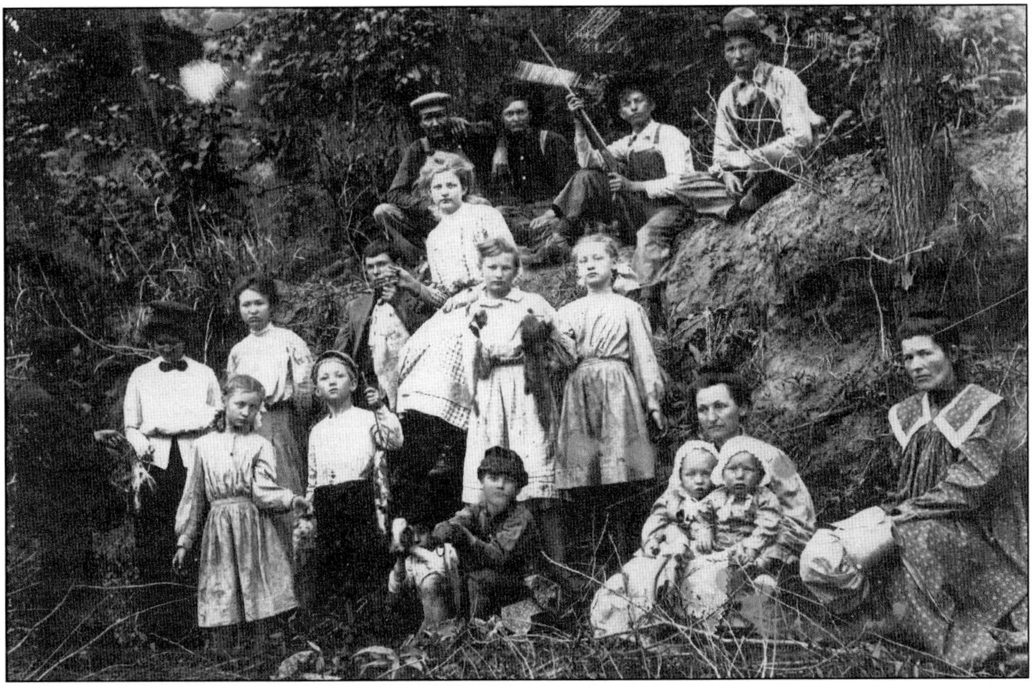

With a large variety of catfish, bass, and other native fish, the Red River also provided a good food source, as can been seen in this photograph of the McGaughy family. Several family members are proudly displaying the day's catch. The young man seated on the boulder holding the rifle is Henry Clay McGaughy. (Bob Ferguson.)

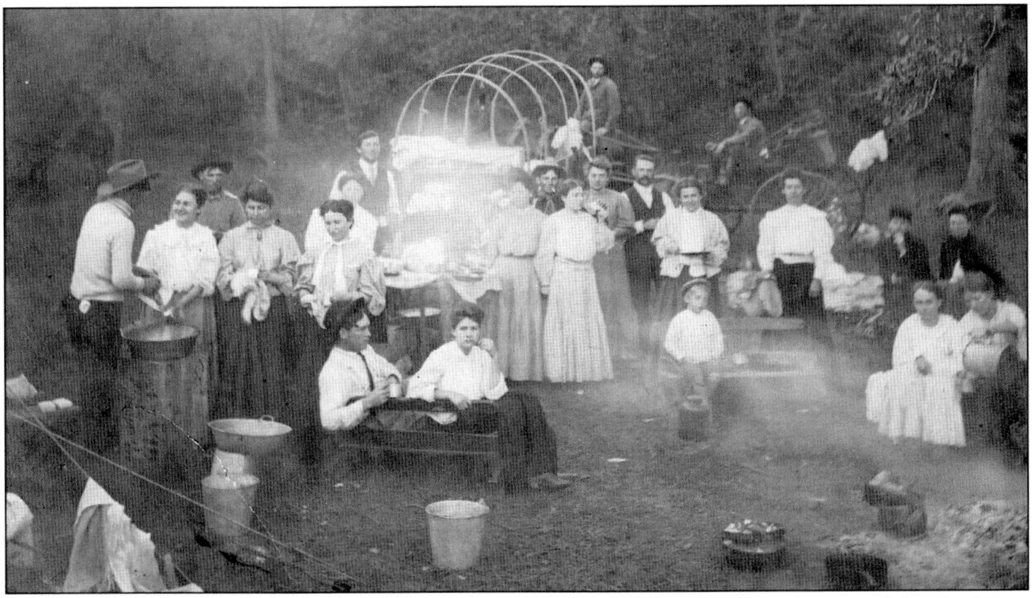

The banks of the Red River also provided the perfect spot for family gatherings, like the King family's fish fry shown in this photograph. Simon King, the patriarch, settled in Nocona in 1890. He and his wife, Hester Ann Ward, raised their children, Benjamin, Charles, Angelica, George, Simon Jr., Thomas, Dock, and John, in Nocona. King owned the gristmill and later the first theater in town. (TNT.)

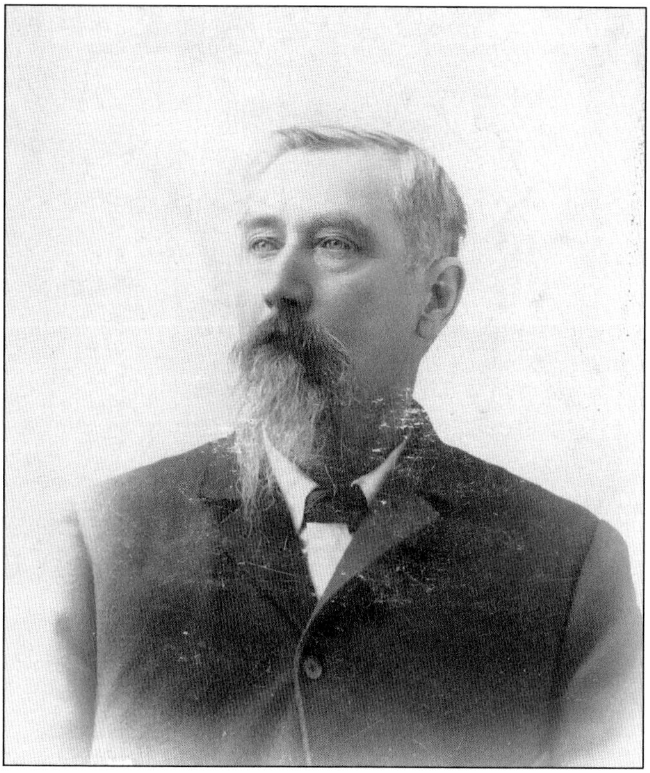

David Crockett Jordan was one of the cofounders of Nocona. Jordan, along with William Broaddus, was responsible for persuading the Missouri, Kansas, and Texas Railroad to choose Nocona as one of its depots. Jordan was born in Kentucky in 1842 and migrated to north-central Texas by the mid-1870s. In 1877, he married Annie Berry. Descendants of the Jordan and Berry families still reside in Nocona today. (TNT.)

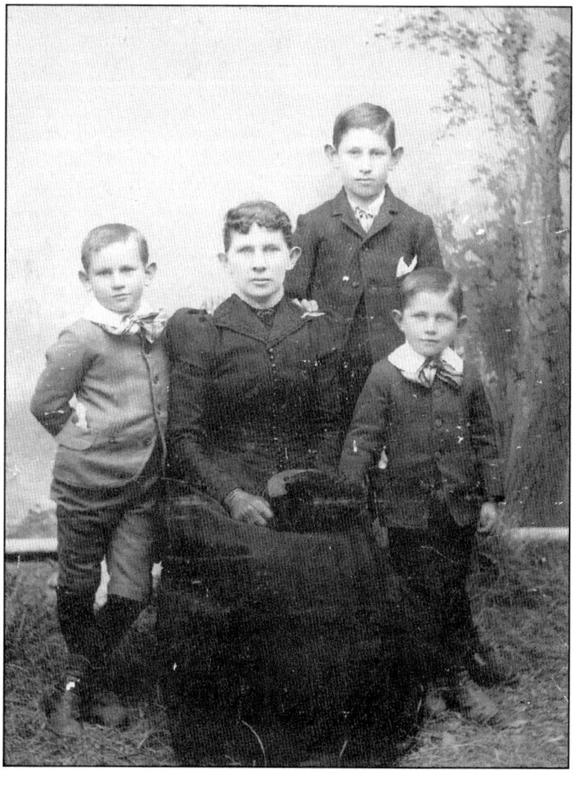

Ann Berry Jordan, the wife of David Crockett Jordan, was born in Grayson County, Texas, in 1860. In the 1870s, the Berry family moved to the Nocona area, where she met and married Jordan. The couple had three boys: from left to right, Thomas "Tink," William, and Dave. Two daughters, Nell and Kitty, were also born to this union, as well as some children who died as infants. (TNT.)

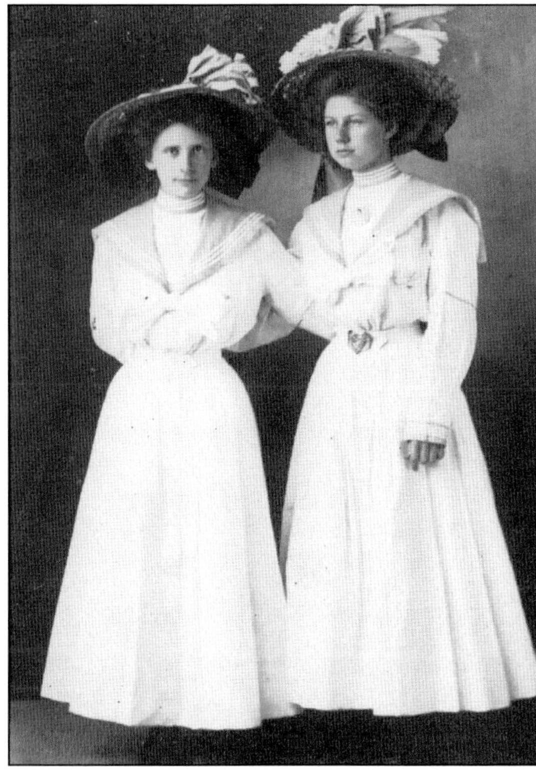

Nell Jordan (left) was the oldest daughter of David and Annie Crockett Jordan. She and her friend Eva Black, shown here in 1910, were involved in many social events and school-related organizations with the young ladies of Nocona. Jordan married Calvin Phillips Dodson. (TNT.)

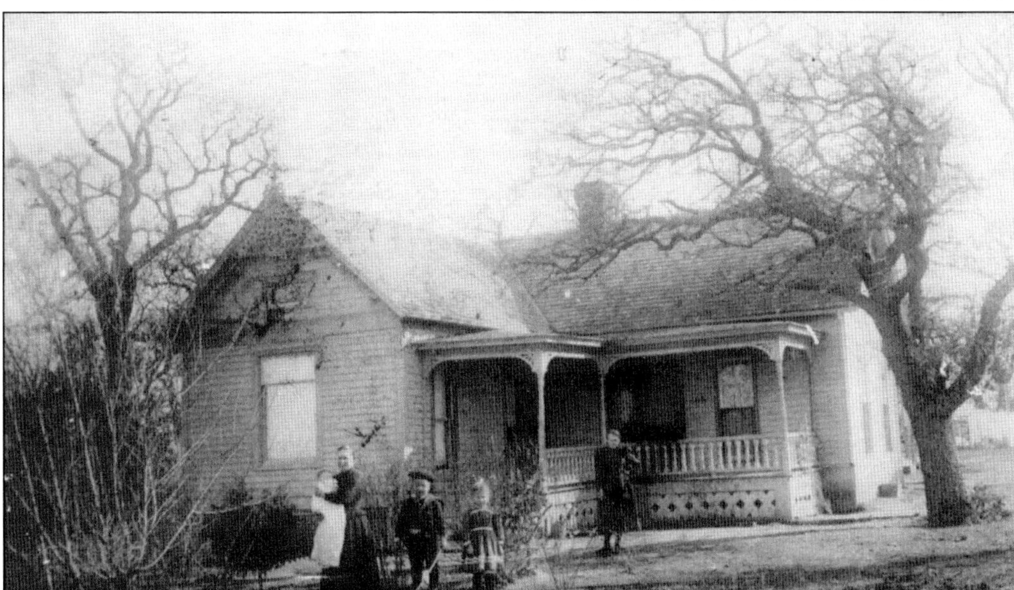

The Jordan home originally sat on the 22,000-acre ranch owned by David Crockett Jordan and William Broaddus. After the dissolution of their partnership in 1891, the ranch was sold off into 25 individual farms, leaving Jordan with approximately 3,600 acres and Broaddus with 4,500. Jordan donated land for Nocona's cemetery, school, and a community park. The park was used to host veteran reunions. (TNT.)

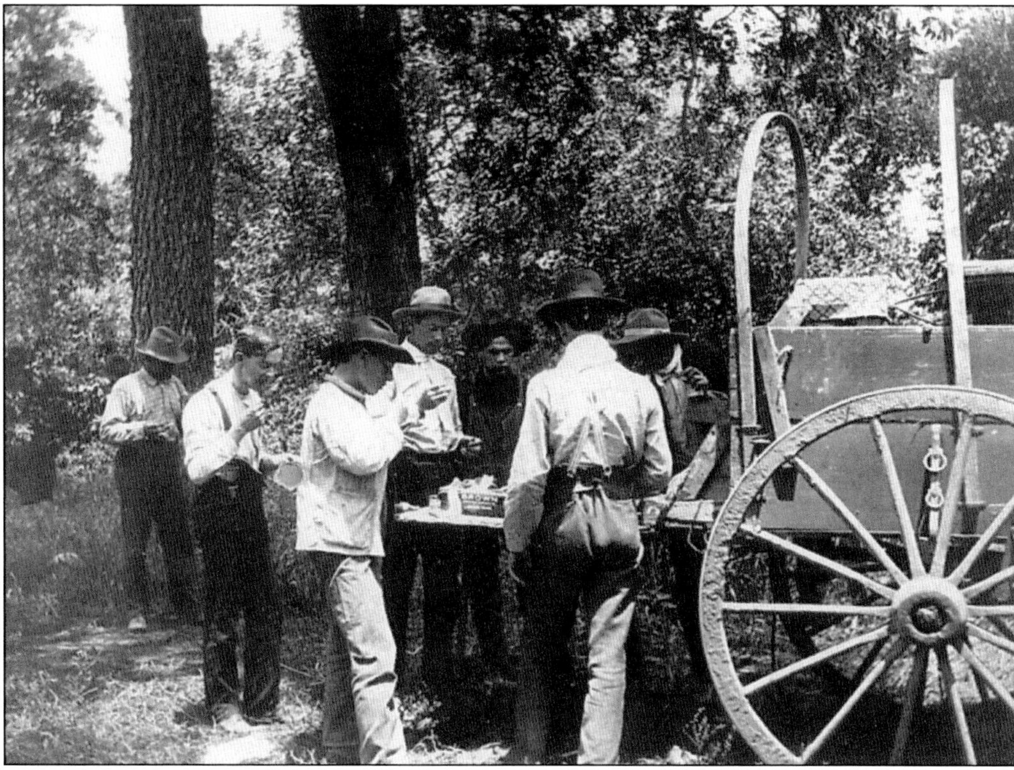

Chuck wagon dinners, like this one on the Jordan ranch, were simple but hearty meals. The cowboys took a few minutes from their grueling work and the hot sun to eat the afternoon meal. The wagon was stocked with all the necessities, including a fold-down tabletop from which the men were served. (TNT.)

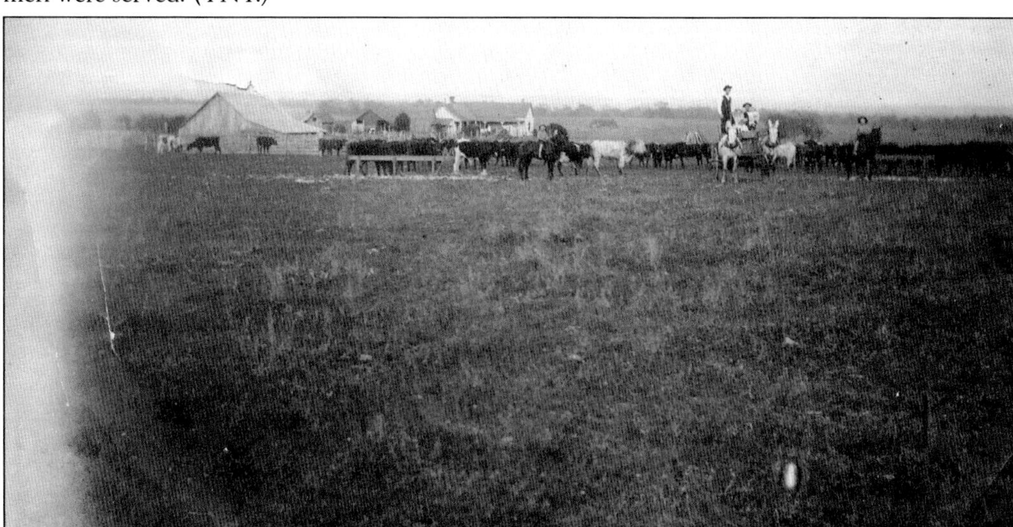

Cornelius Howard and his sons are shown here feeding their cattle in 1902. The Howard ranch was set up in the typical fashion. The family home was located in close proximity to the barn and other out buildings. These buildings housed the horses, wagons, and other implements needed to conduct the daily farm and ranching chores. (TNT.)

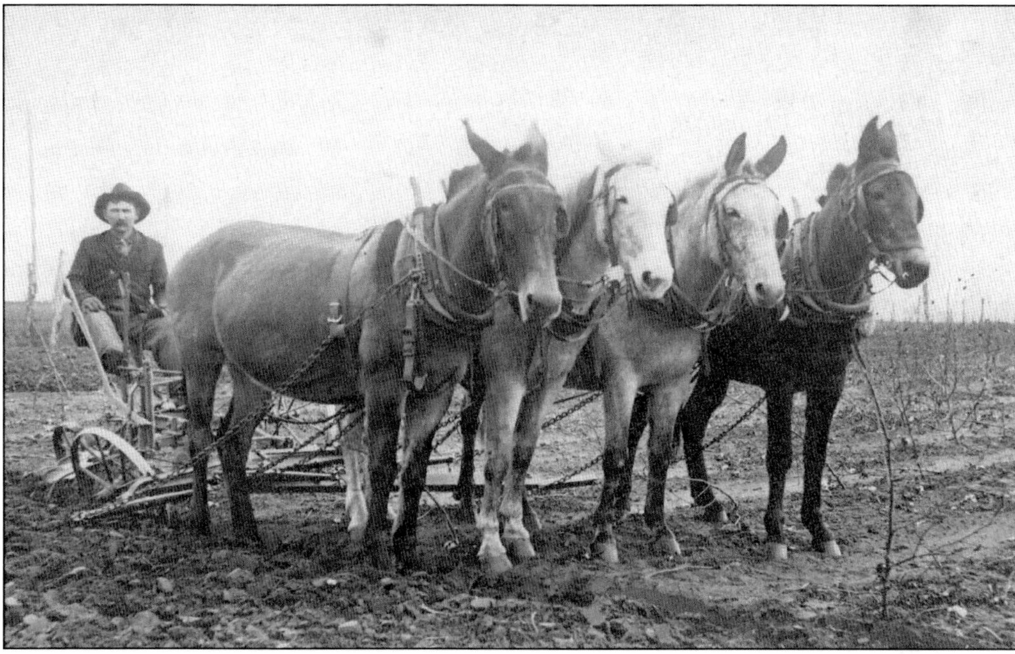

The equipment used for farming at the turn of the century, while effective, was much more labor intensive than the tractors and implements of today. One of the most used tools of the trade was the team-drawn plow. Teams of horses or mules were used to pull the plow while the farmer either rode or walked behind. (TNT.)

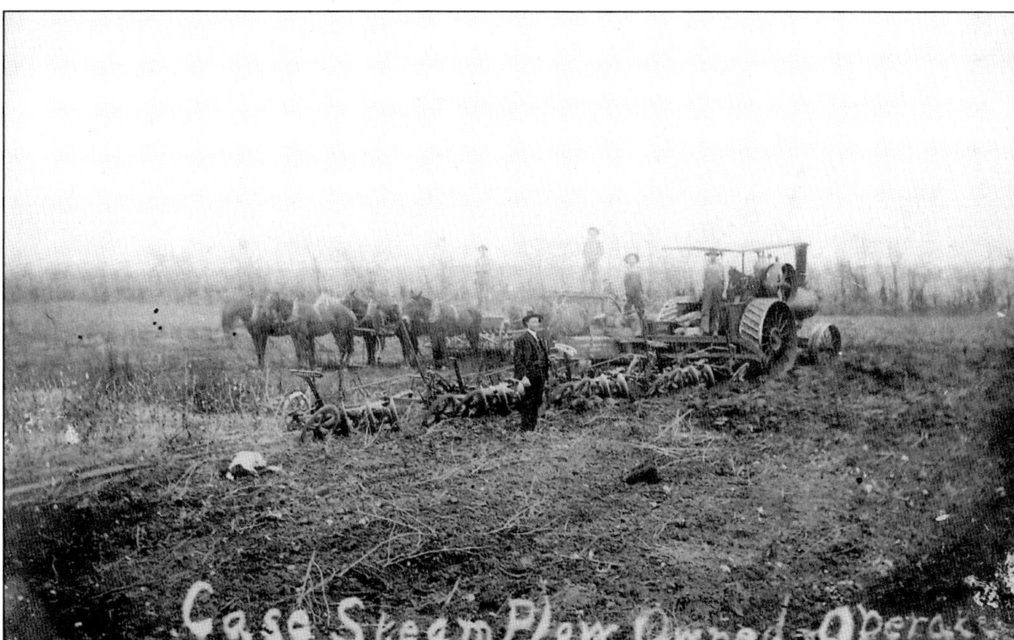

This photograph depicts the team-drawn method of plowing alongside the more modern steam-powered option. Steam-powered equipment quickly gained favor with local farmers. Mr. Grayson owned this Case steam-powered plow. It was purchased from the J.B. March Hardware Store in Nocona. March was one of the town's first proprietors. (TNT.)

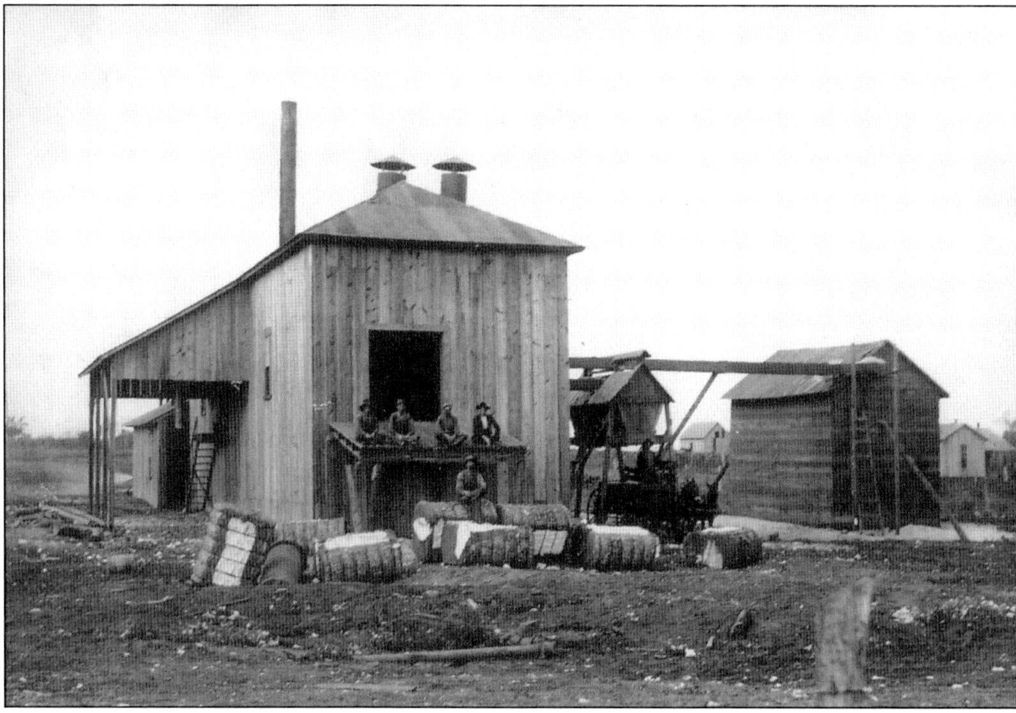

In 1900, cotton was the major crop grown in Nocona. During the time that cotton was king, more than a dozen cotton gins operated in Nocona. The first cotton gin was moved in from Eagle Point and was operated by C.C. Cooper. The last cotton gin was torn down in 1985. (TNT.)

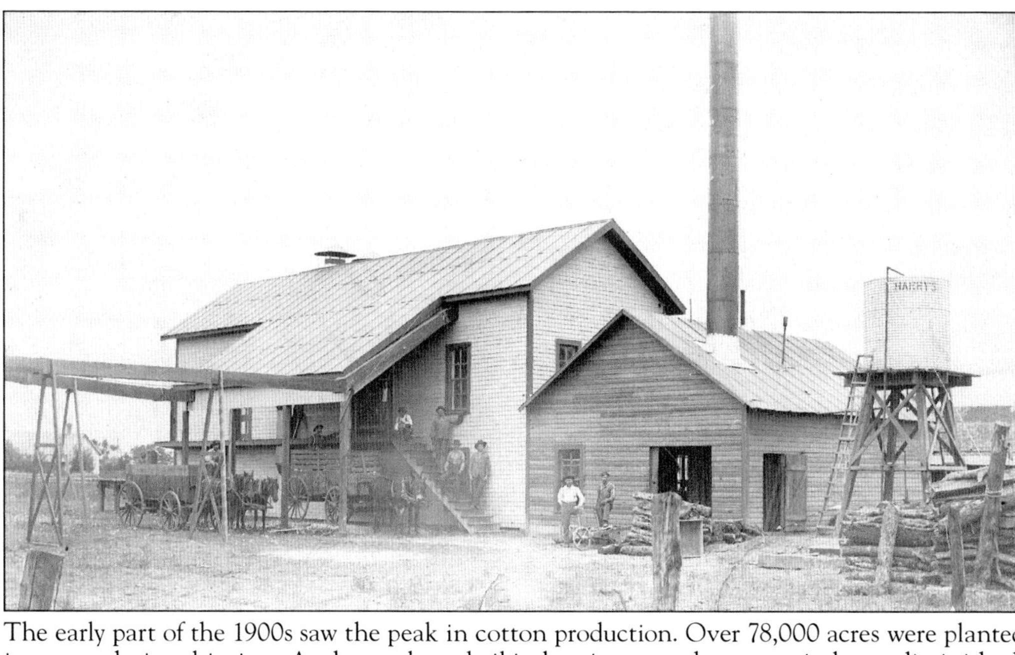

The early part of the 1900s saw the peak in cotton production. Over 78,000 acres were planted in cotton during this time. As the cattle and oil industries grew, the cotton industry diminished. By 1930, approximately 39,058 acres of cotton were planted. It had dropped to 7,130 acres by 1945. (TNT.)

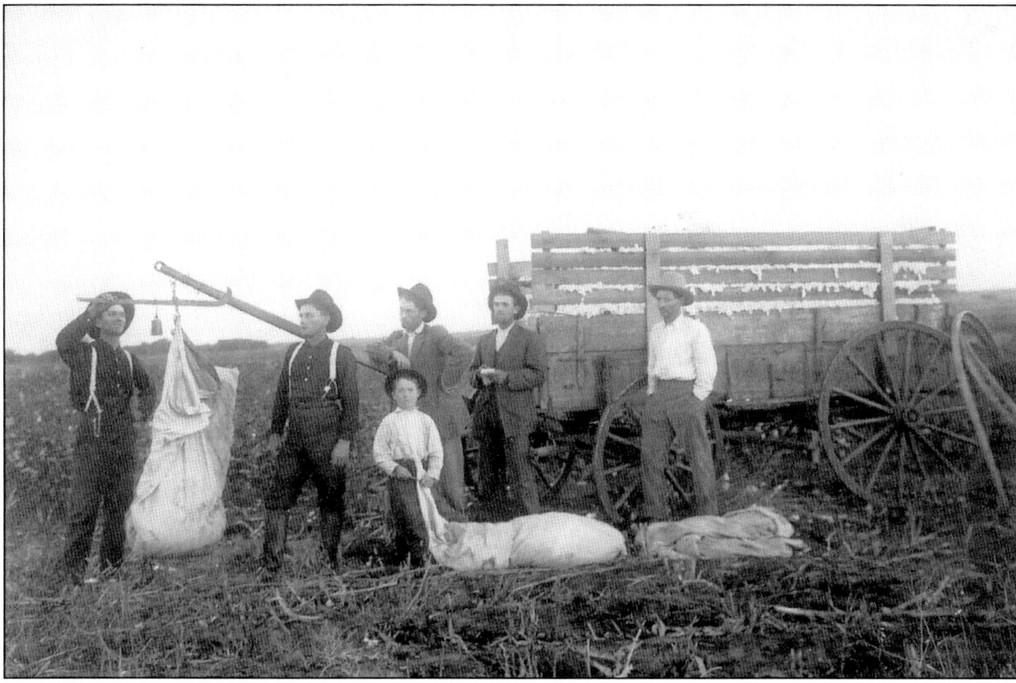

Picking cotton was back-breaking work. All able-bodied family members participated. They walked each row, pulling the bolls by hand and placing them in their tow sacks. Once the sacks were full, or as heavy as the pickers could carry, they were weighed and placed in the wagon to be taken to the gin. (TNT.)

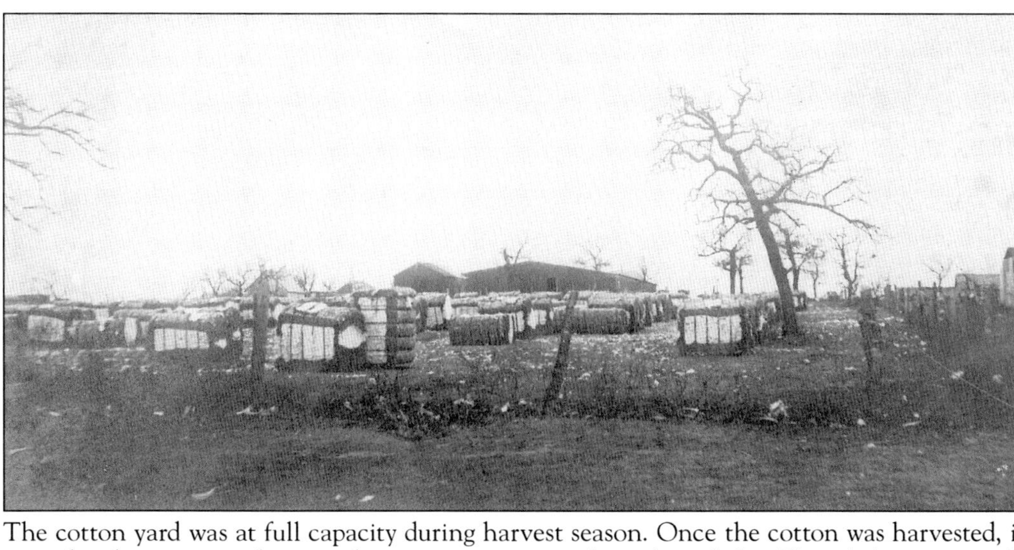

The cotton yard was at full capacity during harvest season. Once the cotton was harvested, it was taken by wagon to the gin, where it was compressed into large bales. These bales were neatly lined up throughout the cotton yard and then loaded on the trains for export throughout the country. (TNT.)

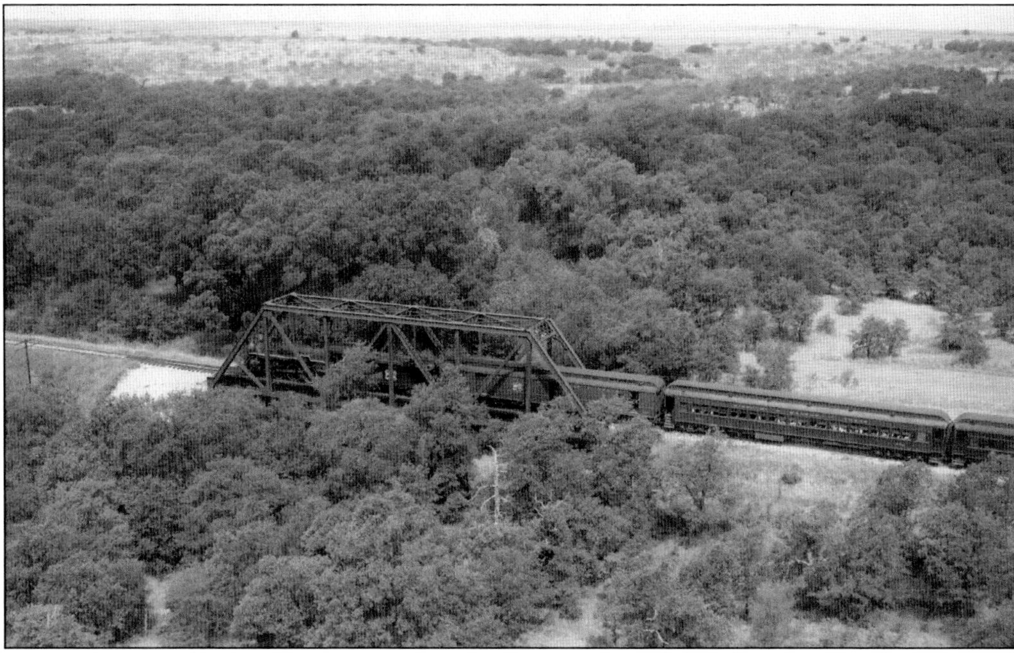

Construction on the section of Missouri, Kansas, and Texas railroad that passed through Nocona was completed in 1887. Due to the wooded terrain, several trees had to be cleared to lay the track. Trestle bridges were also required in many locations to accommodate the streams and creeks that fed into the Red River. (TNT.)

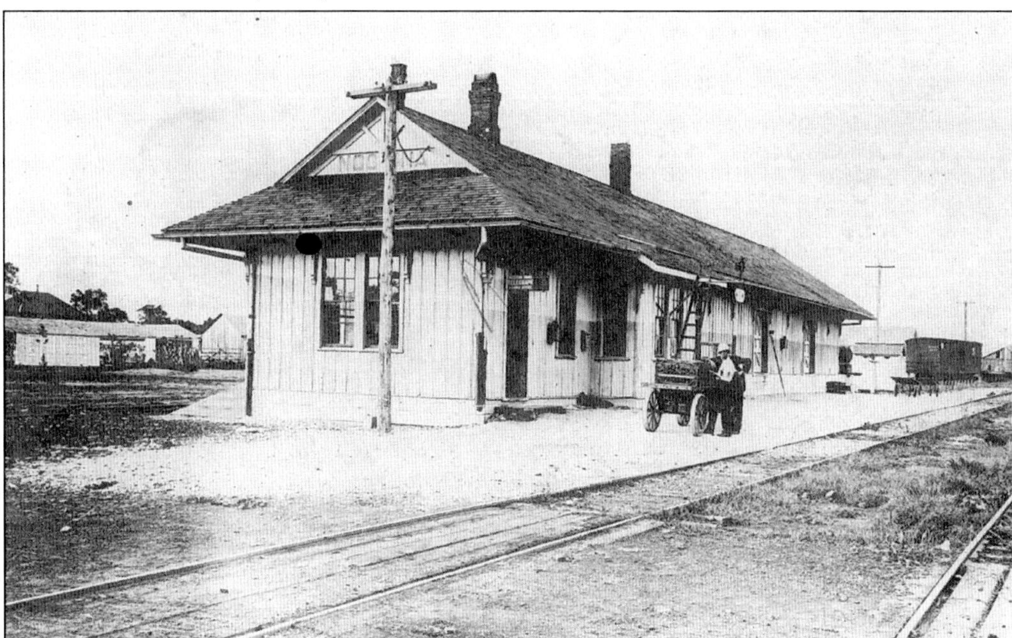

The first train depot was built in Nocona in 1887. The original structure burned. This depot was built in 1898. It was located on Clay Street near present-day Highway 82. Going to the depot to see who was on the incoming train or who was about to travel out of Nocona was a common family outing. (TNT.)

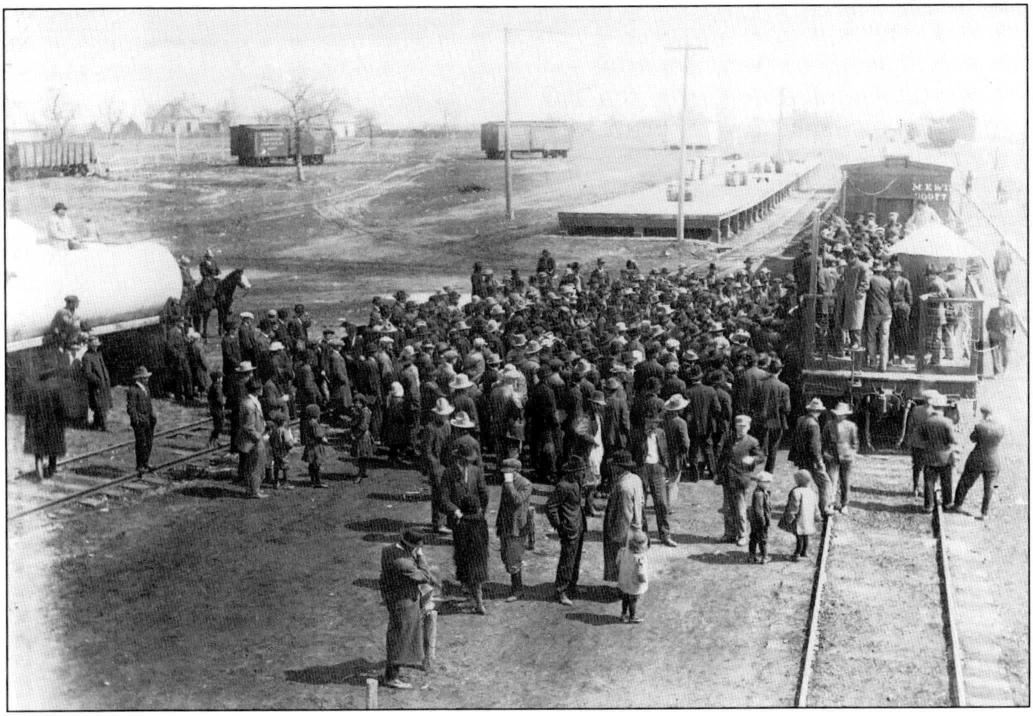

A large group of men and some children gather around the train as it is stopped at the Cooke Street train crossing near the cotton platform. The Nocona Public Library stands today at the platform location. In the distance to the right, the coal and sand chutes are visible. (Montague County Historical Commission.)

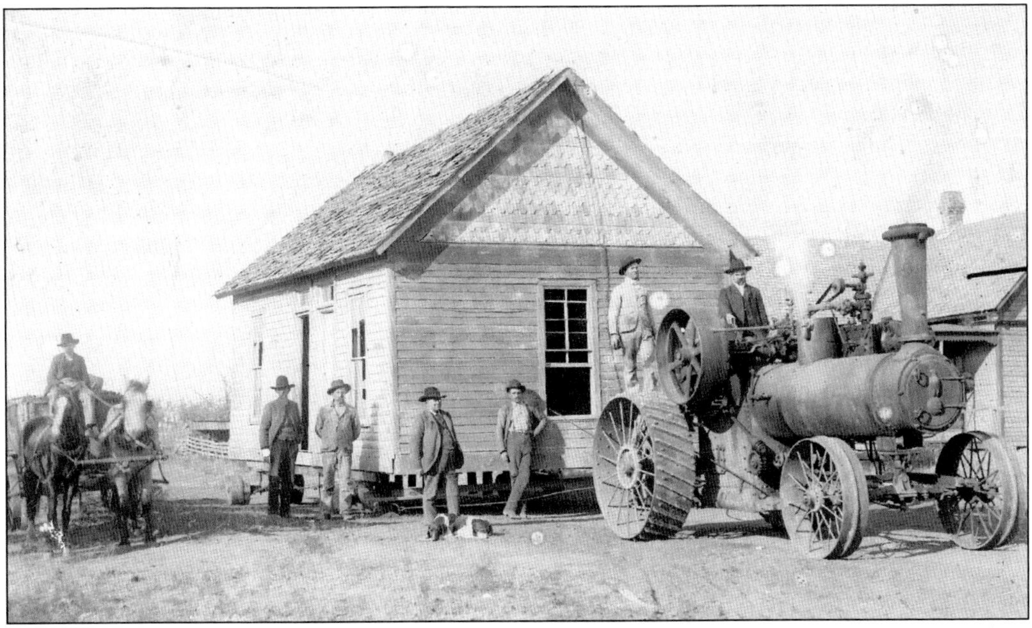

Farm equipment was often called into duty for other purposes. J.H. Cone (right) is seen standing on the steam-powered tractor. Cone, one of Nocona's earliest business owners, with the help of friends, used a steam-powered tractor to move a house to a new location. (Wanda Billings.)

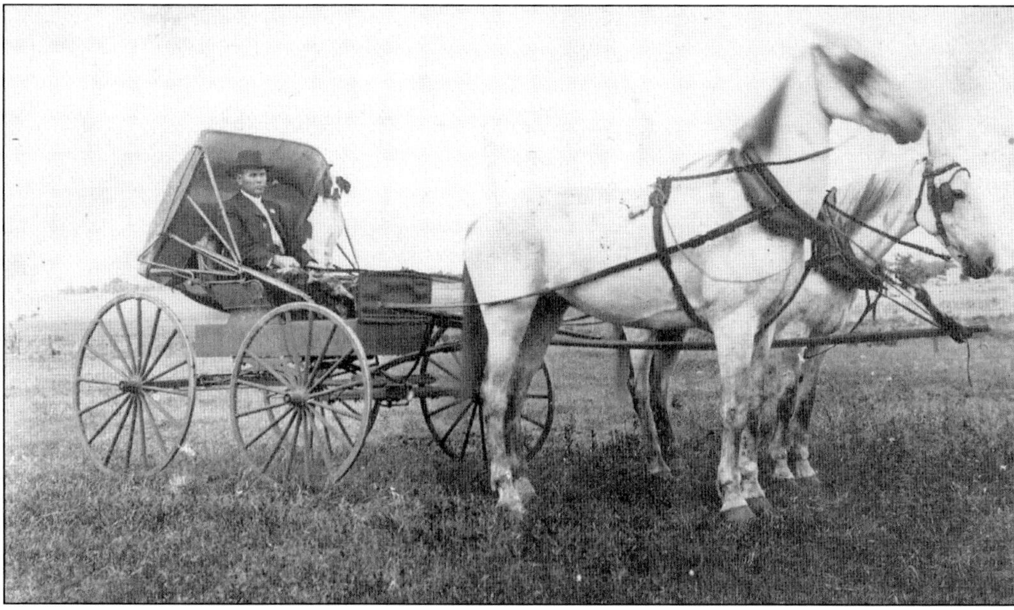

The most common forms of transportation in the early days of Nocona were riding horseback or traveling by way of horse-drawn buggy. Status could often be determined by one's mode of transportation. This gentleman, with his matching team, was probably a man of some means. (Montague County Historical Commission.)

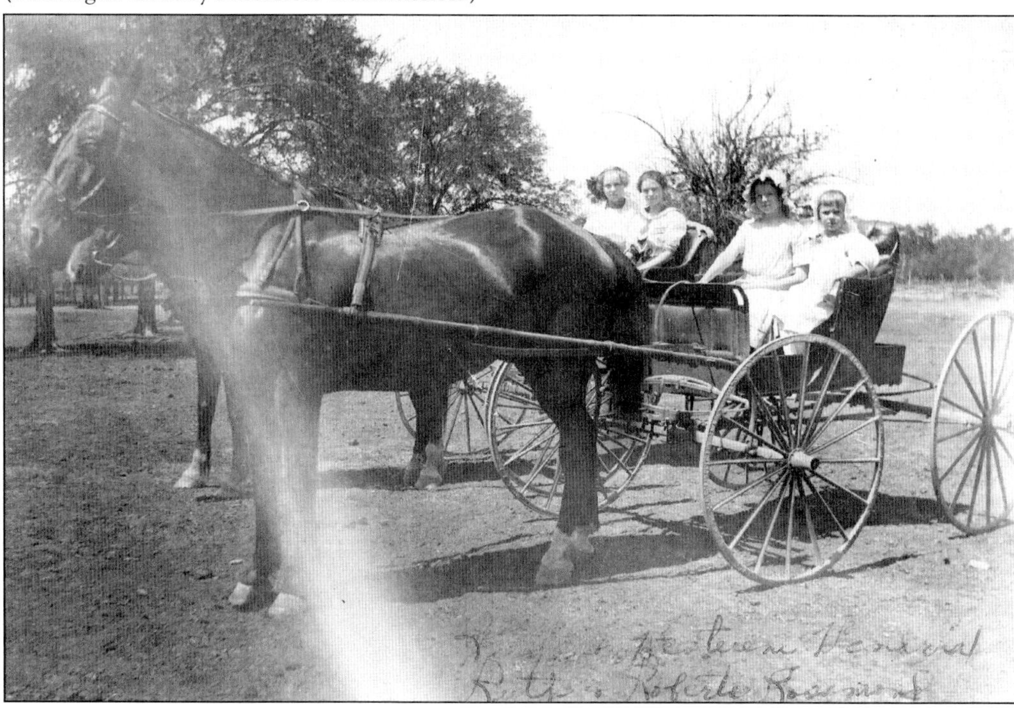

At the turn of the century, entertainment options were somewhat limited. Enjoying an afternoon buggy ride, these young ladies are, from left to right, Rugie Mae (Cone) Daniel, Hortense (LaForce) Hendrix, Ruth (Cone) Billings, and Roberta Rosemond. Billings and Rosemond are wearing their bonnets, as was the custom. (Wanda Billings.)

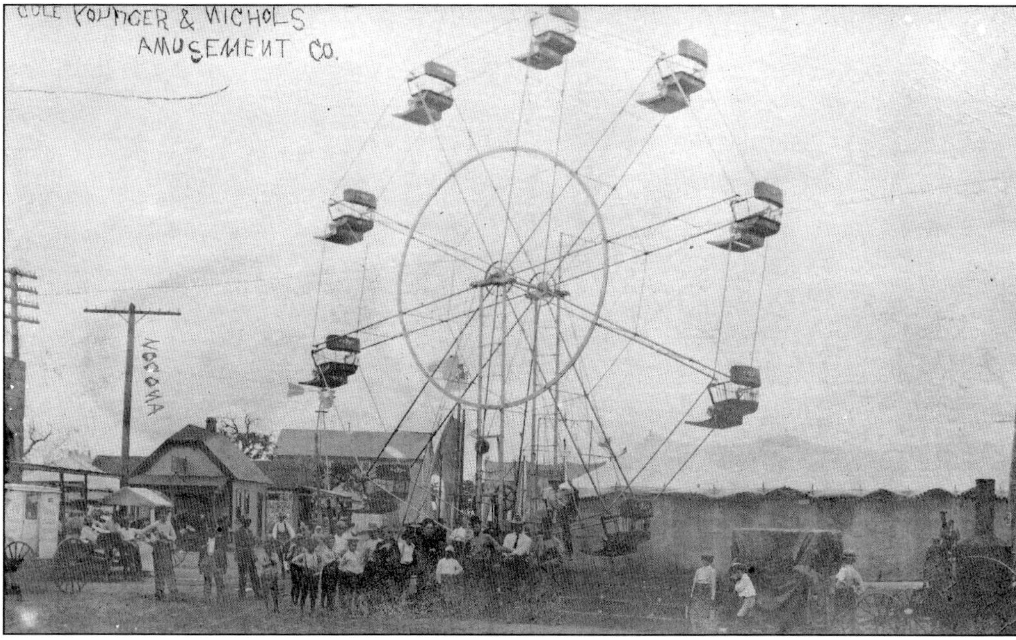

Traveling circuses and amusement parks were popular attractions in rural areas. Around 1908, the Cole Younger and Nichols Amusement Company stopped in Nocona. The 64-year-old Younger, of the James-Younger outlaw gang, opened the attraction after being released from prison in 1901. The amusement company made stops all over the country. (TNT.)

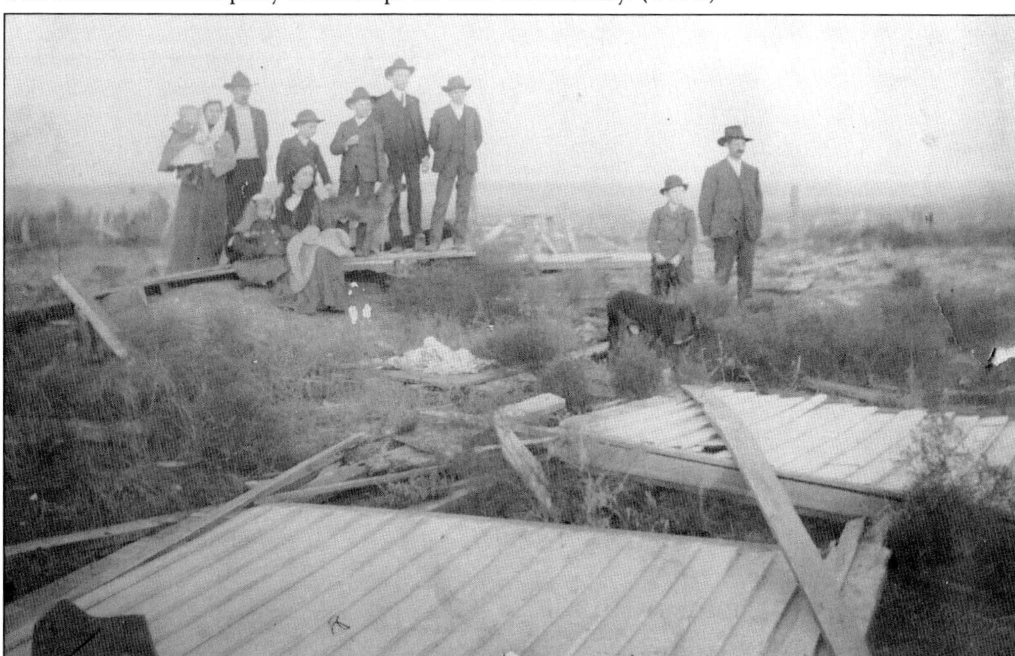

Nocona prospered from its inception, but it was not without its share of tragedies. This photograph shows the damage to Mr. Wood's home after it was struck by a tornado in July 1905. Fourteen Nocona residents lost their lives in this deadly storm. The 1905 tornado was the second tornado of great force to hit Nocona; the first was in May 1896. (TNT.)

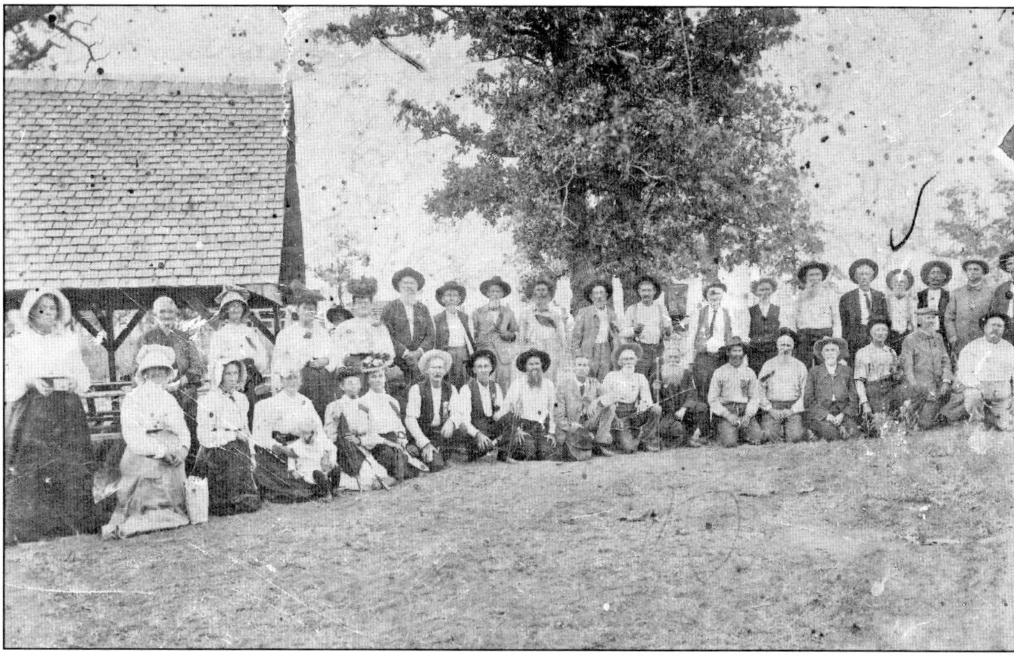

An annual reunion for the United Confederate Veterans (UCV) was held at the Bob Stone Camp UCV No. 93 in Nocona. The Bob Stone Camp was organized in 1880. Dozens of Confederate veterans and their families traveled in wagons to Nocona to attend this event. The meeting lasted several days and included several different activities. This photograph shows the veterans who attended in 1903. (TNT.)

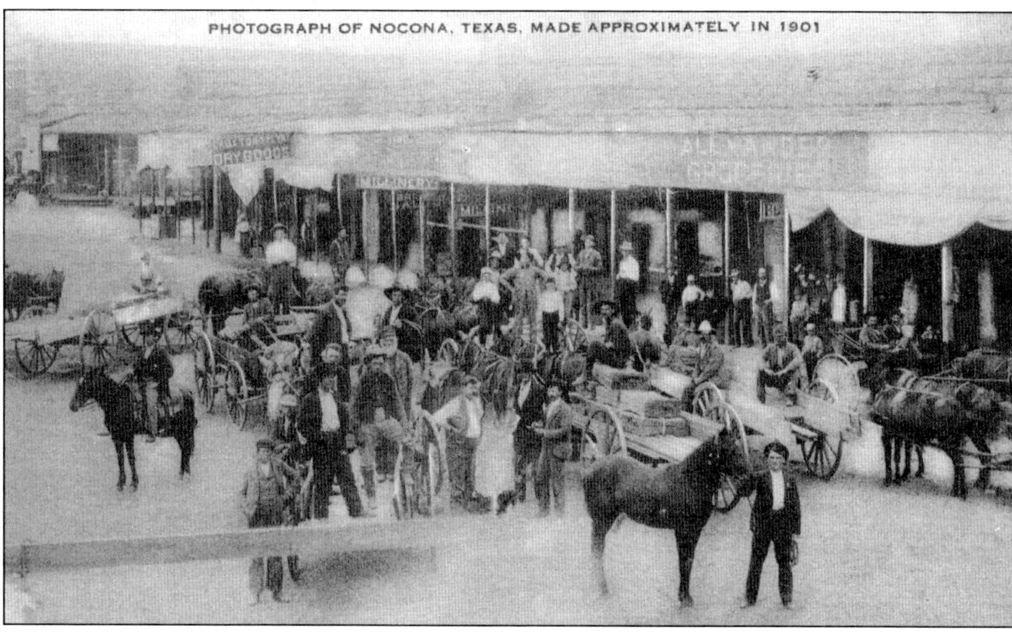

By 1901, Nocona was a bustling town. In this early street scene, the following business establishments can be identified. From left to right are Croxton and Flynt Dry Goods, Miss Lou Harwell's millinery shop, and Alexander's Groceries. A newspaper of the time advertises that Harwell's millinery had an inventory of over 500 hats. (TNT.)

Two

City and Community

New businesses flocked to Nocona to take advantage of the railroad service. With commerce comes growth, so as the number of businesses increased, so did the population. When Nocona incorporated in 1890, the population was approximately 200 citizens; in 1902, there were 961 citizens; and by 1910, the town had grown to 1,338. The oil boom of the 1920s led to an even larger jump in population, so that by 1930, Nocona was home to over 2,352 people.

The majority of the first commercial establishments set up shop along Clay Street, facing south, for the utmost exposure to the railroad traffic. In 1902, Nocona was home to no less than 36 businesses. These fledgling upstarts included dry goods and grocery stores, blacksmith shops, hardware stores, barbershops, and, of course, a few saloons.

Found alongside the stores that provided different types of tangible goods were several that provided services. Nocona had a weekly newspaper almost from the time of its inception. There were several banks that called Nocona home. The two most prominent were the Farmers and Merchants Bank and the Peoples National Bank. Both operated for several decades in Nocona. Several doctors practiced in Nocona over the years, starting with country doctors who made house calls by horse and buggy, which led up to the establishment of a hospital within the city limits.

Nocona citizens were prosperous and hardworking, but they also had a strong social network. Several clubs and organizations were formed to enrich the community. These included fraternal organizations, such as the Masons, and civic organizations, like the chamber of commerce and the Rotary and Lions Clubs. There were also several women's clubs; Thursdays Literary Club and the Maids and Matrons Club were just a couple of groups formed by the ladies of Nocona. Other organizations included the Rodeo Association, the Chisholm Trail Riding Club, the Lone Star Band, and many more.

Whether at work or at play, Nocona residents took pride in their community. The handiwork of these early residents created a successful blueprint for future generations to follow.

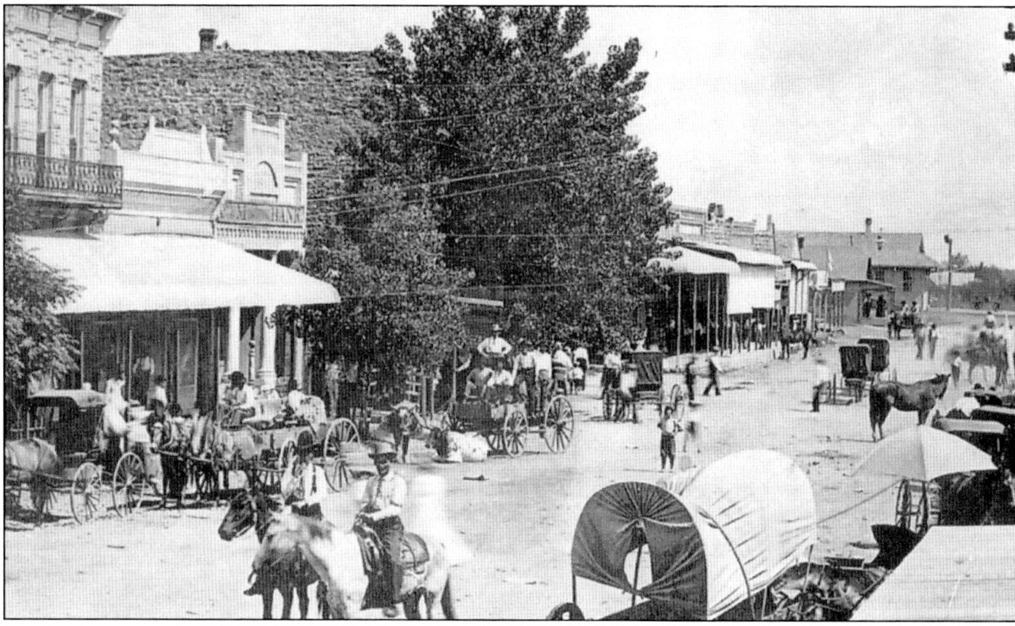

In the beginning, most new businesses set up along Front Street in order to be adjacent to the railroad. Soon, however, the business population outgrew Front Street and expanded to include Clay Street. This early 1900s photograph of Clay Street illustrates a typical day in downtown Nocona. The Farmers and Merchants Bank (third from left) was in the heart of the business district. (TNT.)

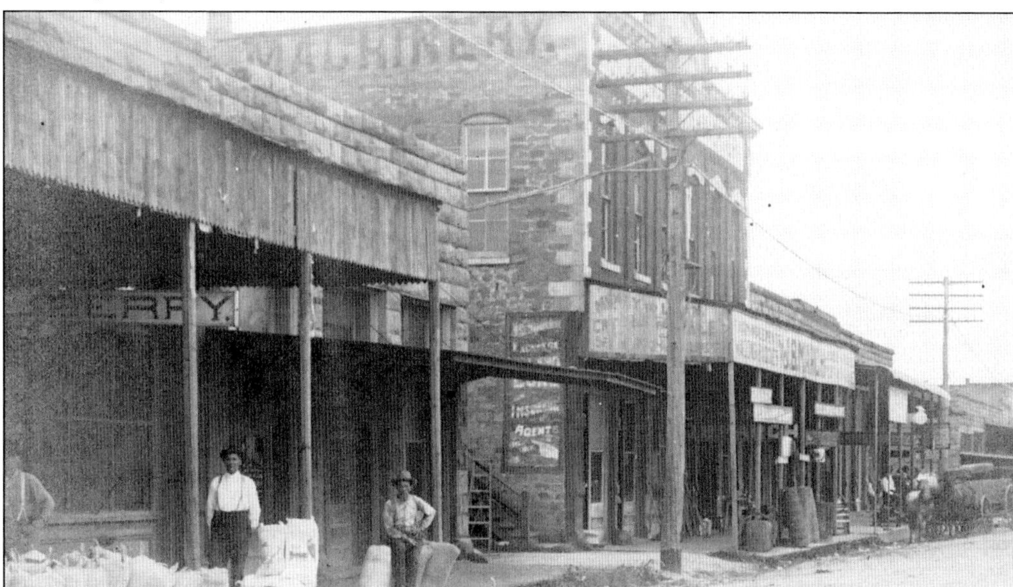

Two early businesses in Nocona were the J.J. Berry grocery store and flour mill and the J.B. March Hardware and Furniture Company. March handled everything from cook stoves to farm implements. The J.B. March Opera House was located on the second floor of the hardware building. The opera house closed in the 1910s, but the hardware store remained a staple in Nocona for several more years. (TNT.)

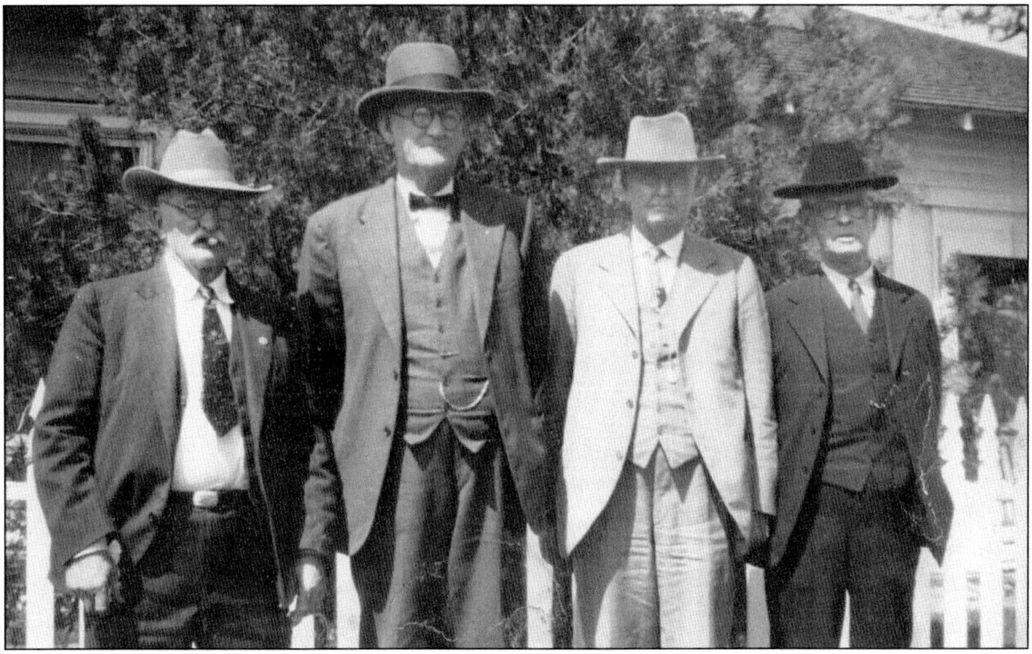

Four of Nocona's first businessmen were, from left to right, Sam McCool, J.B. March, Chris Quillen, and Tom Hoben. McCool owned a feed store. March owned furniture, hardware, and funeral businesses. Quillen was one of Nocona's first bankers. Hoben was a rancher and the stepson of Nocona cofounder William Broaddus. (Montague County Historical Commission.)

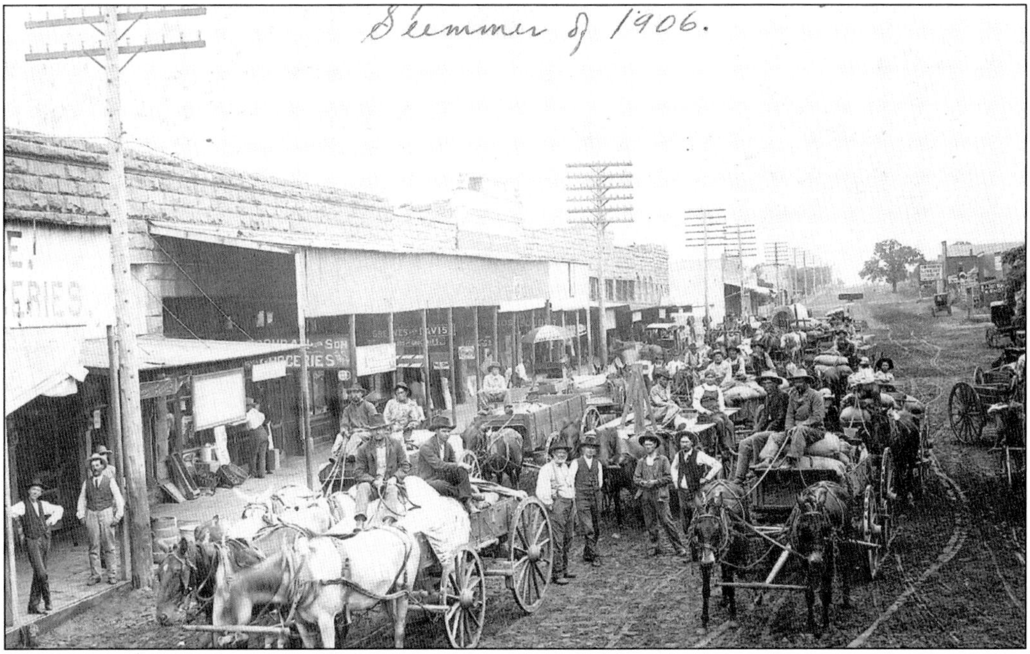

A fire destroyed more than a block of west Clay Street on December 12, 1891. The businesses seen in this photograph are of stone and brick construction. After the fire, bricks were desired to reconstruct the buildings. The lime plant southeast of town provided the large brick stones that were used for the new buildings. (TNT.)

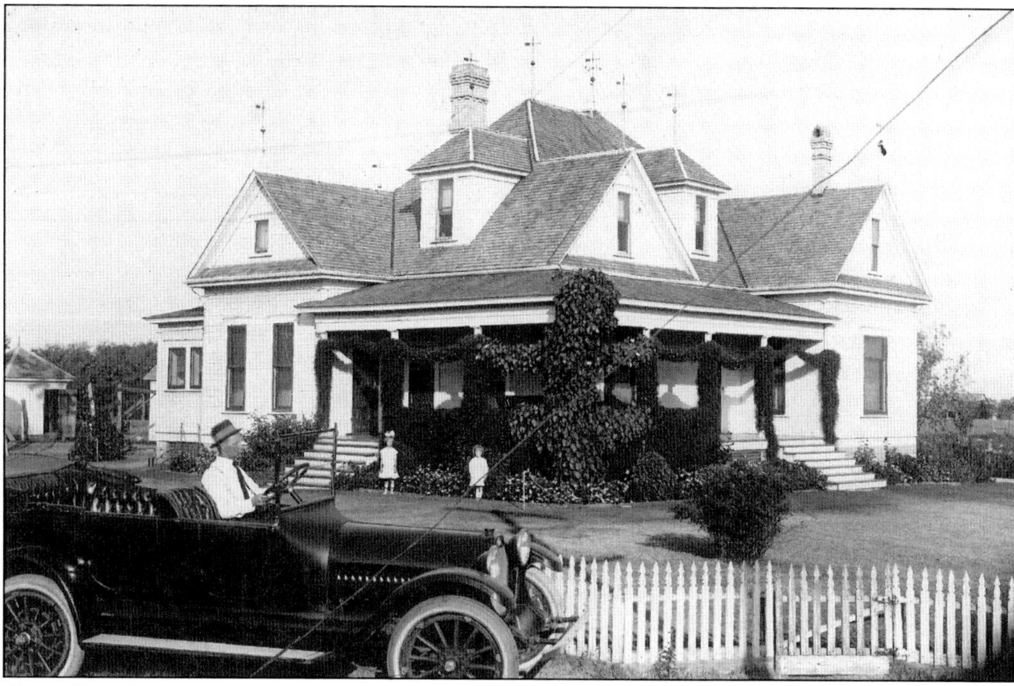

One of Nocona's early residents and merchants was J.H. "Bus" Cone (seated in car). He brought his family to Montague County in 1891. In the summer of 1906, he built this new home, located at 803 Clay Street. Playing in the yard are two of his daughters, Rugie Mae (left) and Ruth. (Wanda Billings.)

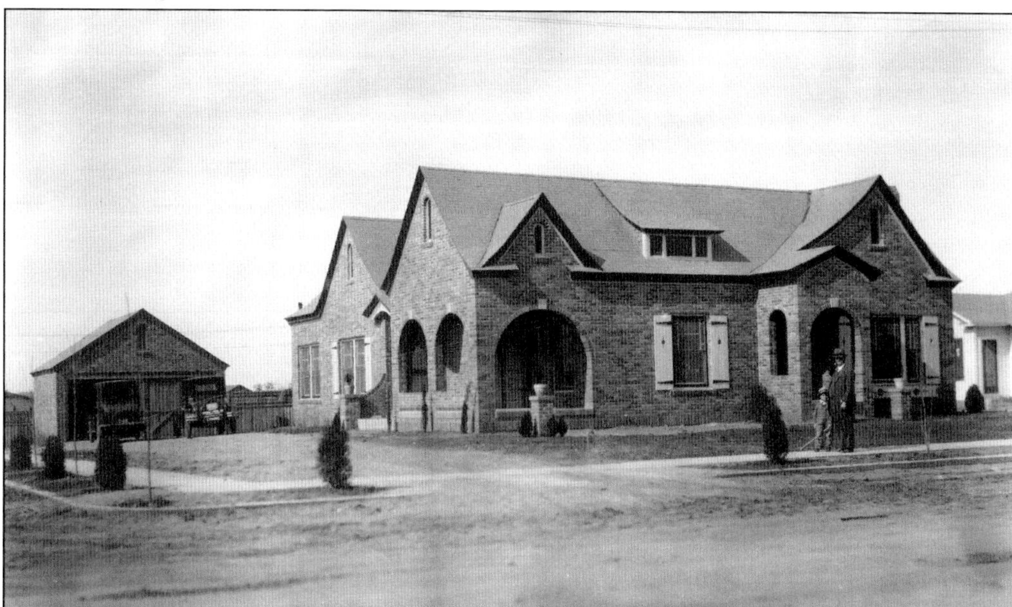

In the late 1920s, Bus Cone built this modern home for his family. He is standing in front next to his grandson Billy Joe Billings. Upon arriving in Nocona, he went to work as a clerk in the J.B. March Hardware and Furniture Store. Later, after opening his own hardware business, Cone and March shared a healthy rivalry that lasted for years. (Wanda Billings.)

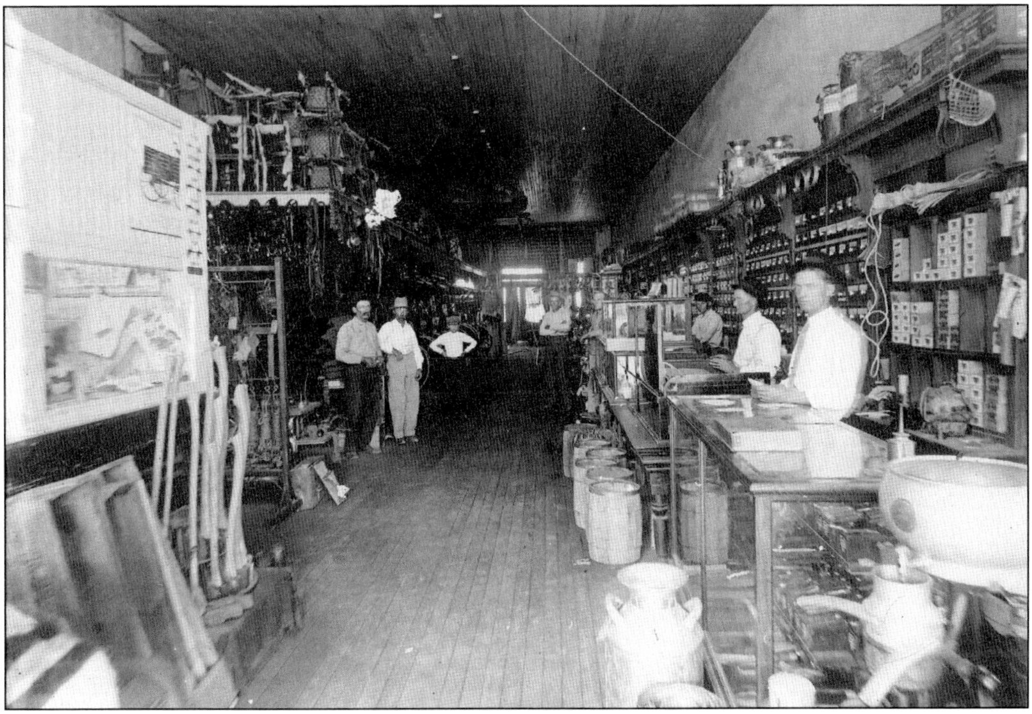

Bus Cone stocked a large variety of items in his hardware store. Notice the cigars in the glass display case and the Winchester ammunition on the shelves above the case. In front of the display are barrels of horseshoes. In the back (left) is large selection of buggies. Cone owned this store until 1941, when he sold out to the Scott brothers of St. Jo. (Wanda Billings.)

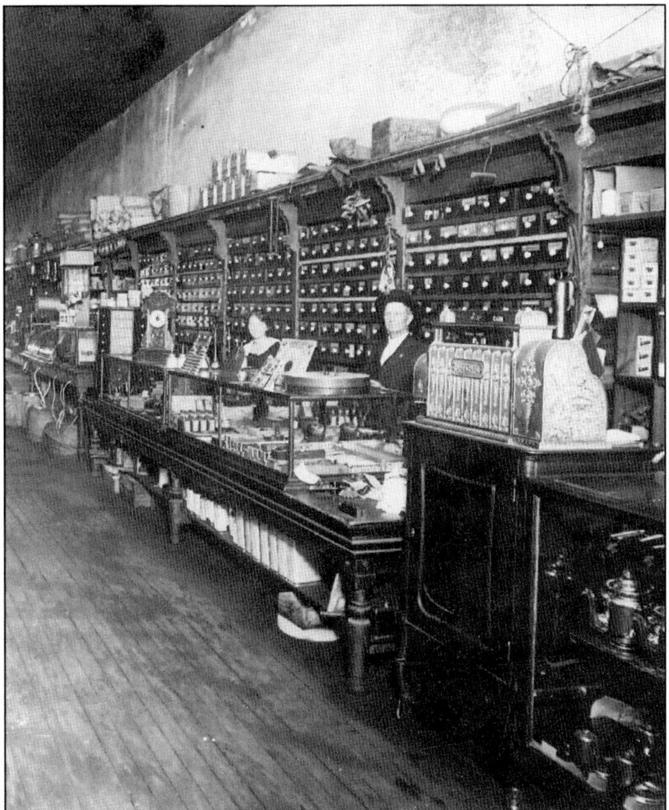

In 1911, Bus Cone purchased an existing hardware business from Barlow and Harbour. The Cone Hardware store was located on the corner of Clay and Oak Streets. This photograph is of the interior of Cone's store. In 1918, he opened and operated a funeral home in conjunction with his hardware business. (Wanda Billings.)

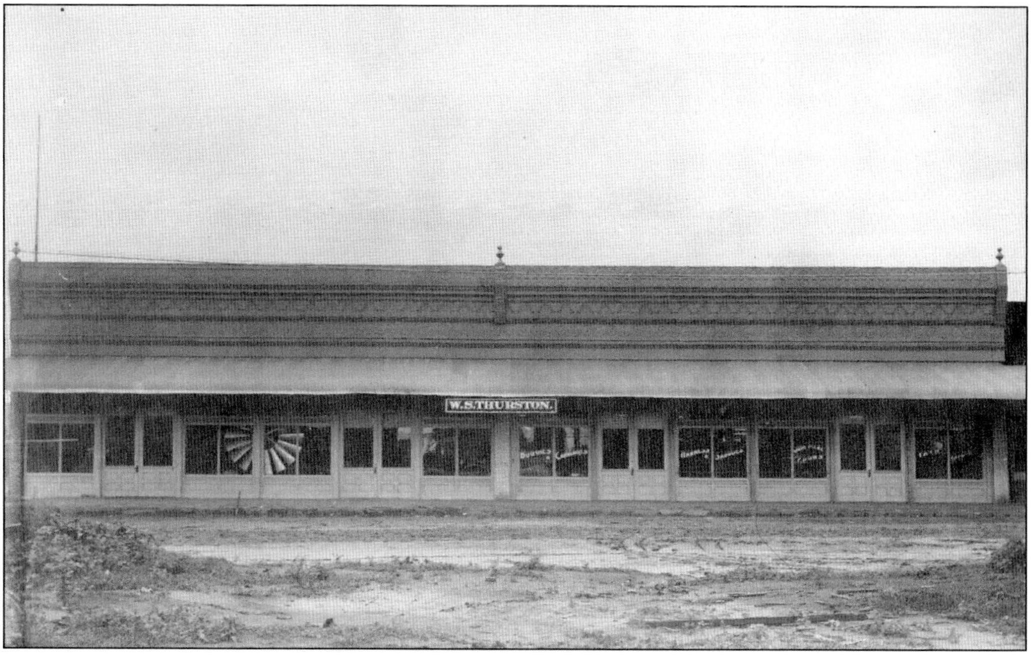

W.S. Thurston came to Nocona in 1885 from nearby Red River Station. His store was located on the corner of Clay and Elm Streets, and his home was located at 509 Pecan Street. He opened a large hardware and farm implement store. He dealt in John Deere farming equipment. The signage on the windows in this photograph reads, "Buggies, Carriages, Harness, Saddles, and Plows." (TNT.)

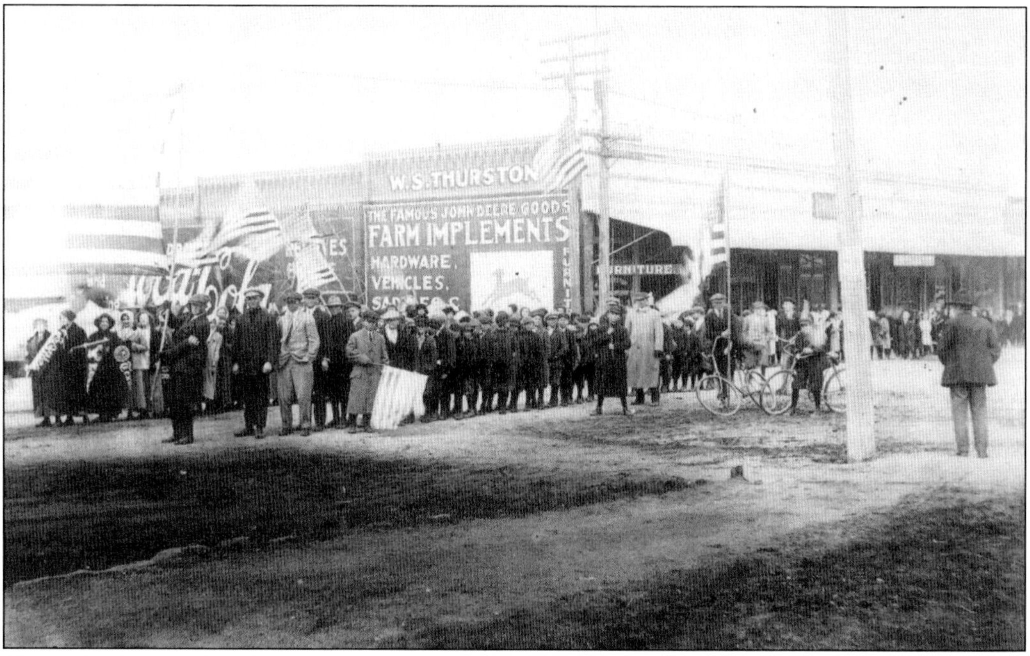

The W.S. Thurston Building is the backdrop to this 1917 parade. The advertisement on the side of the building hawks John Deere implements, hardware, vehicles, saddles, and furniture. Near this corner of Clay and Elm Streets was the public water well. (Montague County Historical Commission.)

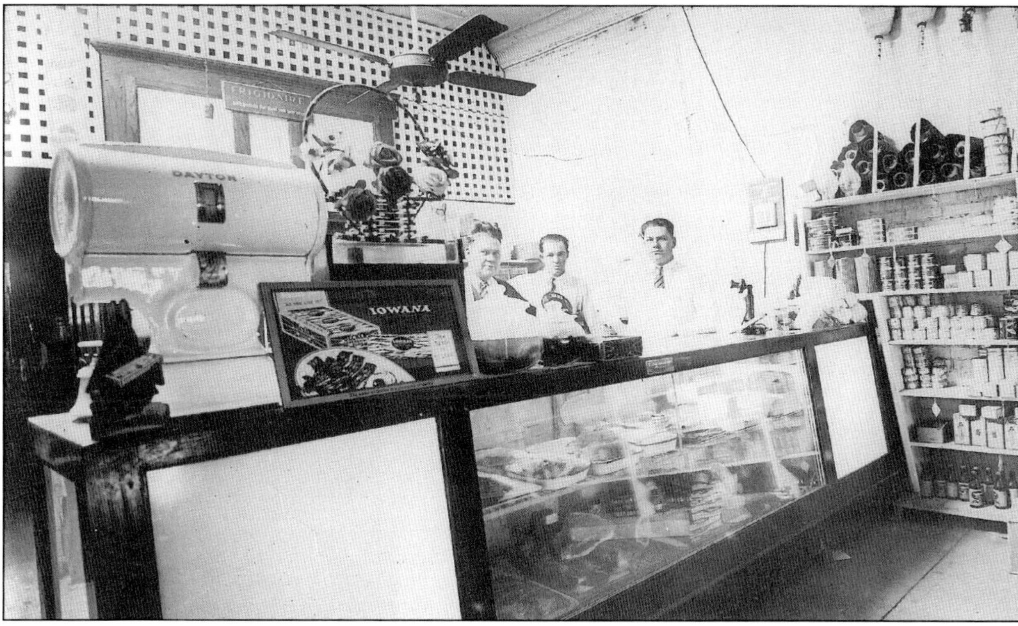

The Nocona Cash Grocery Store was opened in 1924 by Sam Arnold (left), his wife Gertrude, and his two brothers Oscar (center) and Alvin (right). The store was located on the second block of Clay Street. The Depression hit the company hard. Good-hearted Sam Arnold extended approximately $40,000 in credit to his customers during the trying economic times, causing the business to go bankrupt. (Dan Fenoglio.)

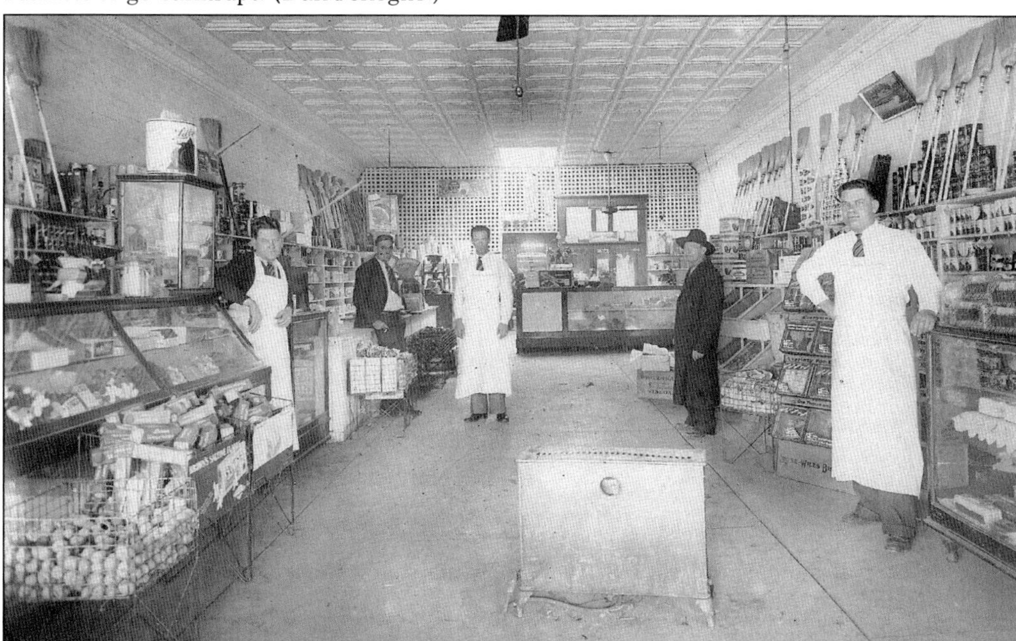

Shown in this photograph of the Nocona Cash Grocery Store are, from left to right, Sam Arnold, Oscar Arnold, George Steagall (Red Steagall's grandfather), Dave Maddox, and Alvin Arnold. Sam Arnold's grandson Dan Fenoglio has purchased the original building and restored it with flair. Daddy Sam's is a great entertainment venue today. (Dan Fenoglio.)

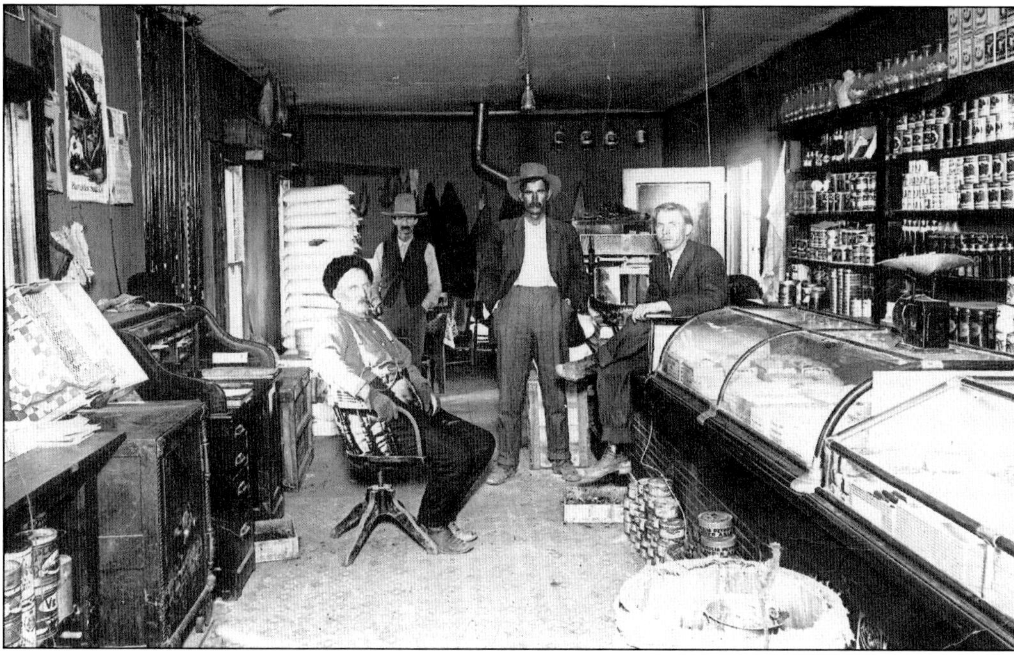

James A. Fooshee (seated) established a dry goods store in 1887. Upon close examination of this photograph, one can make out syrup buckets hanging along the back wall and flower vases and corn flakes on the top shelf on the right. There is a selection of fishing poles behind the desk, with a large safe located in front of the desk. (TNT.)

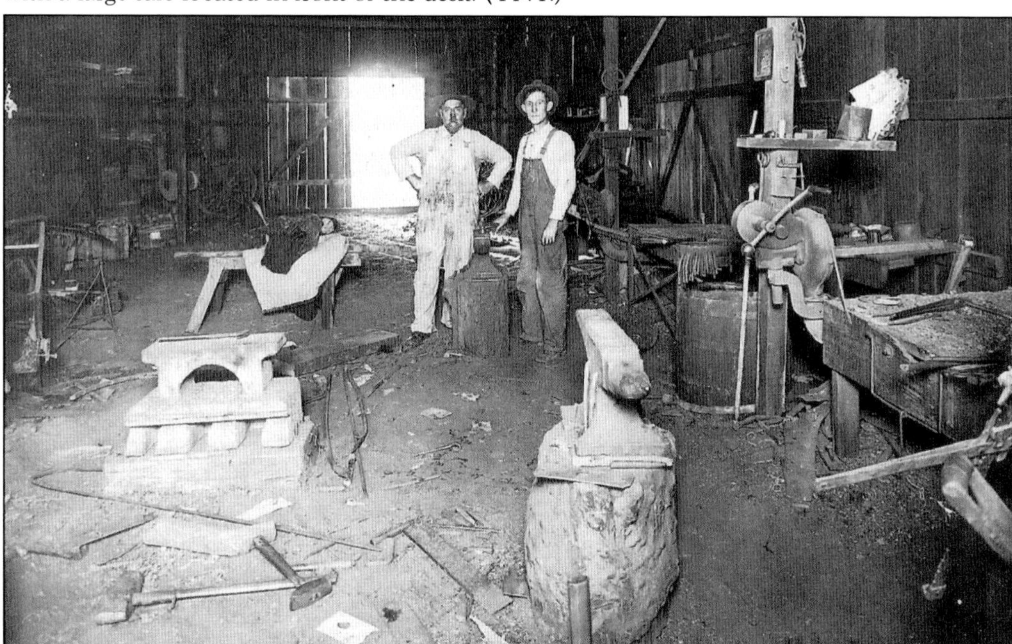

The local blacksmith was essential to any rural area settlement. This photograph is of one of the early 1900s blacksmith shops in Nocona. It was located at 201 Main Street. Working at the anvil are Finley Nelson (right) and Lee Holcomb. Lying on the ground around the other anvils are several tools of the blacksmithing trade. (TNT.)

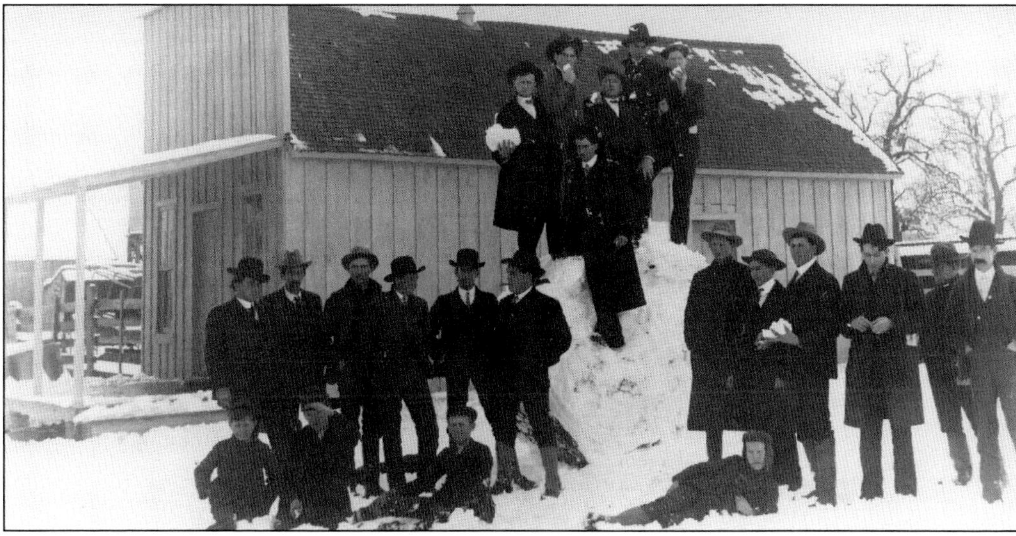

These snowy photographs were taken in February 1905 outside of Daddy Woods's store. This store was a place where many of the local merchants and businessmen of the day congregated in the mornings to visit. The gentlemen enjoying the snow (above) are, from left to right, (first row) Otis King, Marvin Matlock, and unidentified; (second row) Dr. S.T. Humphreys, unidentified, Bruce Barlow, Bill Pribble, George Mullins, Roy Berry, Gill Utt, James Foster, and Newton Pribble. The last three are unidentified. The young man above, with the large snowball, is John L. Biter. The Central Christian Church (below) can be seen in the background. (TNT.)

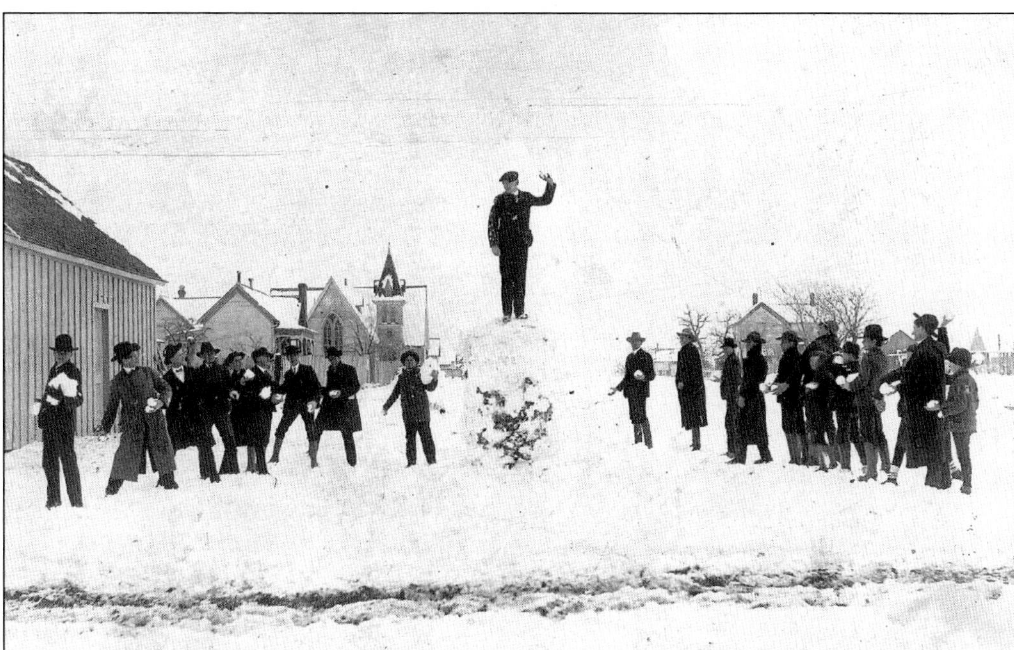

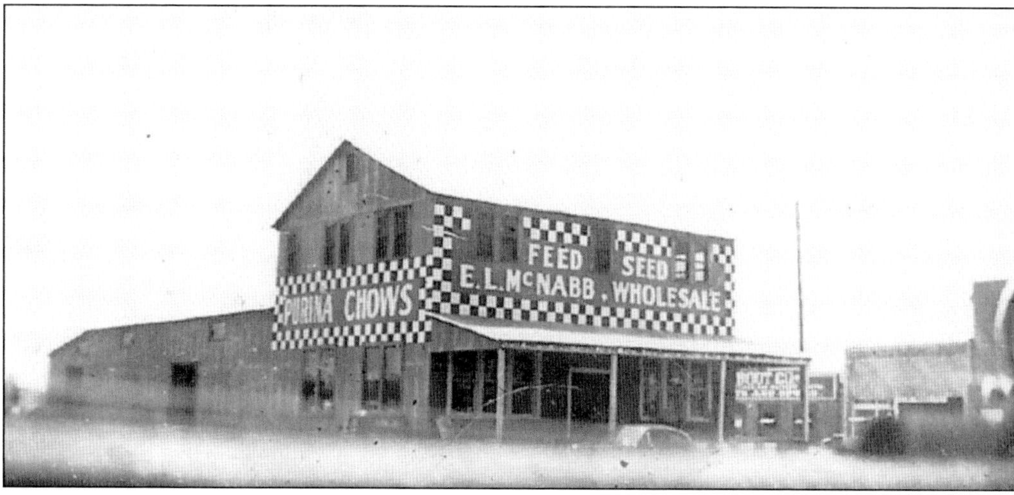

E.L. McNabb moved with his parents to Nocona in 1903. His father, Wash McNabb, ran a wagon yard in the early days of Nocona. Later, as automobiles became more popular, he ran a taxi service. E.L. McNabb established his feed store in 1929. The feed store is still in operation and owned by the McNabb family. This photograph shows the building in the 1930s. (TNT.)

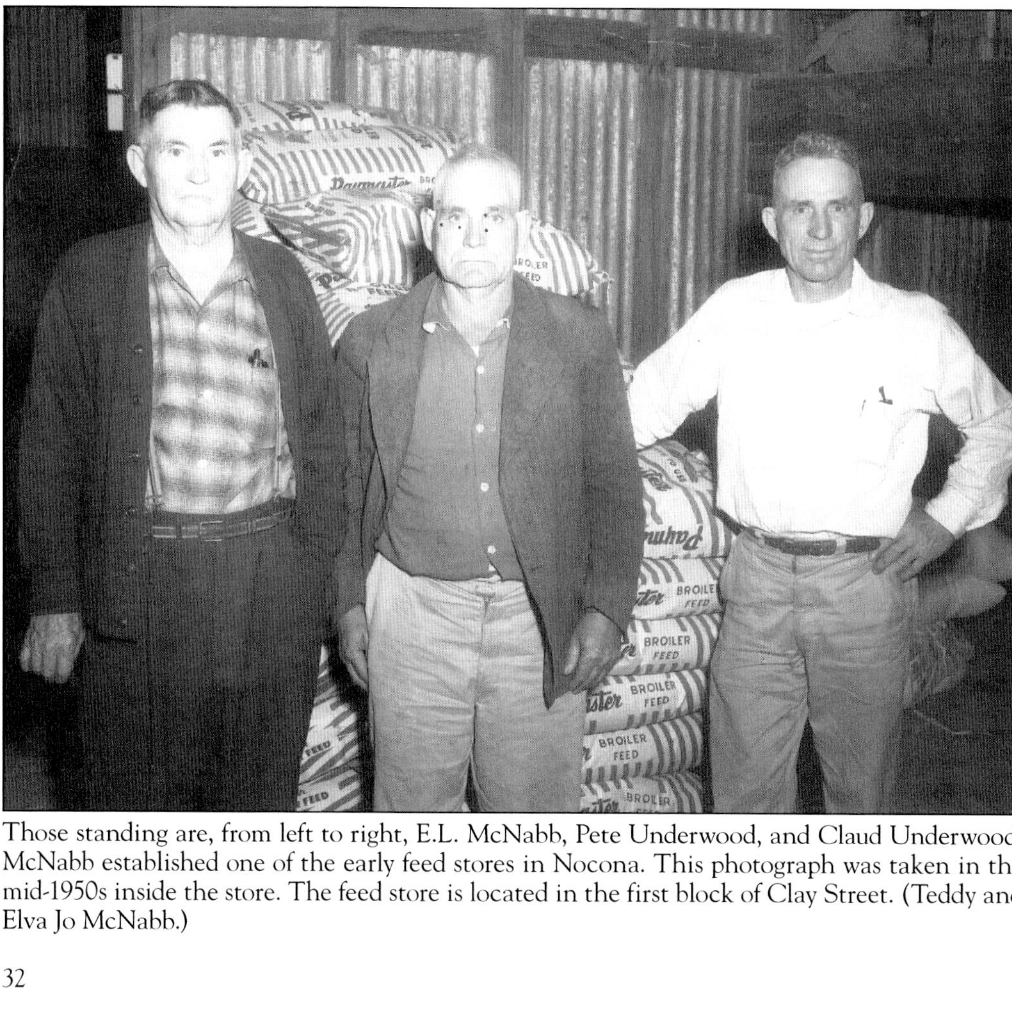

Those standing are, from left to right, E.L. McNabb, Pete Underwood, and Claud Underwood. McNabb established one of the early feed stores in Nocona. This photograph was taken in the mid-1950s inside the store. The feed store is located in the first block of Clay Street. (Teddy and Elva Jo McNabb.)

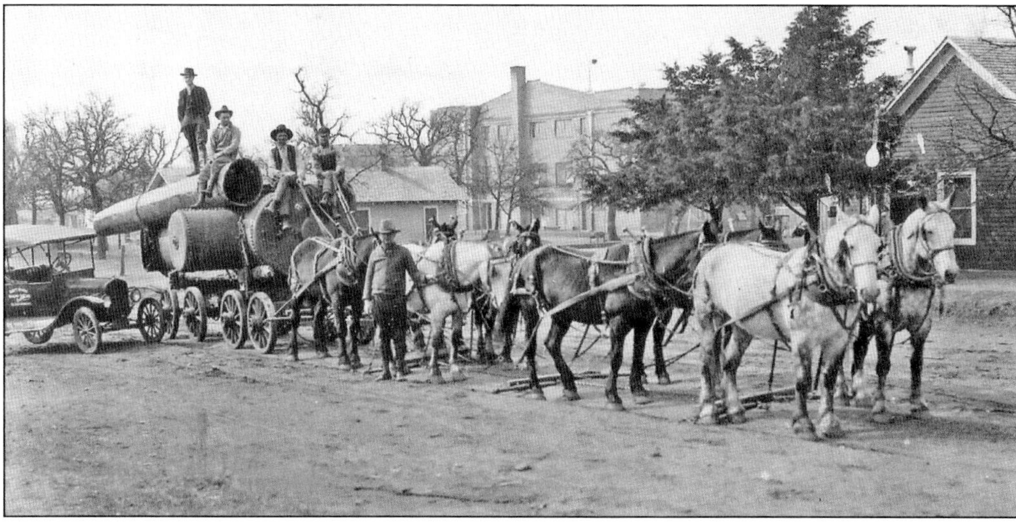

A group of men are moving a boiler, possibly to install it in one of the businesses located in downtown Nocona. Using an eight-horse team indicates that the boiler was extremely heavy. This photograph was taken just after they had maneuvered around a tricky corner. The large building visible in the background is the high school. (TNT.)

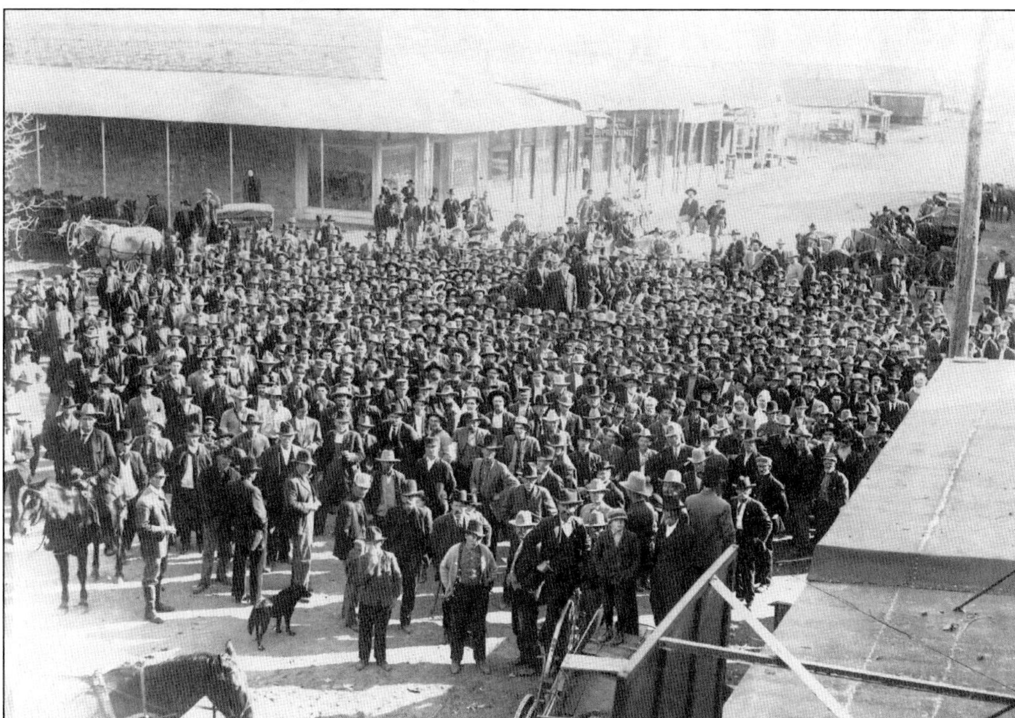

This photograph was taken at the corner of Clay and Oak Streets looking west down Oak Street. The men of Nocona had gathered for a political campaign. The building on the right side of the photograph is the Farmer's Union Grocery store. On the opposite corner is the Fooshee General Store. The building with the "Job Printing" sign is the Nocona News Building. (Montague County Historical Commission.)

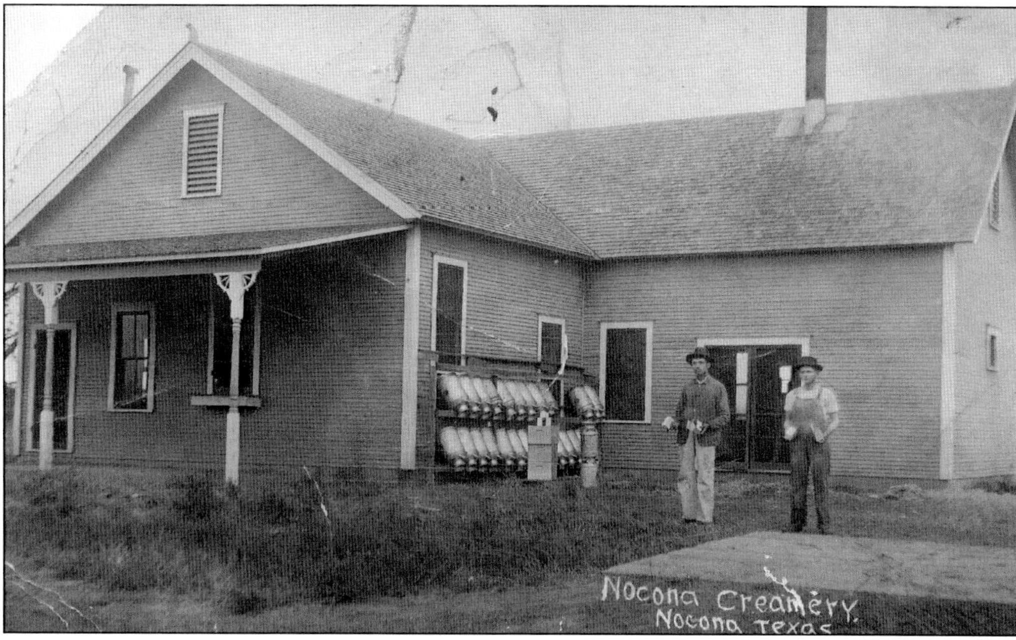

Bill Robinson (left) and his employee Newt Pribble are shown standing in front of the Nocona Creamery. The creamery was established in 1910 by Robinson and his wife, Pearl. It was located on the Montague Highway. Several milk cans are stored in the racks against the building. (TNT.)

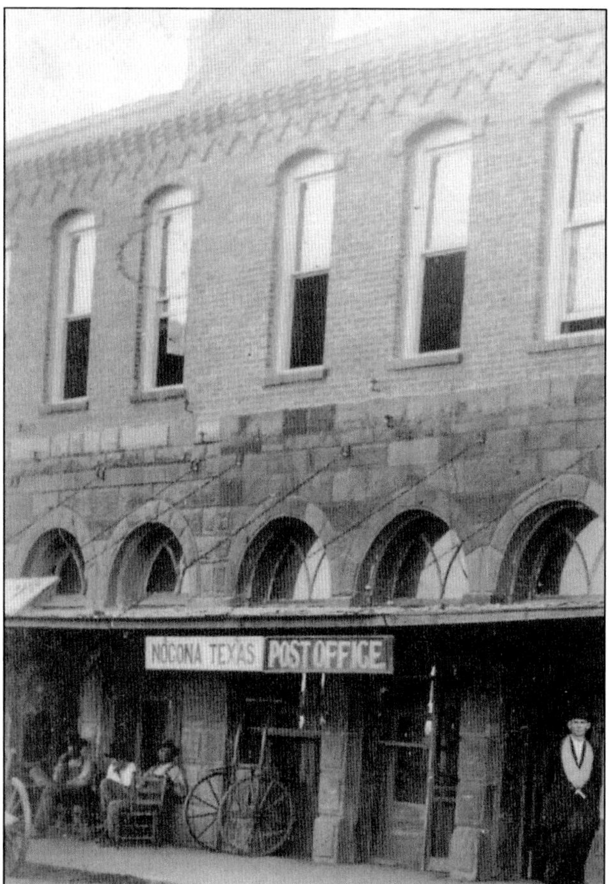

The post office opened in 1887 with the arrival of the railroad. It was originally located on North Front Street, which is known as Willow Street today. Notice the handcart on the front porch that was used to haul the mail from the post office to the delivery wagons. (Montague Historical Commission.)

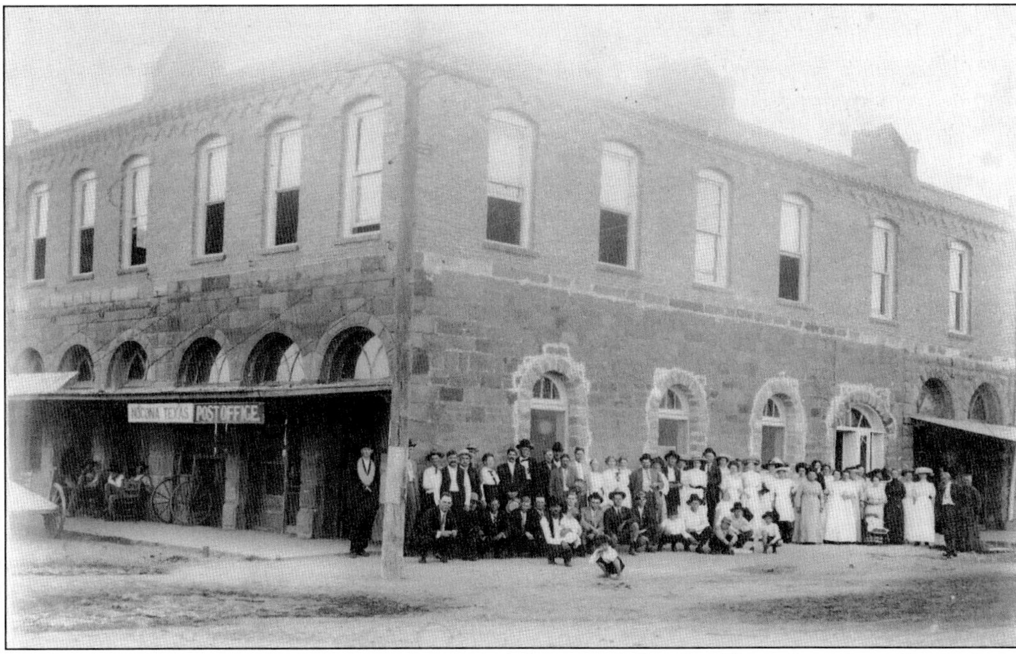

This photograph provides a wider-angle view of the Post Office Building. Standing alongside are members of the Nocona AF&AM. The local Masonic lodge met in the upstairs portion of this building. The gentleman leaning on the post is John Wood, and the first man in the first row is Sam Hodges. (Montague County Historical Commission.)

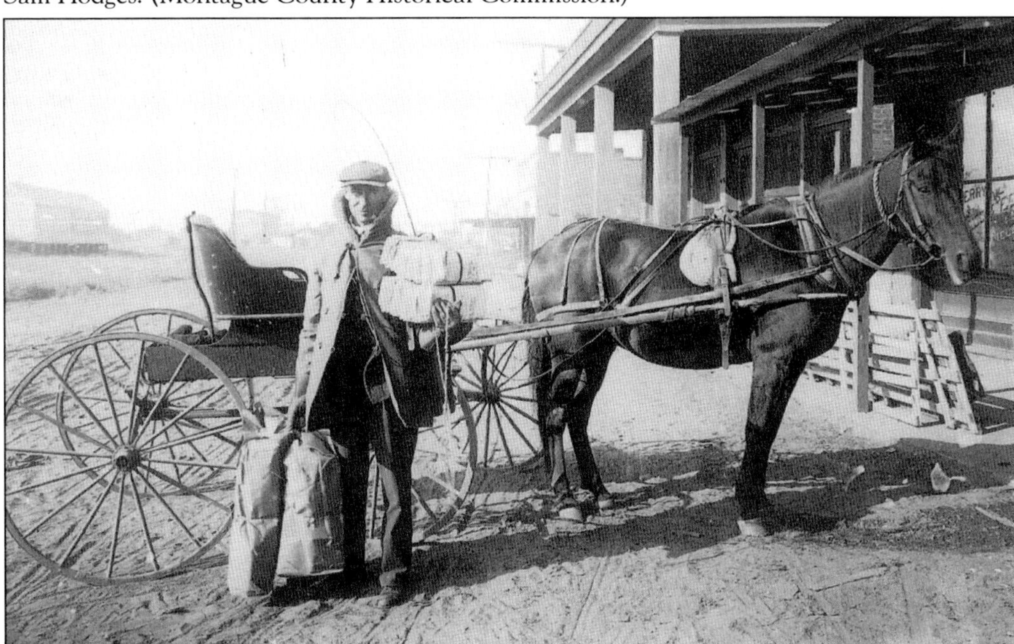

L.C. Stouder (above) was the first rural mail carrier in Nocona. He began delivering the mail to the outlying areas using a horse-drawn buggy in 1905. In 1915, Stouder purchased a motorized mail truck. During the 28 years that he was a rural carrier, he calculated that he opened and closed 85,960 gates and drove 230,250 miles. (TNT.)

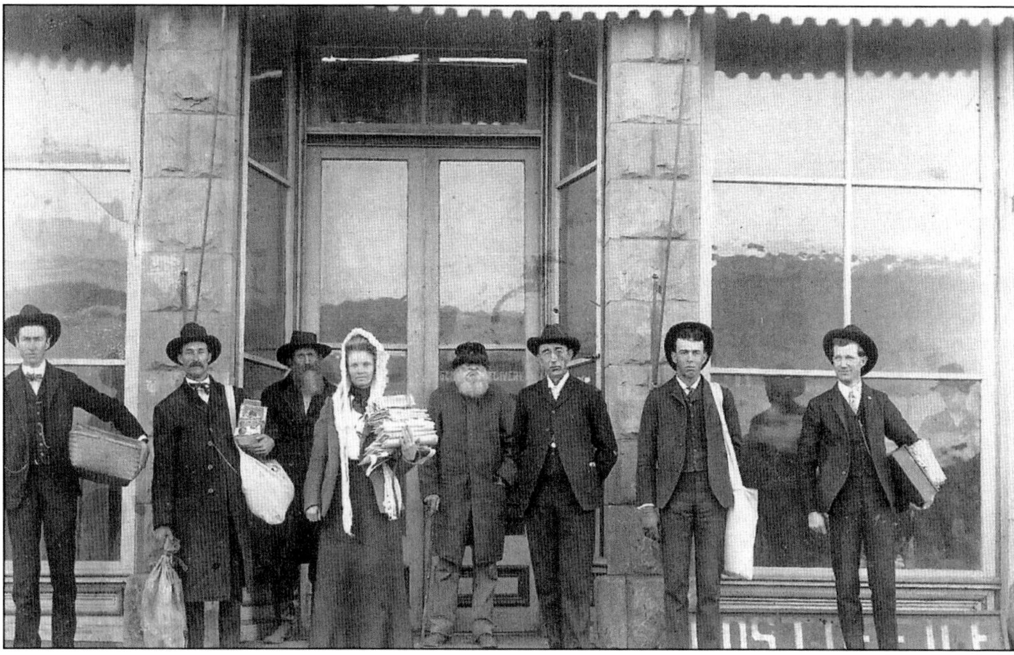

The demand for rural delivery grew enough to hire more carriers. Standing in front of the post office, are, from left to right, L.C. Stouder, rural one carrier; Z.W. Shackelford, route two carrier; James Davis, patron; Maggie Weiss, route three carrier; John McCall, patron; W.N. Merritt, postmaster; Ray Beal, route four carrier; and Ford Frey, route five carrier. (TNT.)

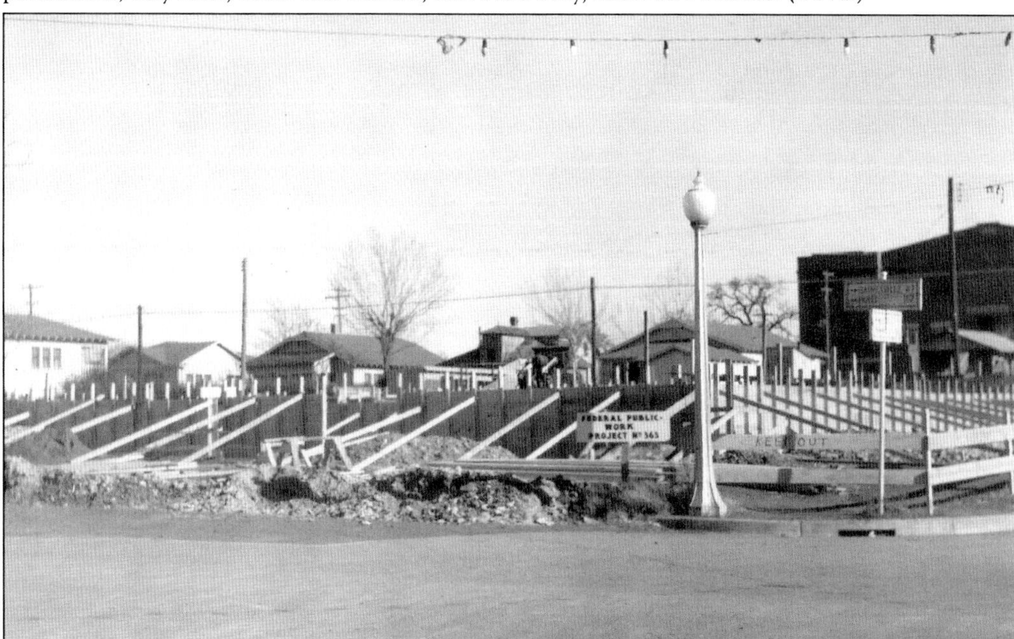

Construction of a new post office began as a Federal Public Works project on December 23, 1935, and was completed on July 23, 1936. The high school building can be seen in the background on the right. The street sign on the corner indicates that Gainesville and Paris, Texas, are located 47 and 152 miles, respectively, to the east. (TNT.)

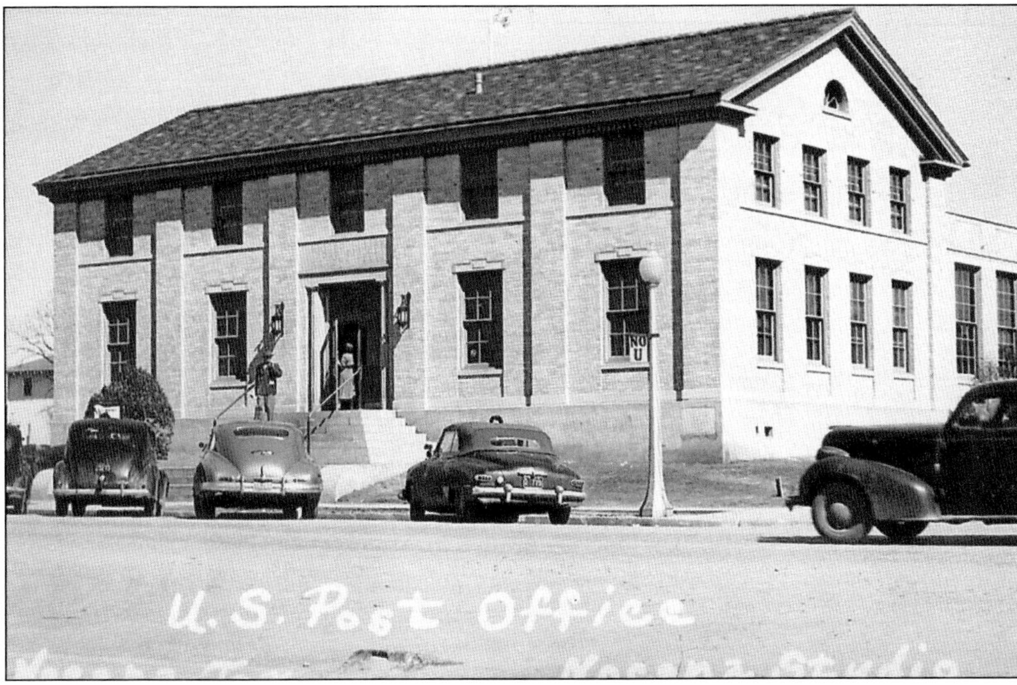

Construction of the new post office was completed on July 23, 1936, exactly six months from the day it was started. This photograph was taken shortly after the building was opened for business. The post office is still in operation in this building. It is located at 400 Clay Street. (TNT.)

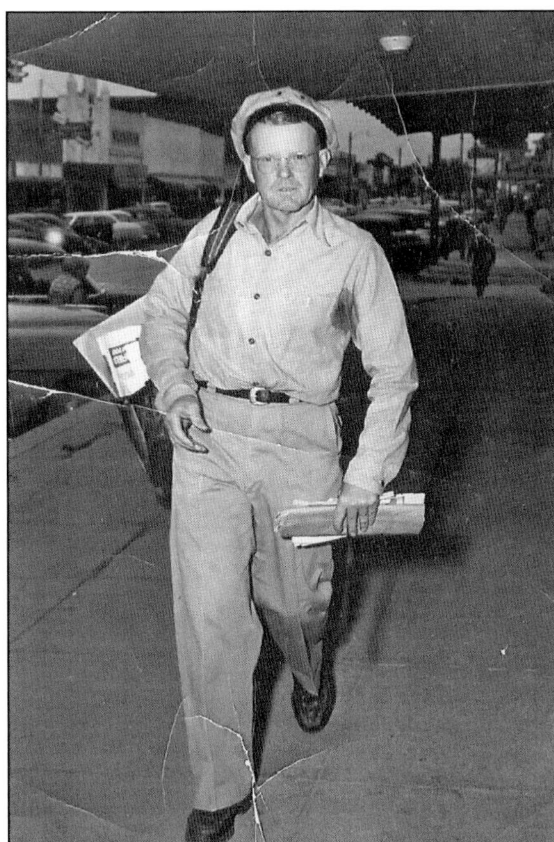

Dave Reed was the first city mail carrier in Nocona. This photograph of Reed was taken on the first day of this new service, October 1, 1949. Reed estimated he walked a total of 17 miles per day. He continued as the city carrier until he was appointed clerk. Reed retired from the post office in 1976. (TNT.)

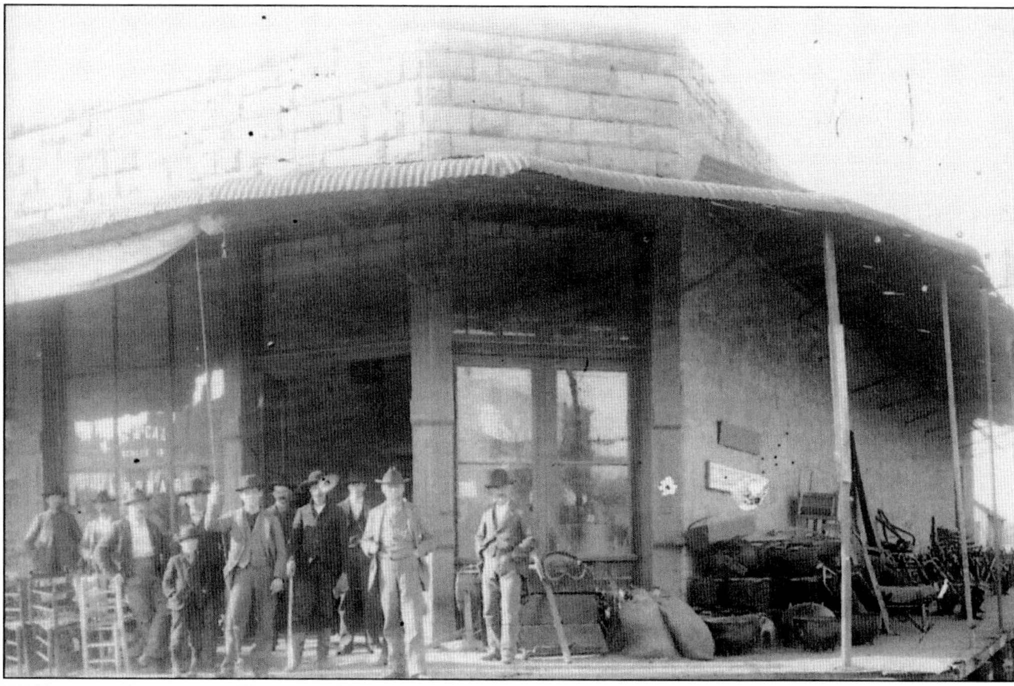

William Asbury McCall originally established his furniture and hardware store on Front Street in 1893. He later built this stone building on the corner of Clay and Oak Streets. Eventually he sold the business to Barlow and Harbour. In this photograph, many of his wares can be seen stacked against the wall. There are large cast iron wash tubs and plows along with several other items. (TNT.)

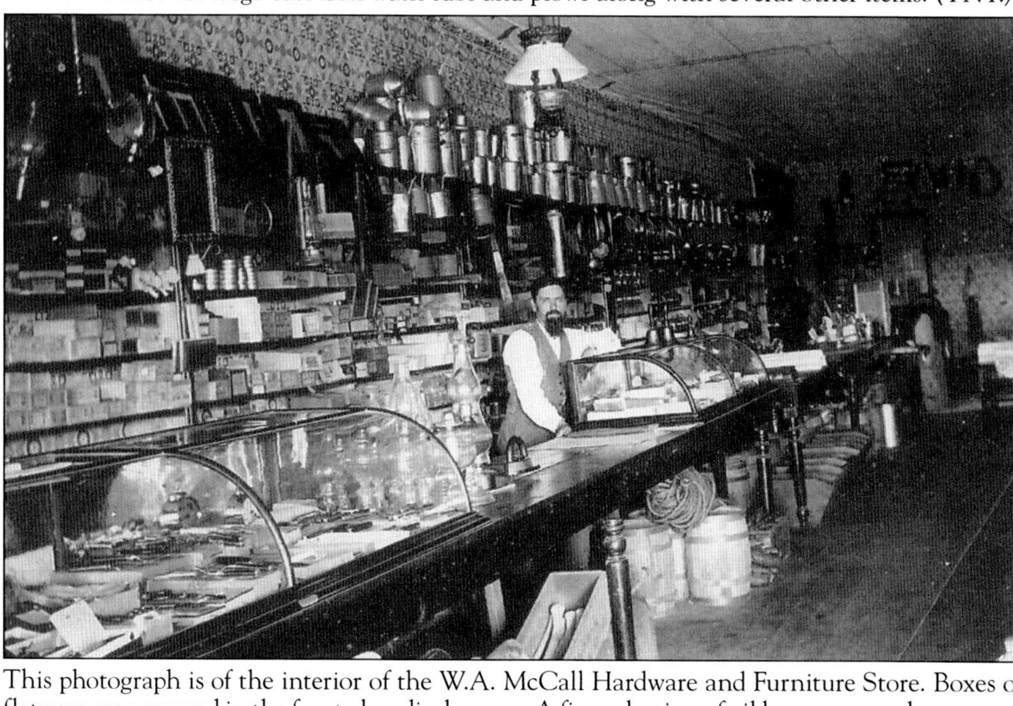

This photograph is of the interior of the W.A. McCall Hardware and Furniture Store. Boxes of flatware are arranged in the front glass display case. A fine selection of oil lamps are on the counter. In the bins and barrels beneath the counter are axes and various other hardware items. (TNT.)

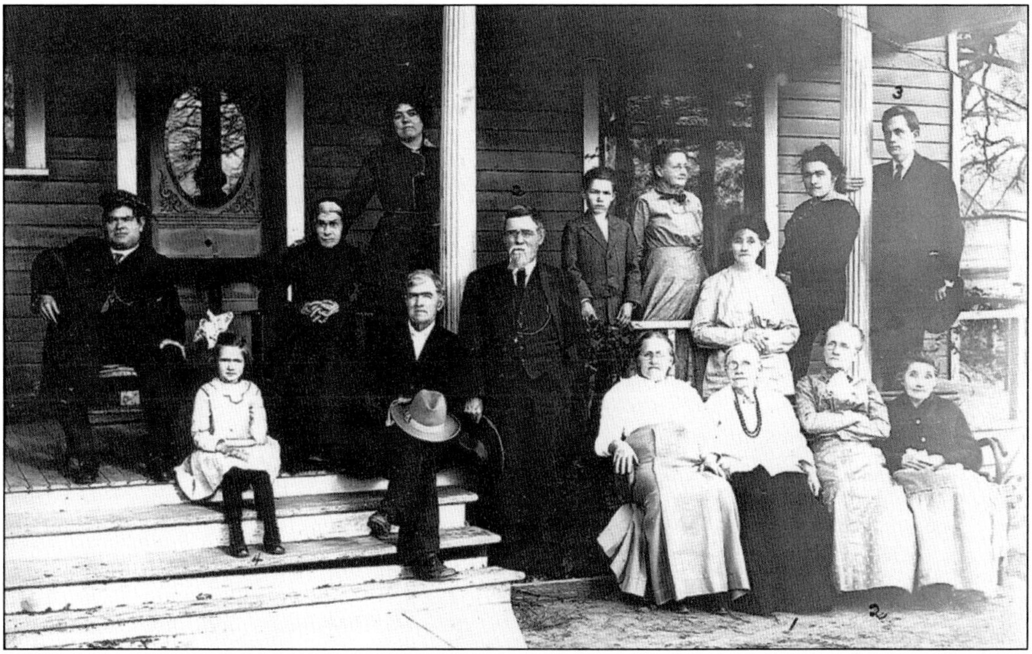

The McCall family came to Nocona in October 1889. The McCalls were extremely instrumental in forming the Farmers and Merchants Bank in Nocona. The family members posed in front of the McCall home are, from left to right, (first row) Ada ?, Mrs. Tobey, Mary Ellen Tobey McCall, and Jennie McCall Black; (second row) Mary Nell McCall Storey, J.N. McElwee, William Asbury McCall, and Nancy McCall McElwee; (third row) Gen. Price McCall, unidentified, Minnie Myrtle McElwee, James W. McCall, Mrs. Davis, Nell McGillicuddy McCall, and Cadmus McCall. William Asbury McCall (right) began buying property as soon as he arrived in Nocona. He purchased the majority of the block along today's Highway 82 bordered by Denton, Sherman, and East Mesquite Streets. Before establishing the bank, McCall owned and operated a hardware store. (Both, TNT.)

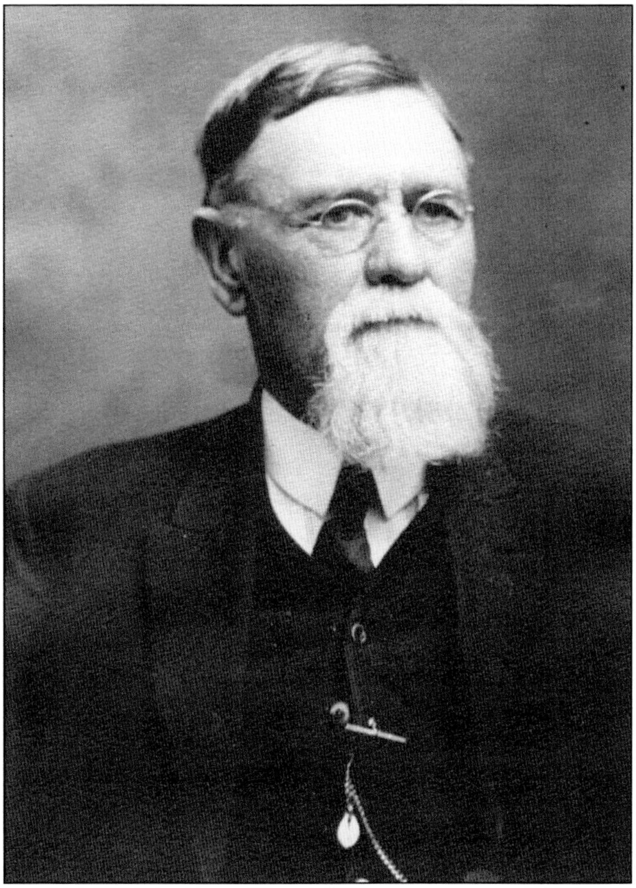

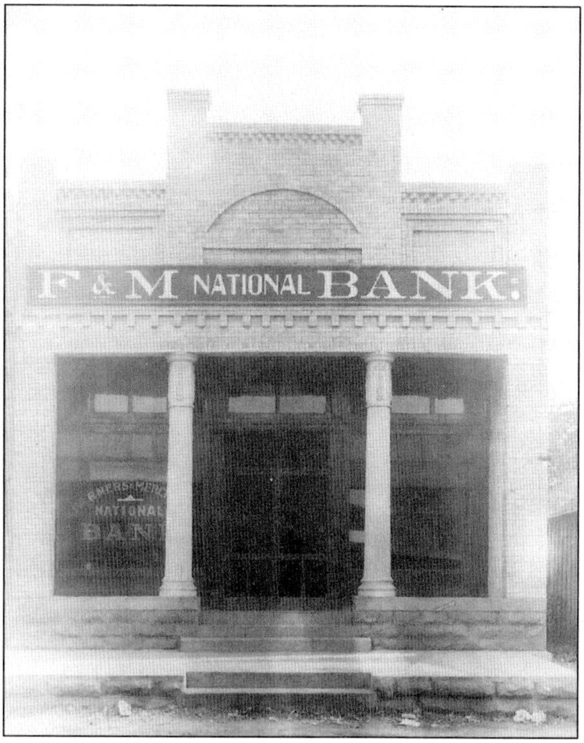

The Farmers and Merchants Bank was organized in 1905 by William Asbury McCall. He was the first president of the bank; his son Cadmus McCall was the vice president. J.A. Fooshee was also a vice president, and J.R. Modrall was the first cashier. The stockholders invested $30,000 in capital. (TNT.)

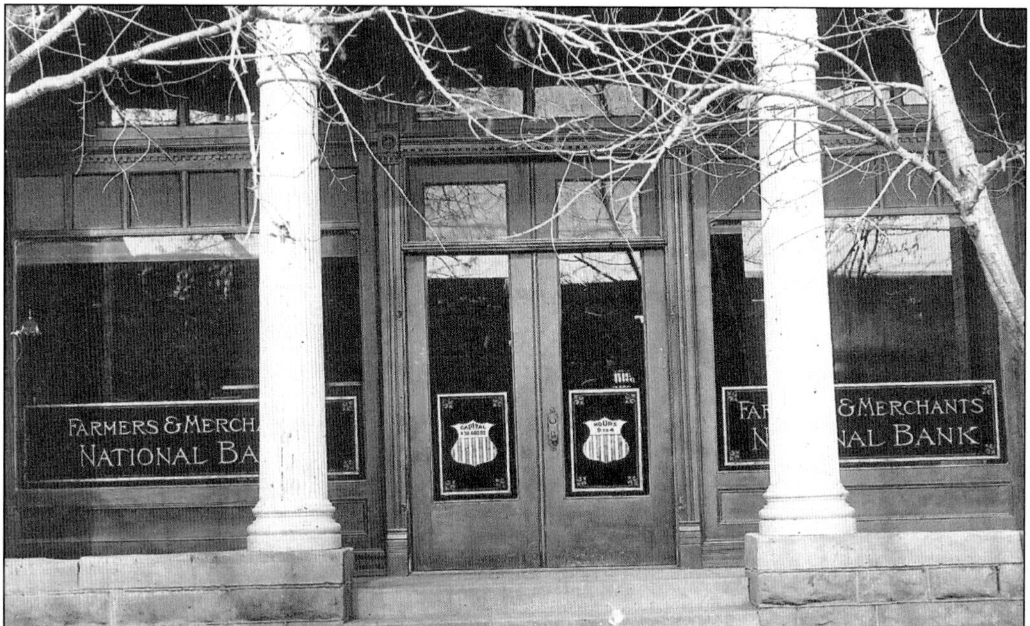

When the doors opened for the first day of business, five individuals and one store made deposits. The individuals were Mrs. J.A. Bartow, J.F. Barlow, Dr. Samuel Humphreys, William Asbury McCall, and J.R. Modrall. Humphreys, McCall, and Modrall were all stockholders of the bank. The one business deposit was made by Warren, Fooshee, and Moody General Store. Co-owner Fooshee was also a bank stockholder. (TNT.)

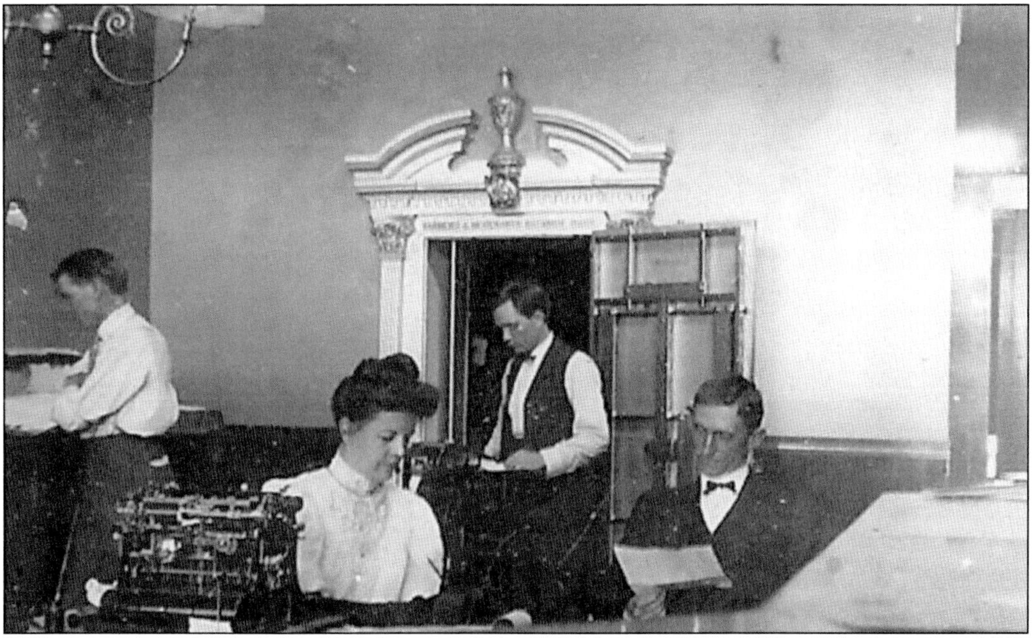

This photograph from the early 1900s shows the interior of the Farmers and Merchants Bank. Cadmus McCall can be seen standing in front of the vault door. J.R Modrall is the gentleman in the bow tie on the right. The woman is sitting behind a state-of-the-art typewriter of the time. (TNT.)

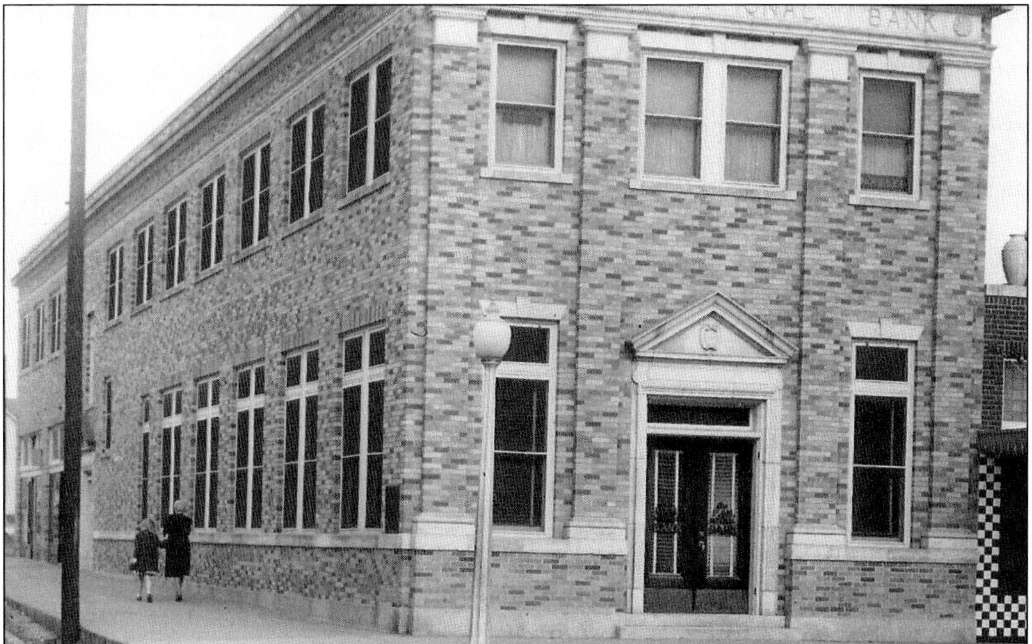

In 1926, the Farmers and Merchants Bank moved to this building. It was located at southeast corner of Elm and Clay Streets. In 1958, the bank occupied a portion of the building along with a beauty shop, an insurance agency, and the offices of Lesh and McCall, attorneys Earl Fitts and Glenn Wilson, Justice of the Peace D.M. Painter, Benton and Holmes, and the Nocona Chamber of Commerce. (TNT.)

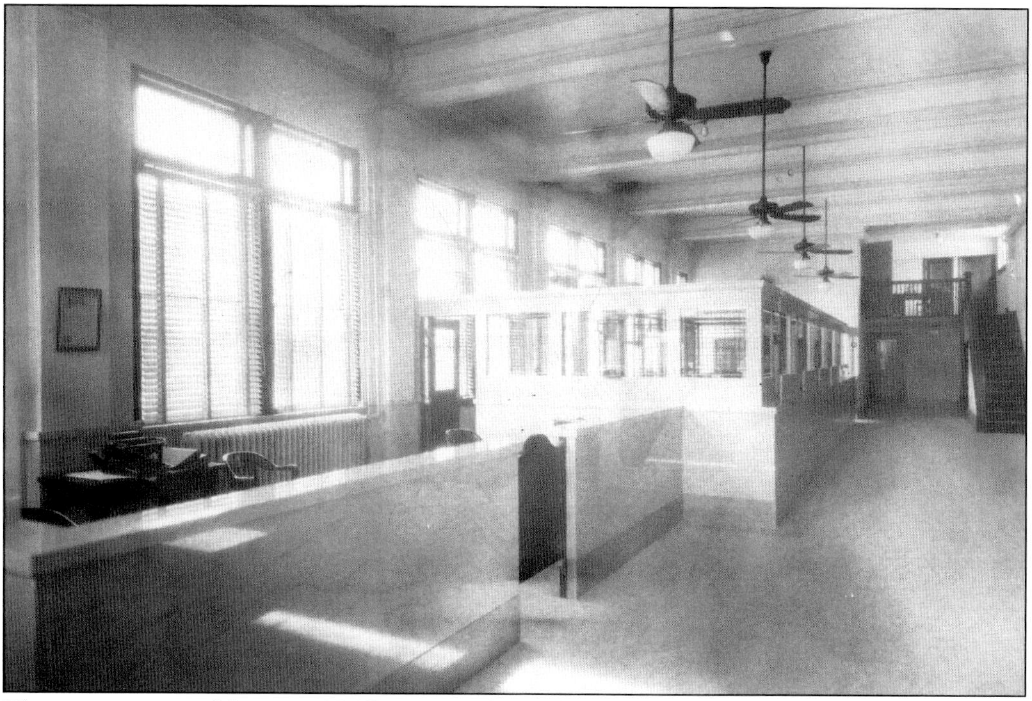

This interior view of the new 1926 Farmers and Merchants Bank showcases the sleek and modern decor after the remodel. The building was cooled and lit by the large ceiling fan light fixtures. Radiators were used to heat the massive building. One radiator is visible under the window in this photograph. (TNT.)

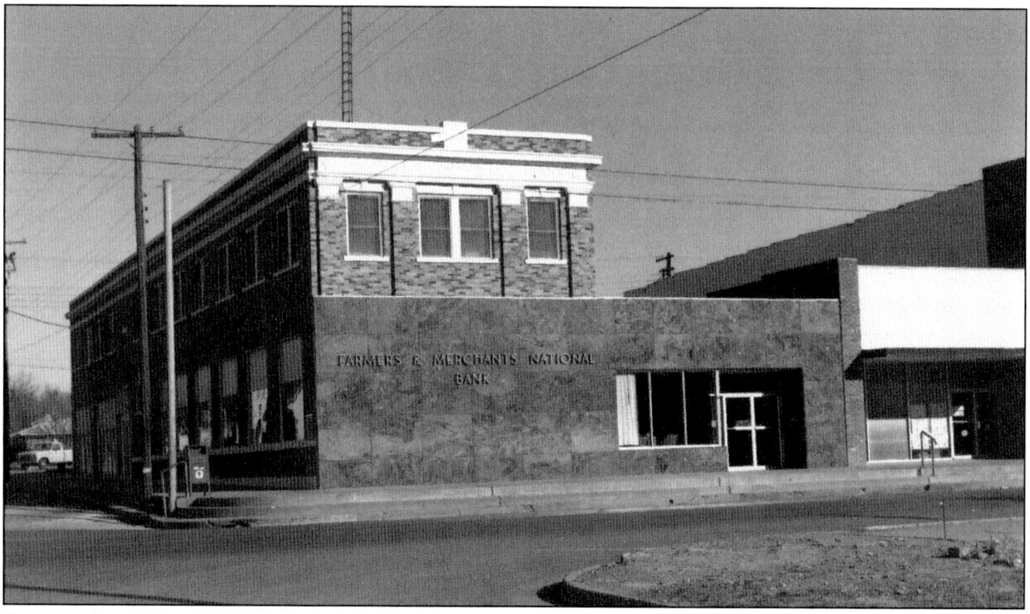

During the 1950s, the Farmers and Merchant Bank Building underwent a huge transformation. A sleek and modern marble facade was attached to the front exterior of the building. Double glass doors and windows were added. The marble was removed in 2006, and the building was restored to its original state. (TNT.)

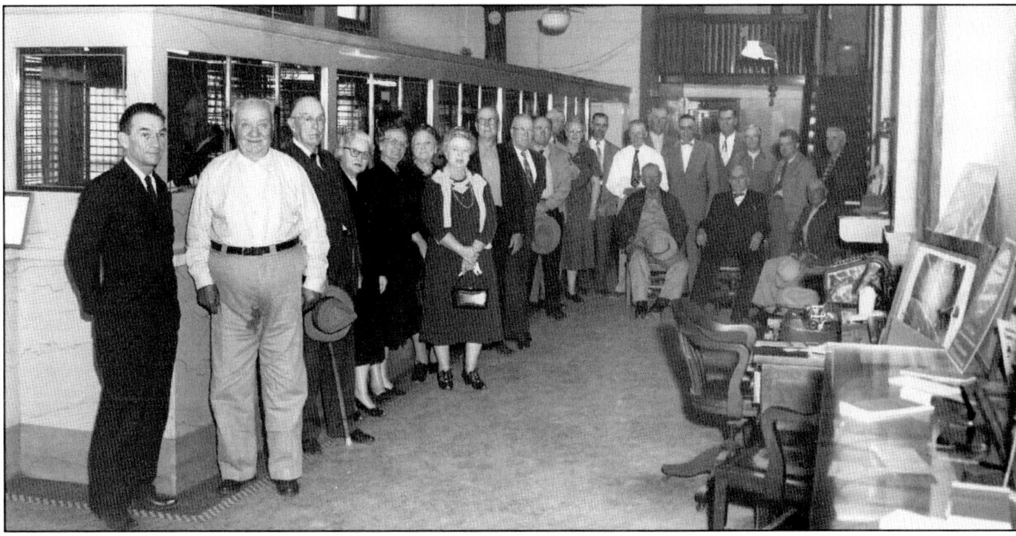

Several bank employees and patrons pose for these photographs. They are, from left to right, J.W. McCall, J.S. York, Ray Beal, Mrs. Ray Beal, Mrs. T.H. Ellis, Sallie Temple, Lena Ruth Gilbert, Grady Fooshee, M.M. Gilbert, Glenn O. Wilson, W.L. Scott, Enid Justin, Willard Grigsby, Atlas Gilbert, Roy C. Fitts, W.F. Leonard, J.D. McElhannon, Hardy Seay, S.W. Driver, and John Reeves. Individuals seated are, from left to right, Ed Hinton, A.D. Lunn, and Bailey Gist (above). Prominent citizen and local businesswoman Enid Justin (below) queues up at the counter to conduct daily business transactions. The gentleman facing the camera is W.L. Scott, and the last gentleman in line is S.W. Driver. (Both, TNT.)

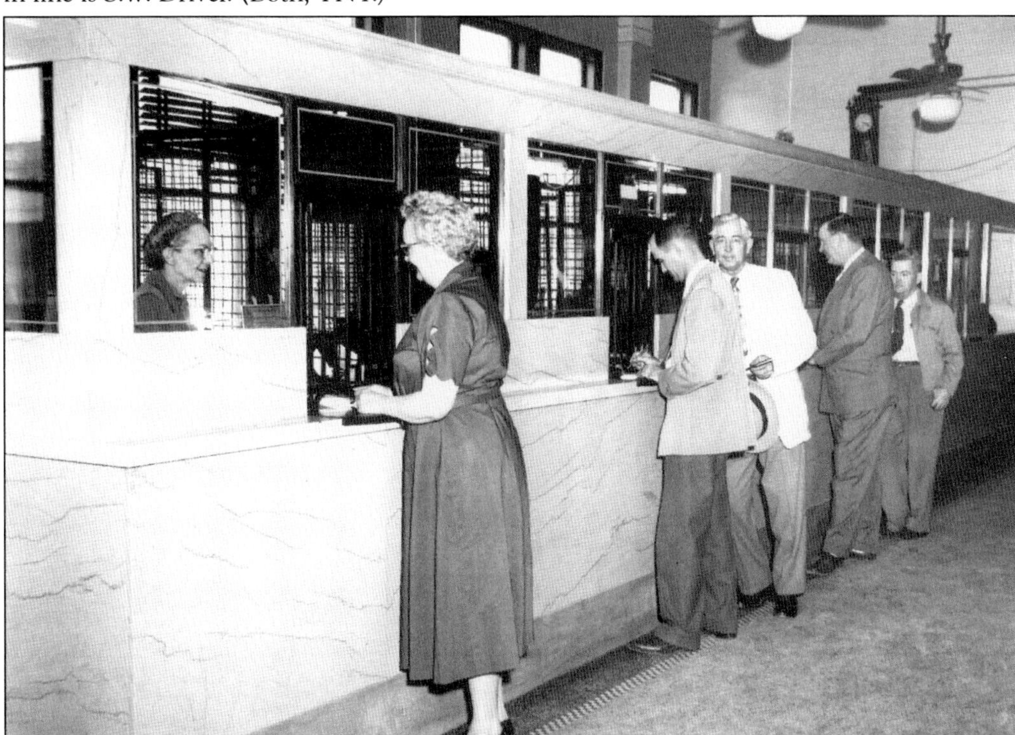

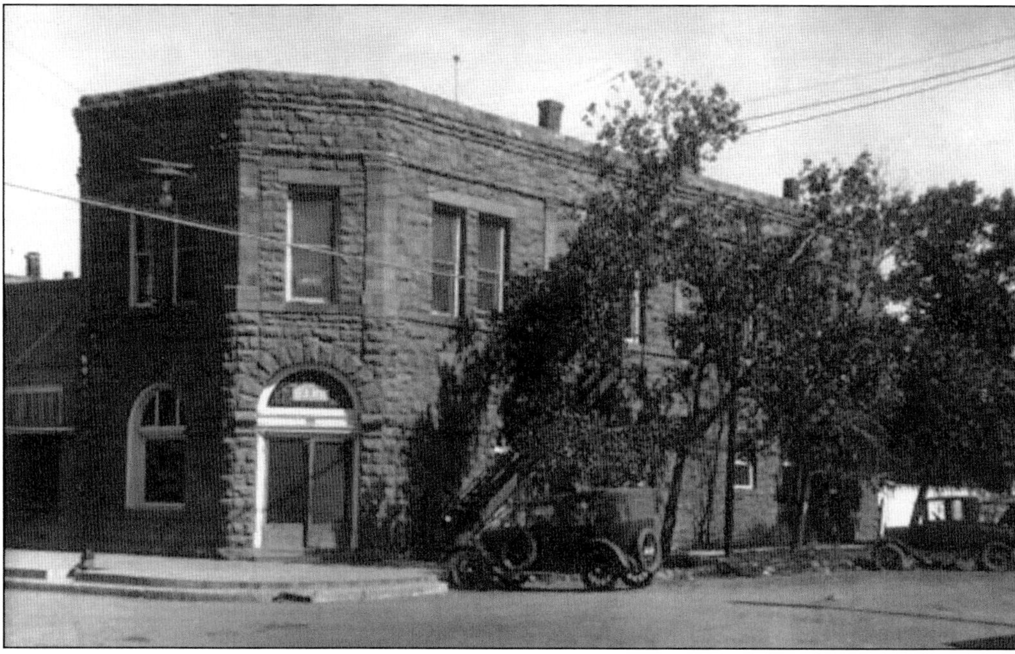

The Peoples National Bank was established in this building in Nocona in 1920. The building is located on the northeast corner of Clay and Elm Streets (above). The bank operated in this structure until 1949, when the second floor was removed, the south and west sides were bricked, and the entire building was remodeled. G.M. Utt was the first president of the bank. In later years, the Peoples National Bank moved across the street from the original building into this more modern facility (below) at southwest corner of Clay and Elm Streets. (Both, TNT.)

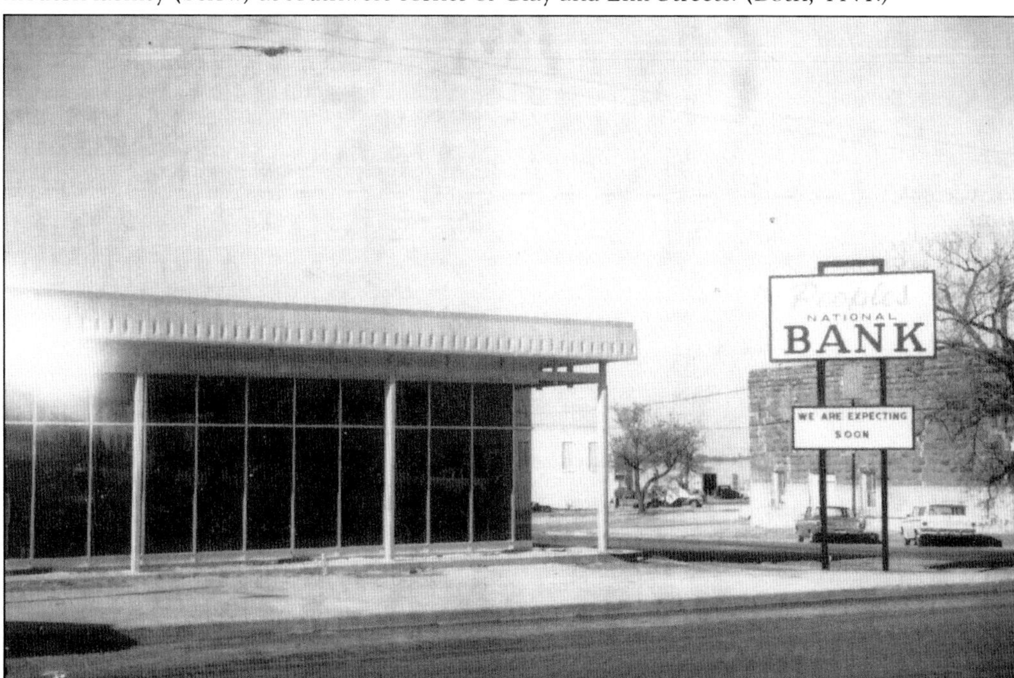

One of the first barbers in Nocona was W.T. Russell (right). Russell later became an attorney and the county judge. He is the barber at the first chair (below). There are many interesting details in the 1900 photograph. The barber chairs are made of wood in very ornate fashion. The cupboard on the back wall holds individual shaving mugs and brushes. The light fixtures on the wall and ceiling are gas lanterns. In the back right corner, the large potbellied stove that was used to heat the building can be seen. (Both, Montague County Historical Commission.)

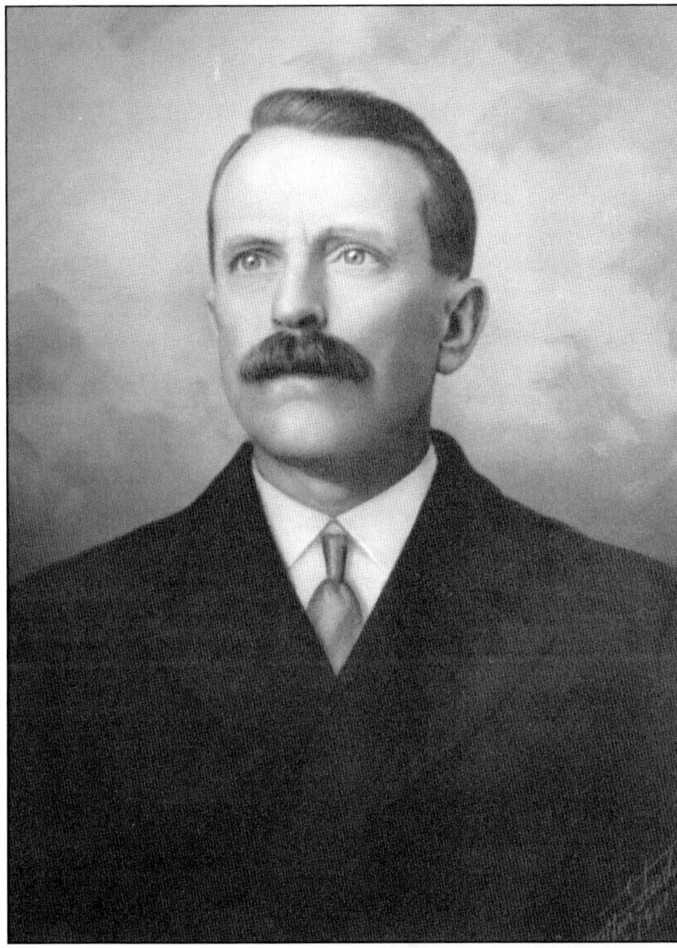

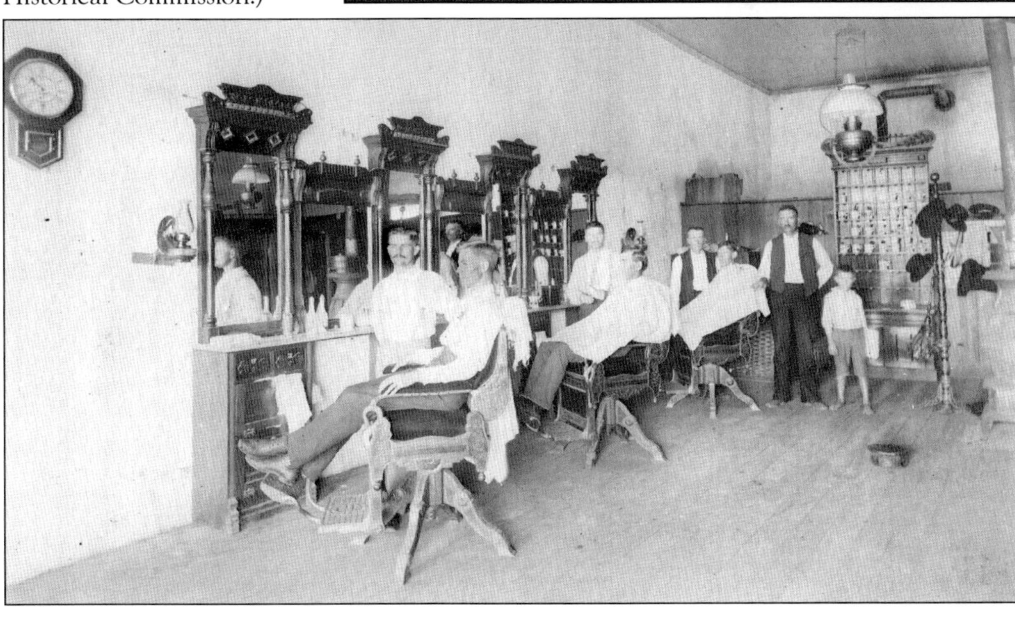

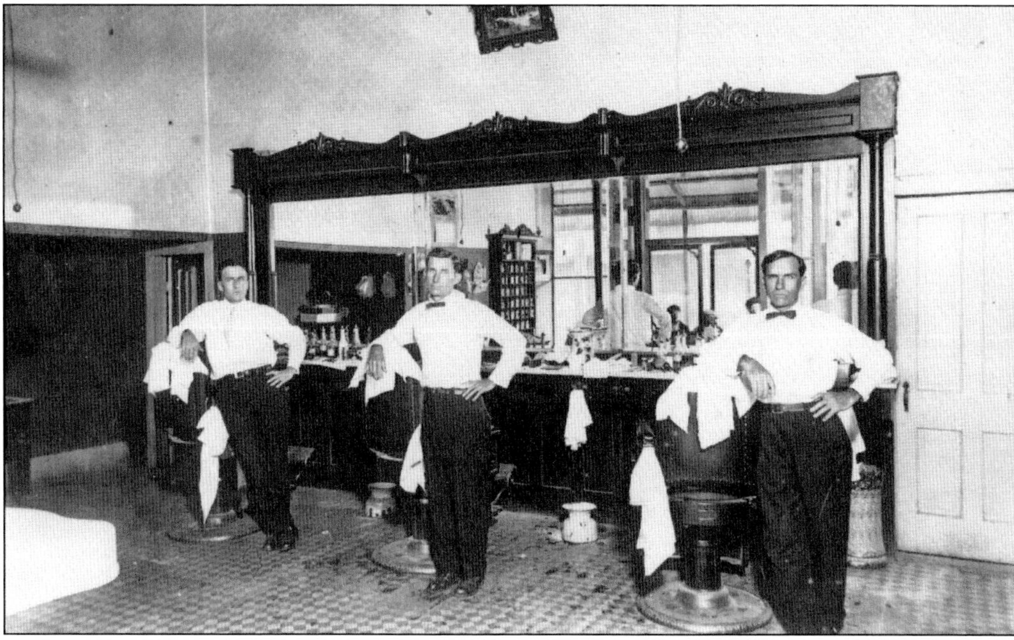

This photograph of a Nocona barbershop is from around 1910. Each barber chair, for the convenience of the shop's patrons, provides spittoons. In the mirror's reflection, customers waiting for their turn can be seen. Also seen in the reflection is the cupboard holding shaving mugs and brushes. The barbers each have a selection of ointments and tonics lined along the counter. (TNT.)

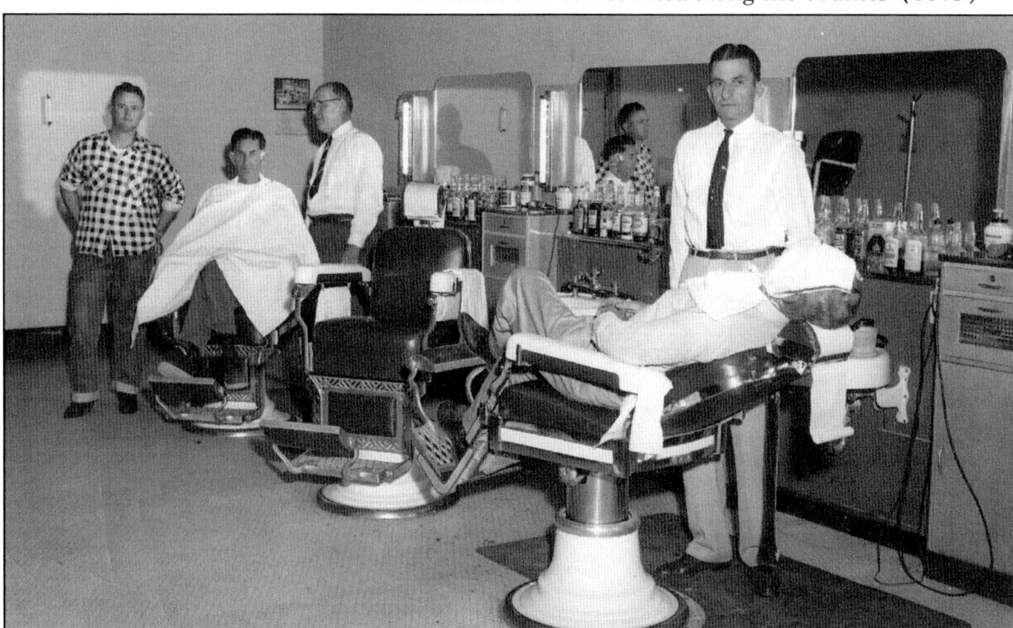

This photograph shows the interior of the City Barbershop, owned by B.T. "Fat" Edward. This was a full-service establishment, offering haircuts as well as shaves. The barbershop operated for many years on the ground floor of the Fillmore Hotel on Clay Street. The barbers and patrons shown here are, from left to right, Bobby Ray Pollard, unidentified, B.T. Edwards, Gude McClanahan, and unidentified. (TNT.)

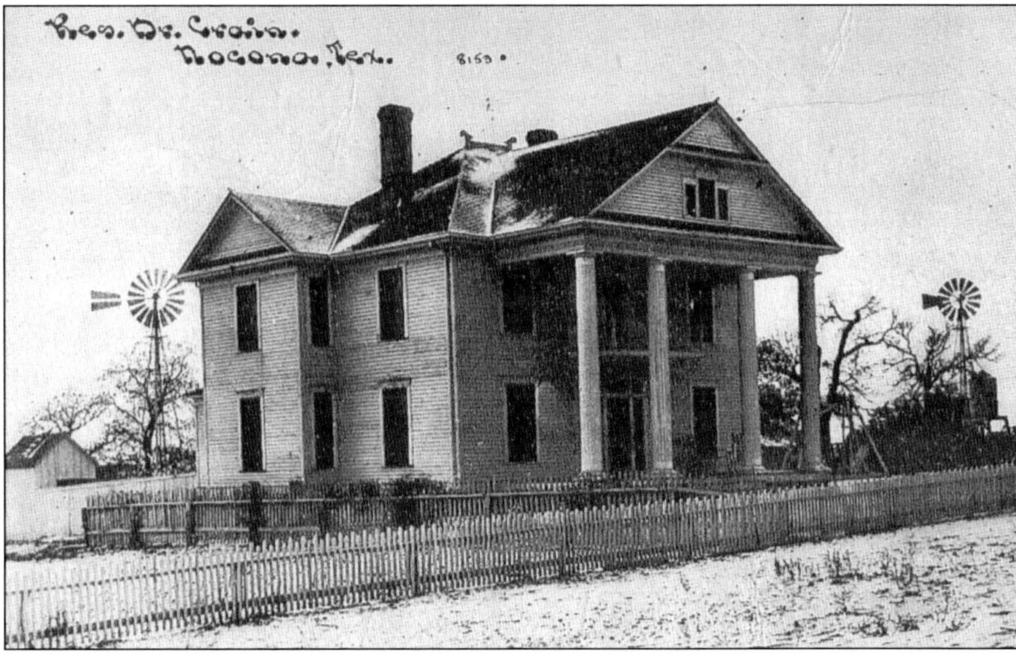

This photograph shows the residence of Dr. Newell Walton Crain. Dr. Crain graduated from Missouri Medical College in 1889. He had a medical practice in Denton, Texas, before moving to Nocona in 1906, when he joined forces with Dr. Henry F. Wilton. The doctors remained business partners until 1920. Dr. Crain served as the county health officer for a number of years. (TNT.)

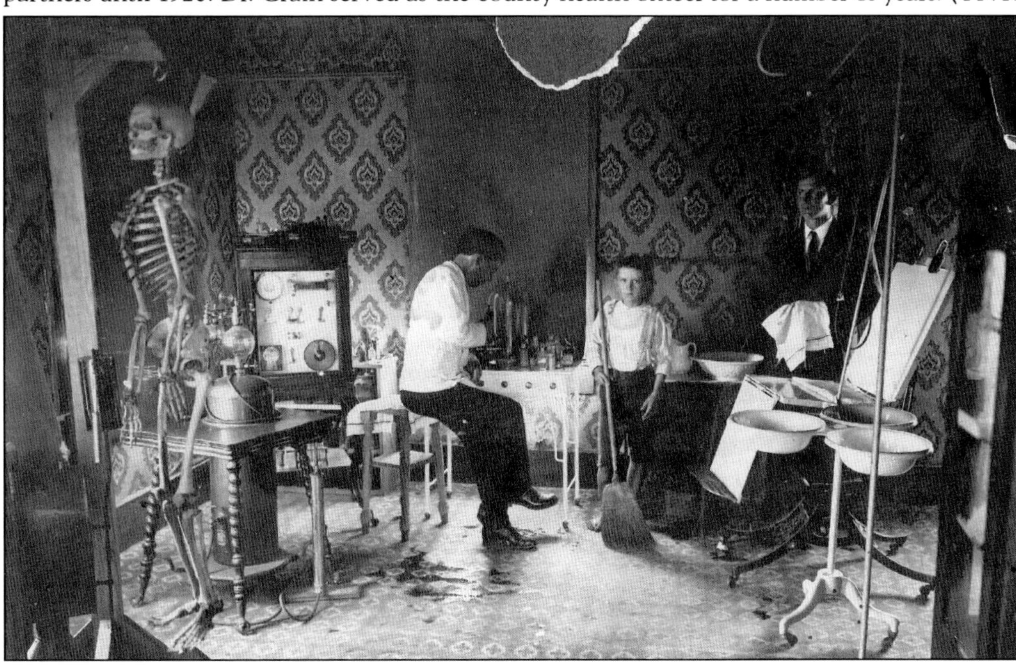

Dr. Samuel Thomas Humphreys (seated) came to Nocona in 1895 after finishing medical school. This photograph shows the interior of his examining room. The identity of the young boy is not known. Dr. Miller can be seen standing in the back right corner. In 1934, Dr. Humphreys died while performing a tonsillectomy, and Dr. D.W. Gunn was called in to complete the procedure. (TNT.)

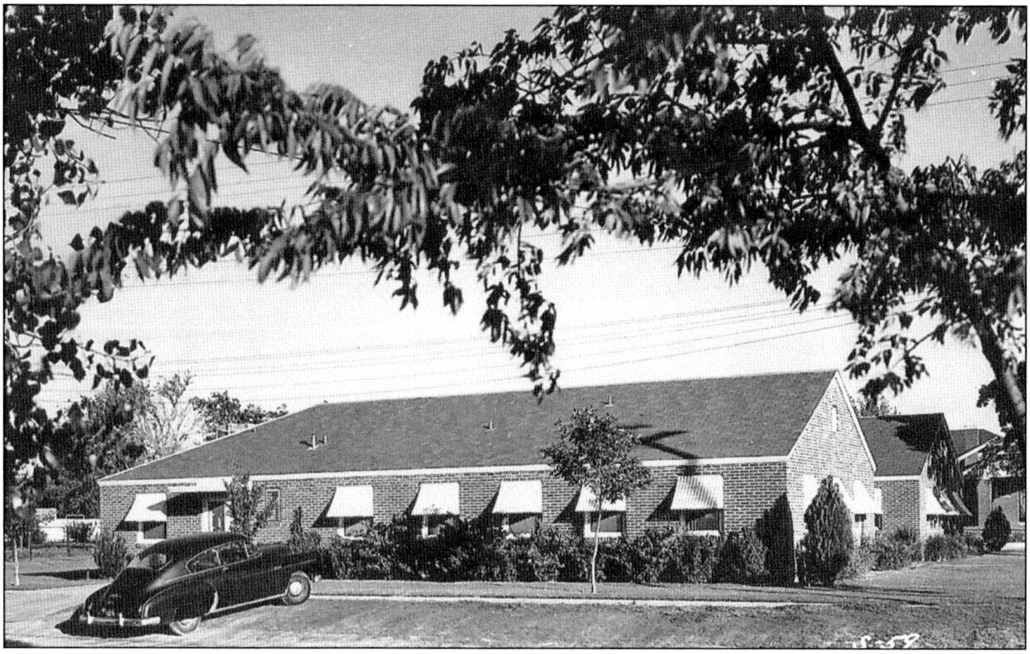

The Major Clinic was established in 1945. Dr. David Major and his four sons, Dr. A.D. Major, Dr. John Major, Dr. Robert Major, and M.H. Major, built the small hospital. It was expanded in 1956 to an 18-patient facility. The hospital was also used as a training facility for new doctors. (TNT.)

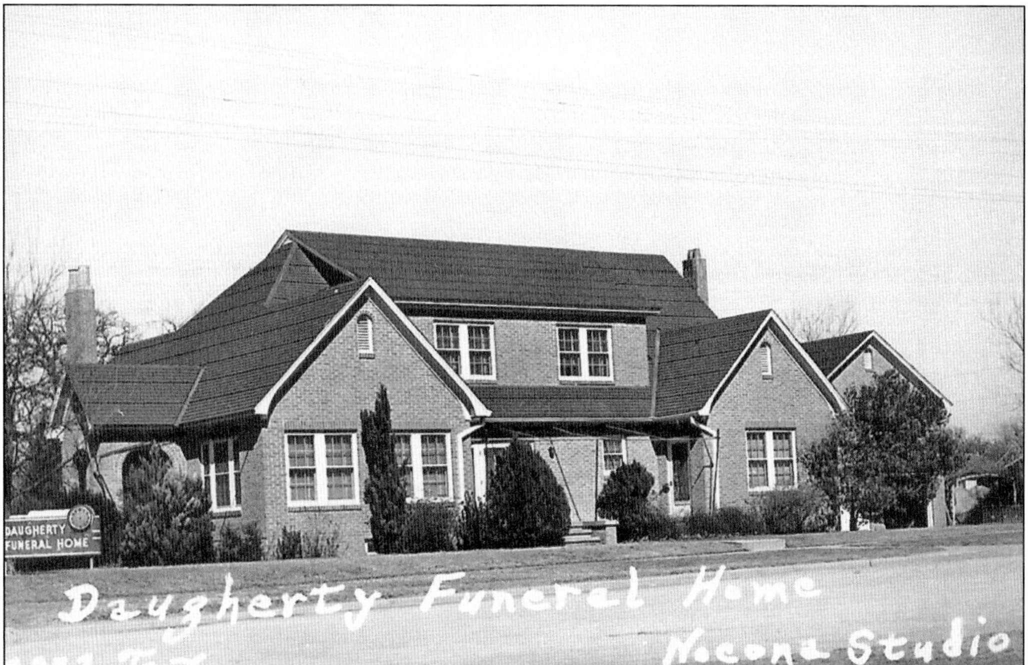

Daughtery Funeral Home was owned and operated by brothers James and Earl Daughtery. The funeral home changed owners in 1968, when it was purchased by James McGaughy. In 1975, Jerry and Paula Wood bought the business. At age 9, current owner Wood worked for Daughtery, the original owner, mowing the lawn at the funeral home. (TNT.)

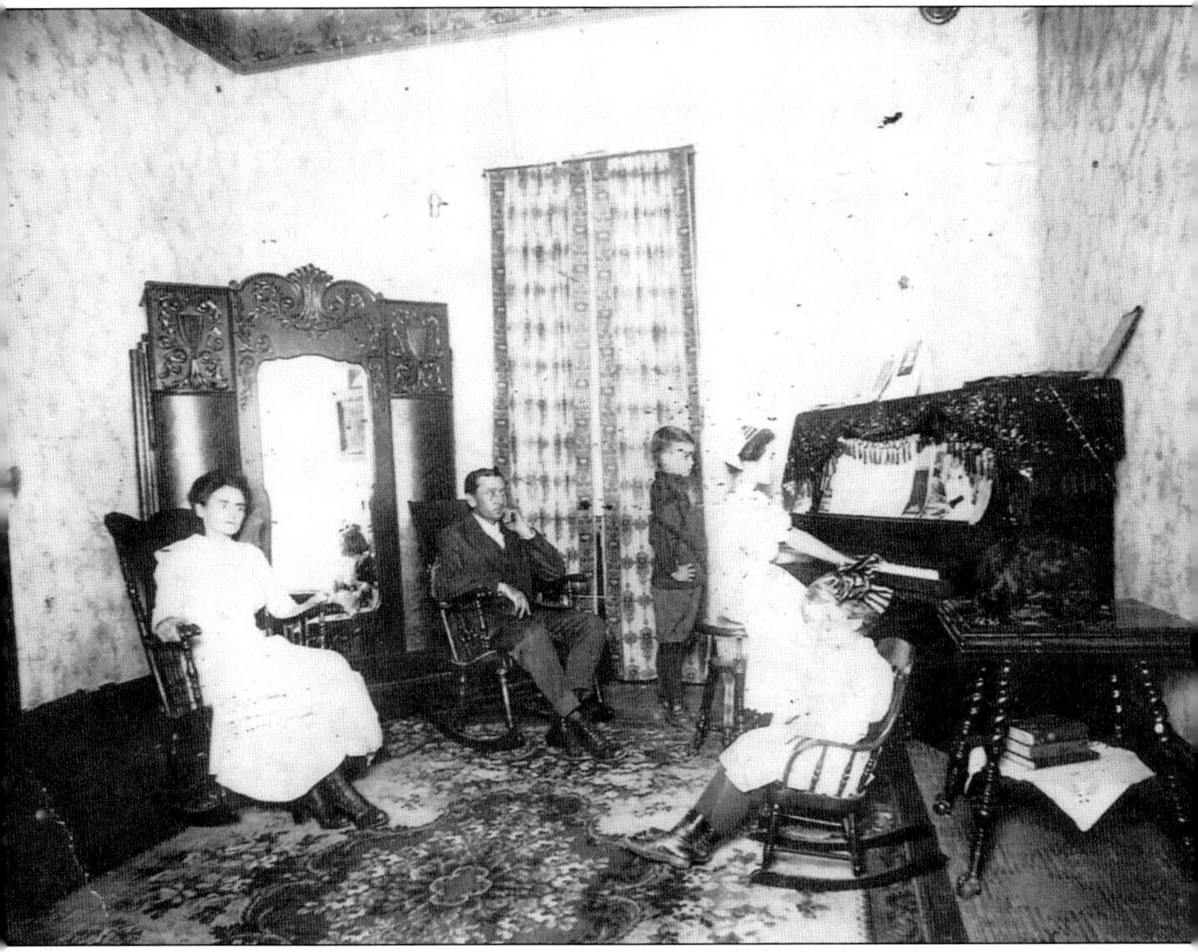

This photograph shows the interior of the Virginia House, which was built in 1888. The Virginia House was a hotel owned by the Pribble family. The hotel had 23 rooms that let for a quarter a day. This grand old structure was located on the northwest corner of Clay and Elm Streets. It was destroyed after it fell into irreversible disrepair. (TNT.)

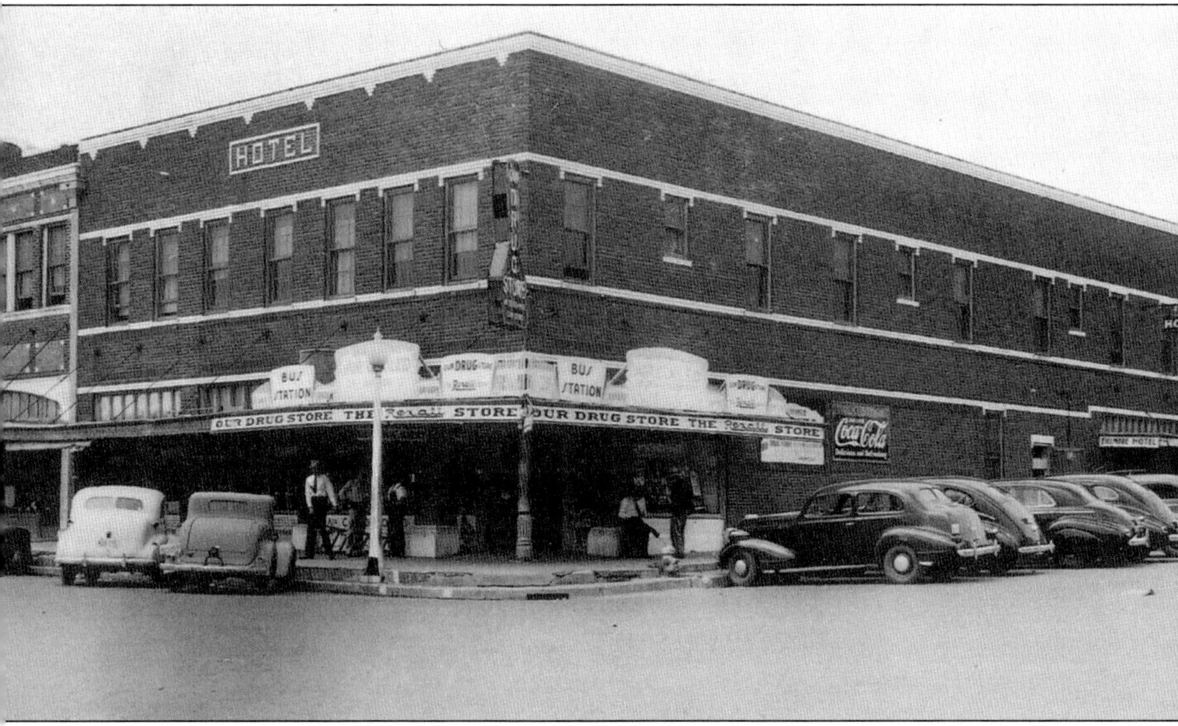

Millard Fillmore Ball opened the Fillmore Hotel on November 18, 1924. It was located on the southeast corner of Clay and Elm Streets. The hotel was equipped with all of the latest state-of-the-art conveniences, such as steam heat, electric lights, and hot and cold running water. The Ball family lived in the hotel. Ball's grandson Cecil Fenoglio was born in room No. 1 in the hotel. (TNT.)

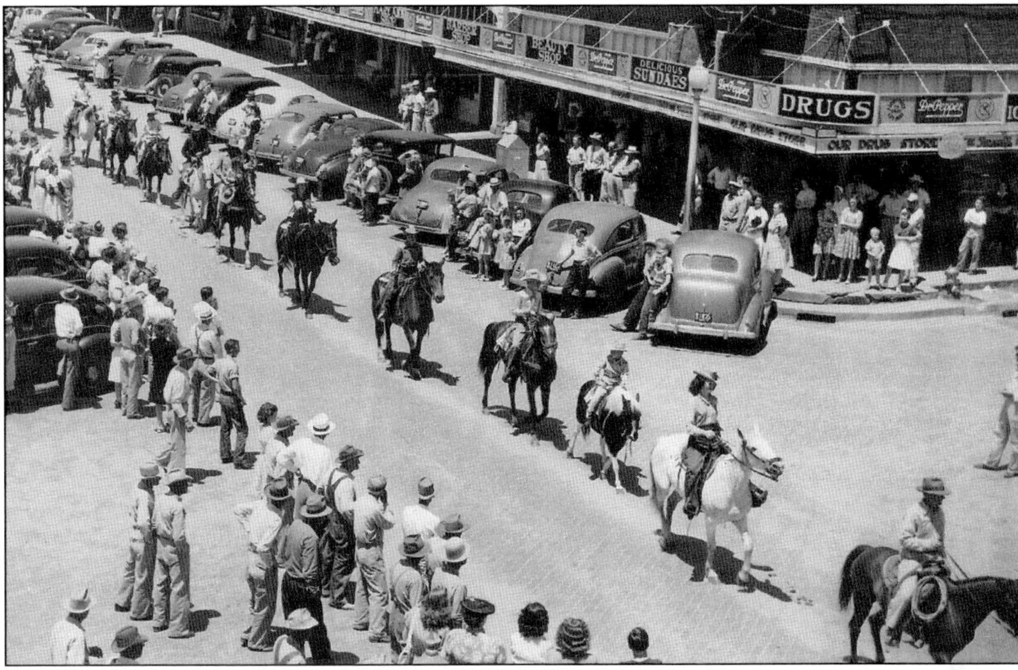

The massive ground floor of the Fillmore Hotel housed more than just the hotel's lobby. B.T. "Fat" Edwards's barbershop and A. Billings's drugstore were located there as well. Later, Mary Ann's Beauty Shop operated from there, too. The large corner on which the hotel was located made it an excellent vantage point from which to watch parades. (TNT.)

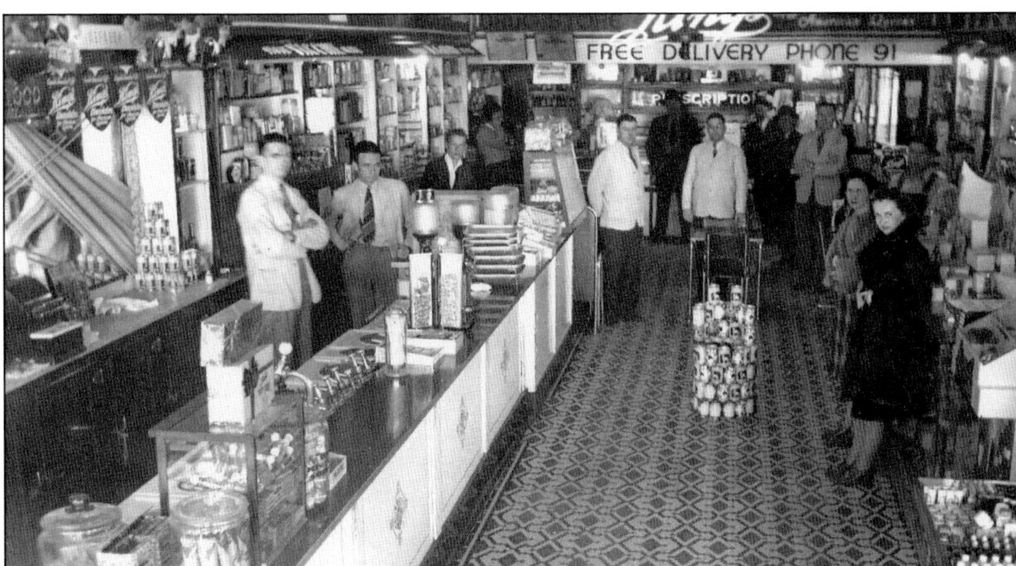

A. Billings owned and operated Our Drugstore on the first floor of the Fillmore Hotel. As the sign reads in the back of the store, the Our Drug offered free delivery by calling phone 91. The drugstore also had a soda fountain. The trays stacked on the counter were used to deliver meals to cars waiting curb side. (TNT.)

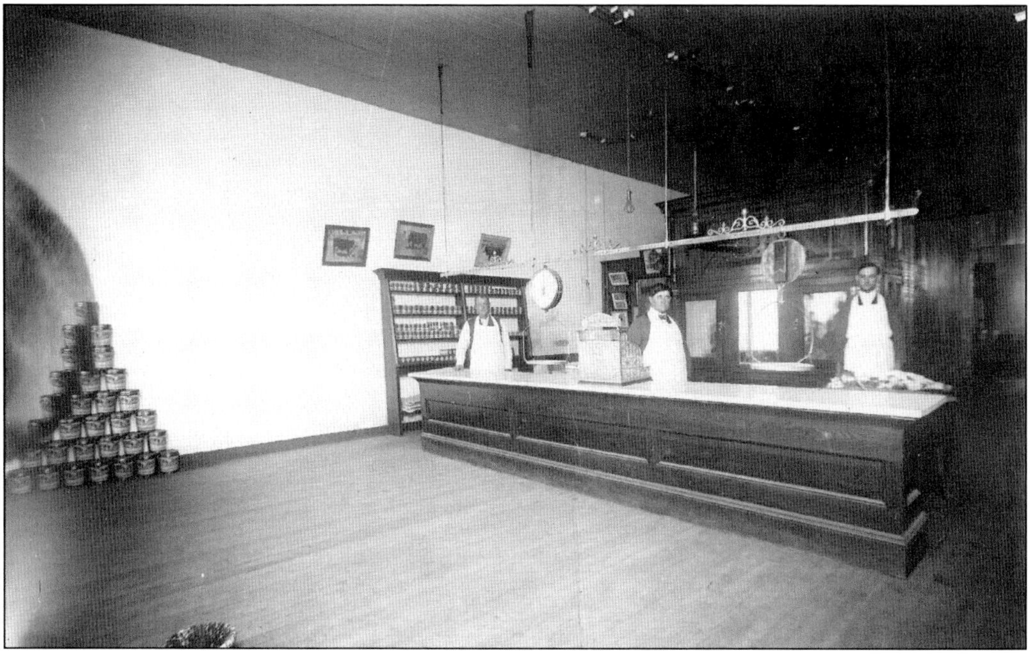

Millard Fillmore Ball (center) established a meat market in Nocona in the early 1900s. It was located at 309 Clay Street. The spittoon was placed in the middle of the floor to eliminate the possibility of accidently hitting the meat counter. The two scales hanging over the counter were used to weigh meat for the customers. (Cecil Fenoglio.)

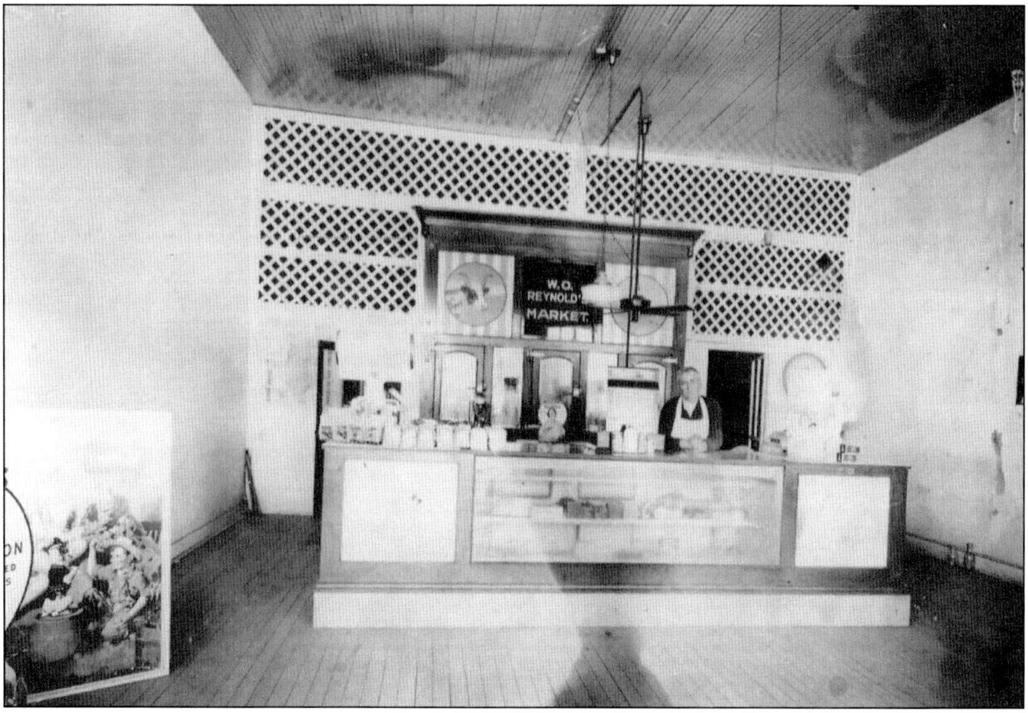

W.O. Reynolds also owned and operated a meat market, believed to be on Clay Street. On the counter are heavy scales for weighing portions of the clientele. (Dan Fenoglio.)

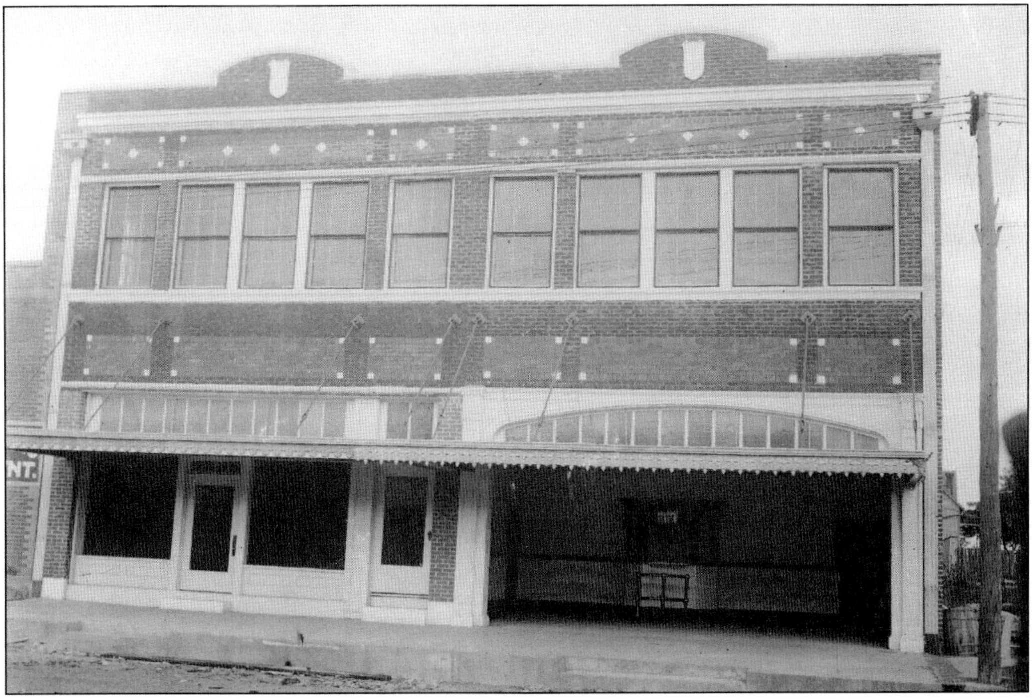

In 1920, Millard Fillmore Ball built the Millstone Theater on Clay Street. Ball's family had operated a mill in Eagle Point prior to moving to Nocona. When Ball constructed the new theater, he had a portion of the millstone imbedded in the pavement in front of the building. The millstone is still visible today. (Cecil Fenoglio.)

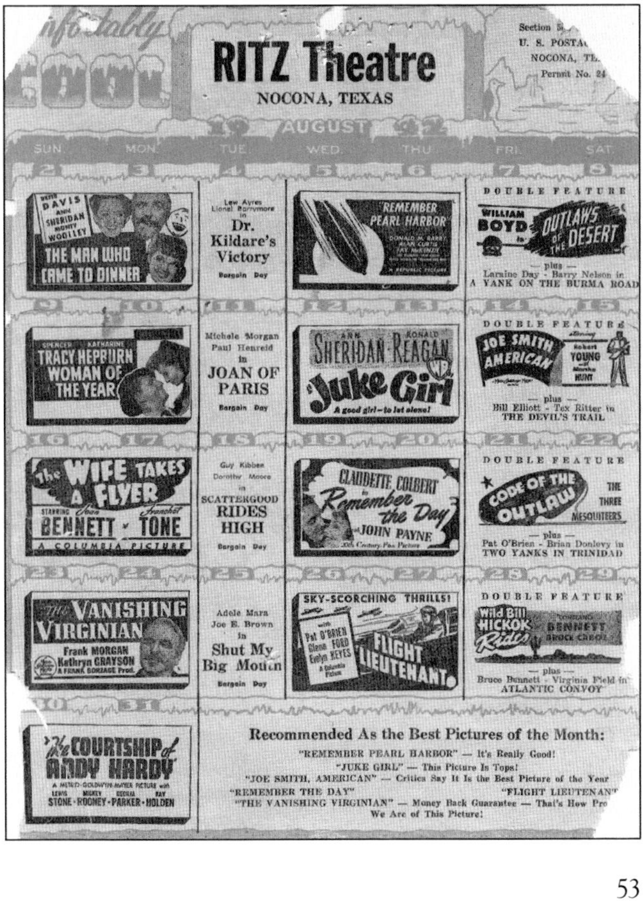

The Ritz Theater was opened on November 10, 1939. It was managed by Jerry and Bonnie Stout and owned by Clinton Bailey. This August 1942 advertisement lists picture shows starring big names such as Bette Davis, Spencer Tracy, and Katherine Hepburn. On Friday and Saturday, the Ritz offered double features. (TNT.)

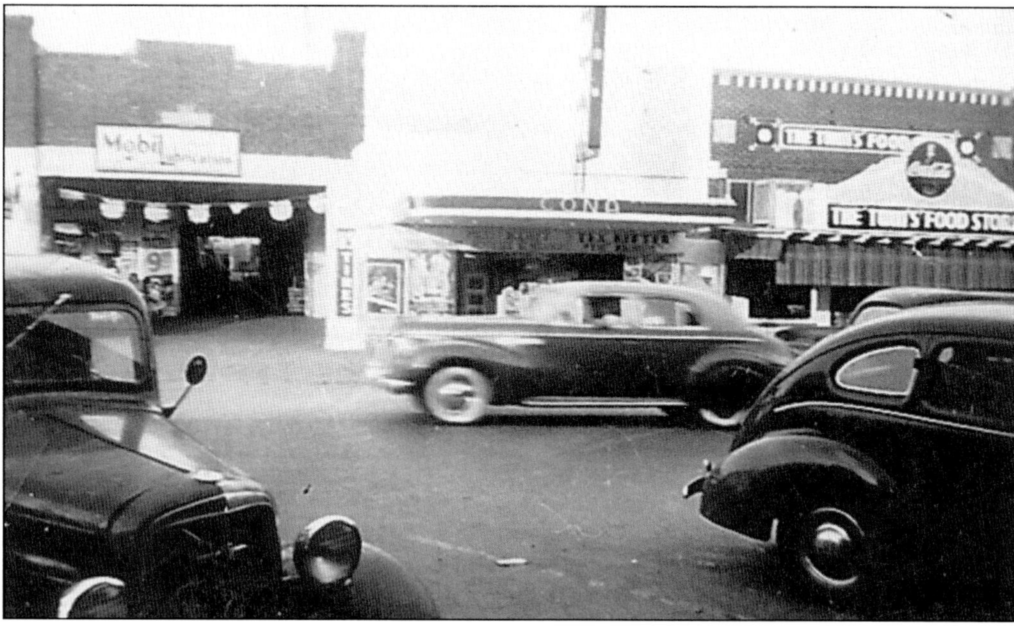

The Cona Theater was located on Clay Street. It was also owned by Clinton Bailey. Bailey owned and operated the Ritz, Roxy, and Cona Theaters simultaneously. Bailey, along with C.E. Campbell, built the Chief Drive-in Movie in 1949. The drive-in was in operation through the early 1970s. (TNT.)

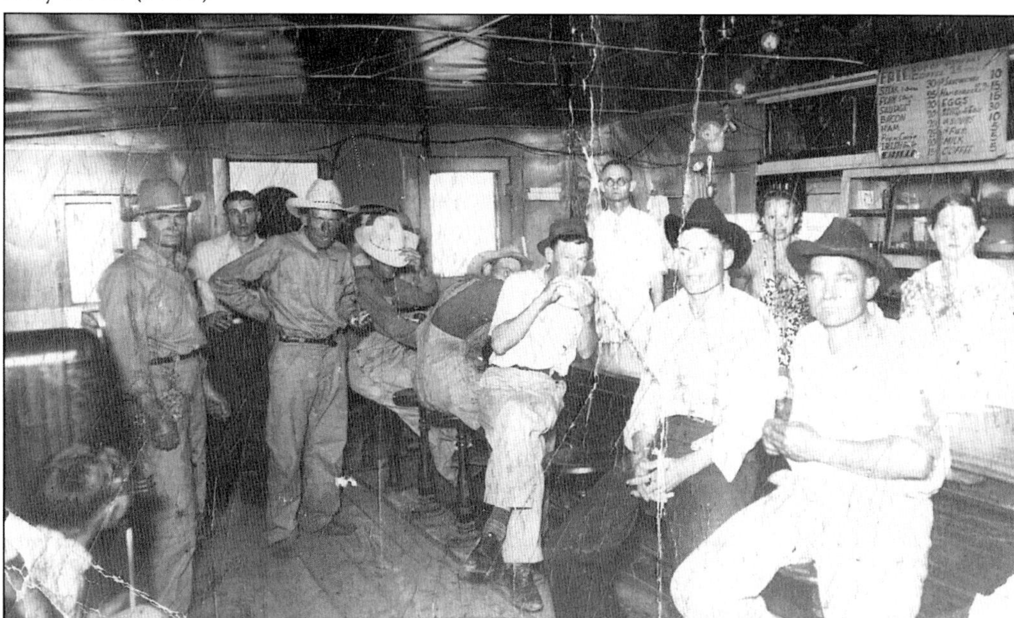

This 1940 photograph depicts the interior of the Walter Shelton's Chinatown Café. The prices on the wallboard menu reflect the Depression-racked economy. One could purchase a T-bone steak for 30¢ or a hamburger for 15¢. Those patronizing the café that day were, from left to right, Wade Shelton, unidentified, Birdie Rich, three unidentified, Mose Cochran, Walter Shelton, two unidentified, and Blanche Howell. (Wade Shelton.)

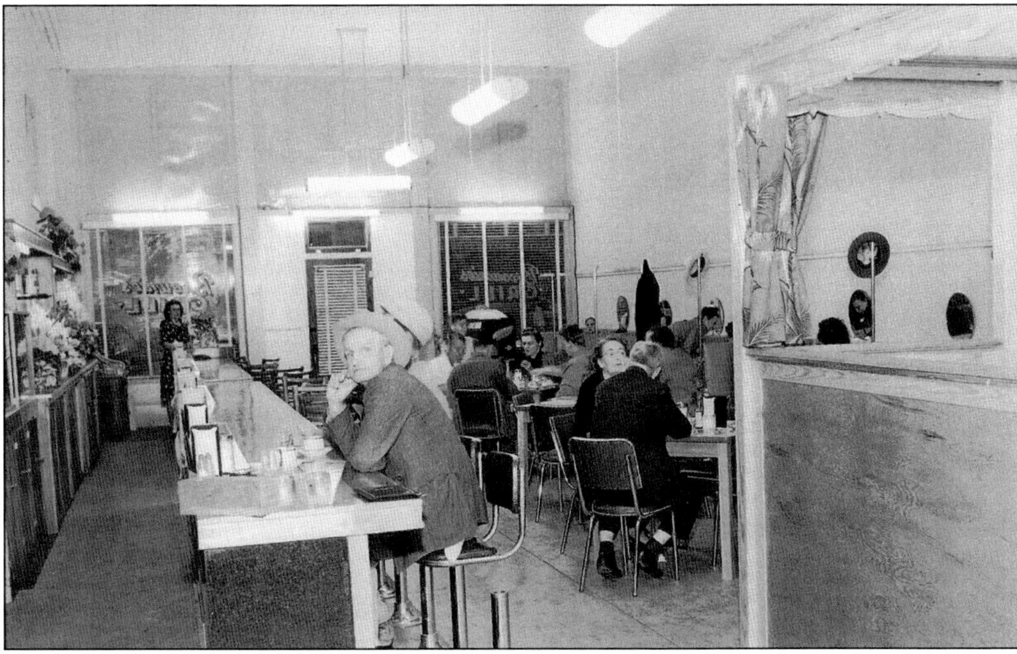

Brownie's Grill was owned and operated by Hoyt and Bonita Brown. The small café was located on Clay Street. Each booth had a pole for the gentlemen's hats. The gentleman sitting at the lunch counter is Oliver Gann. The Roberts E. Storey family can be seen at the back right table enjoying their meal. (TNT.)

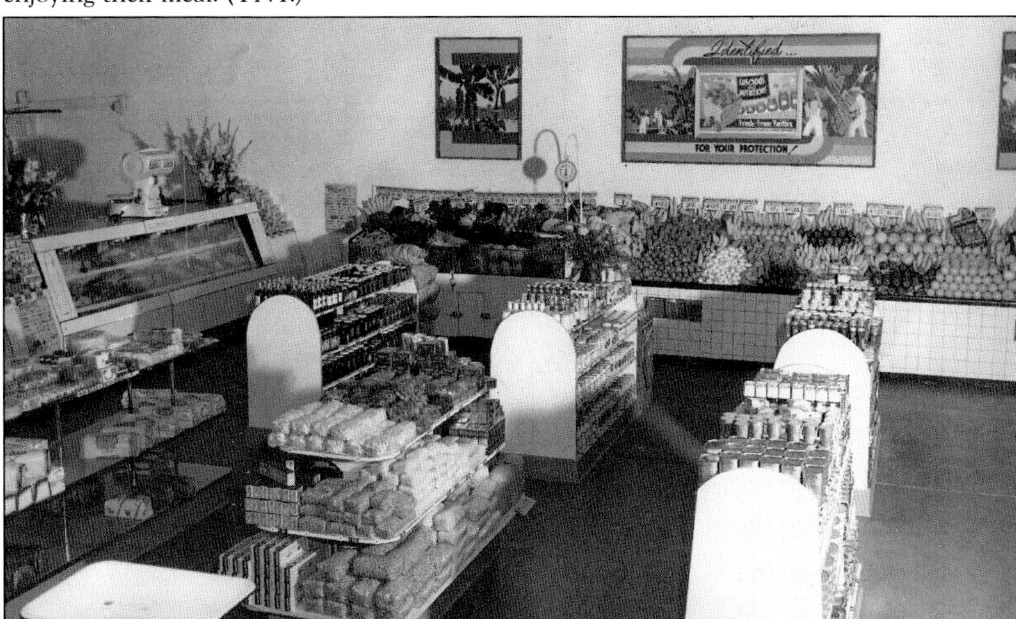

Identical twins Worth and Willard Grigsby opened the Twins Food Store on August 8, 1938. They offered a payroll check cashing service, allowing area factory workers whose shift ended after the banks closed the opportunity to cash their check on Friday evening. The store was the first in Nocona to have a refrigerated produce counter. (Billie Grigsby.)

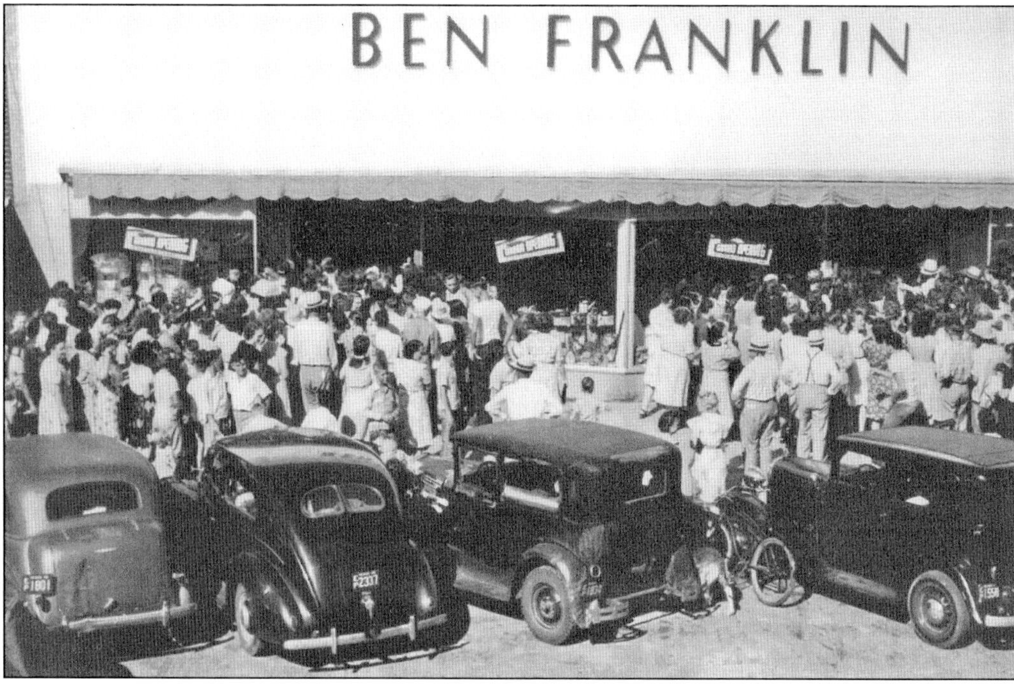

The Ben Franklin Store was a popular shopping venue for the old and young alike. Awaiting the store's grand opening, the huge crowd of people shown in this photograph had gathered out front in the mid-1930s. (TNT.)

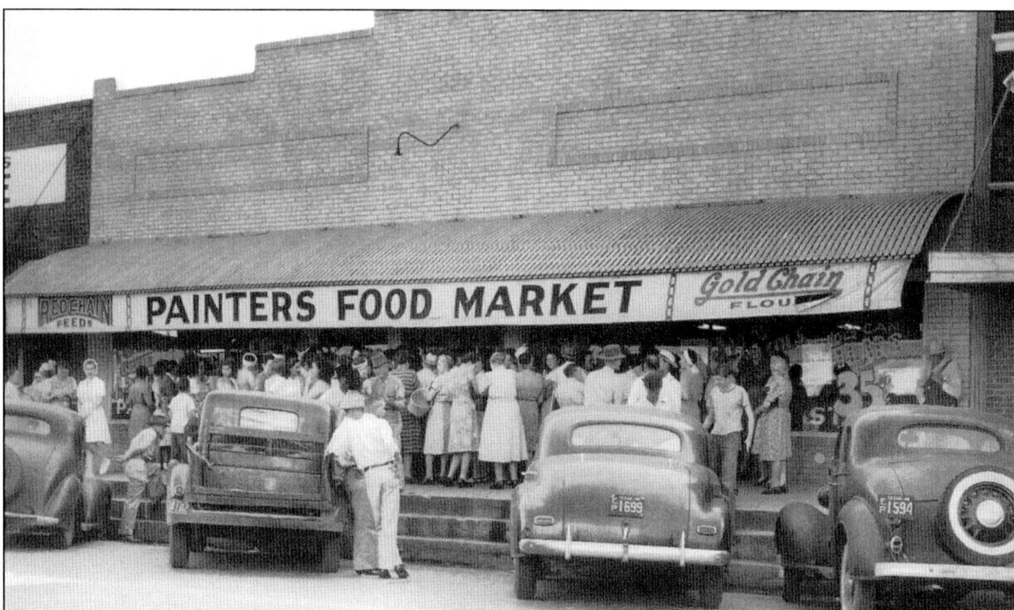

Hubert Painter and his wife, Ruby, opened Painters Food Market on June 10, 1944. The store was a combination grocery store and meat market. The name eventually was changed to Painter's Food Store and became an affiliated food store in the early 1970s. Hubert Painter was named Nocona's Man of the Year in 1969. Ruby Painter was named Nocona's Woman of the Year in 1970. (TNT.)

The Scott Brothers were one of the county's earliest businesses. They owned a hardware store and funeral home in nearby St. Jo in the early 1890s. In June 1941, they purchased the J.H. Cone Hardware Store in Nocona. The store building in this photograph was located on the southwest corner of Oak and Clay Streets. (TNT.)

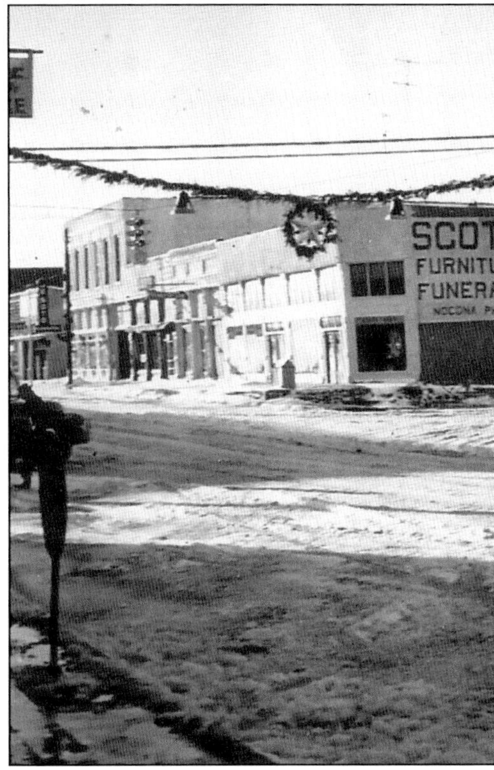

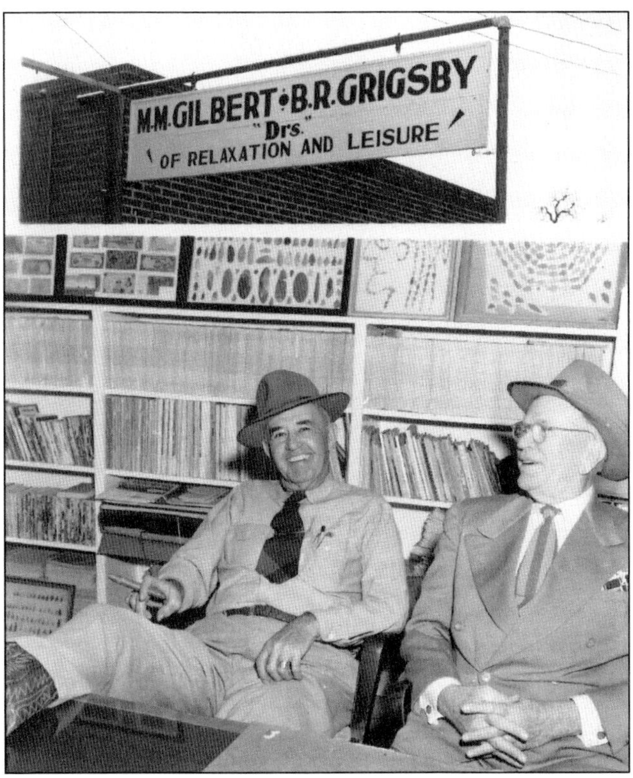

B.R. Grigsby (left) and M.M. Gilbert were prominent citizens in Nocona. After Grigsby had retired from the grocery business and Gilbert from the banking business, they joined forces and became oil lease brokers. The sign above their office read "M.M. Gilbert, B.R. Grigsby, Drs. of Relaxation and Leisure." (Billie Grigsby.)

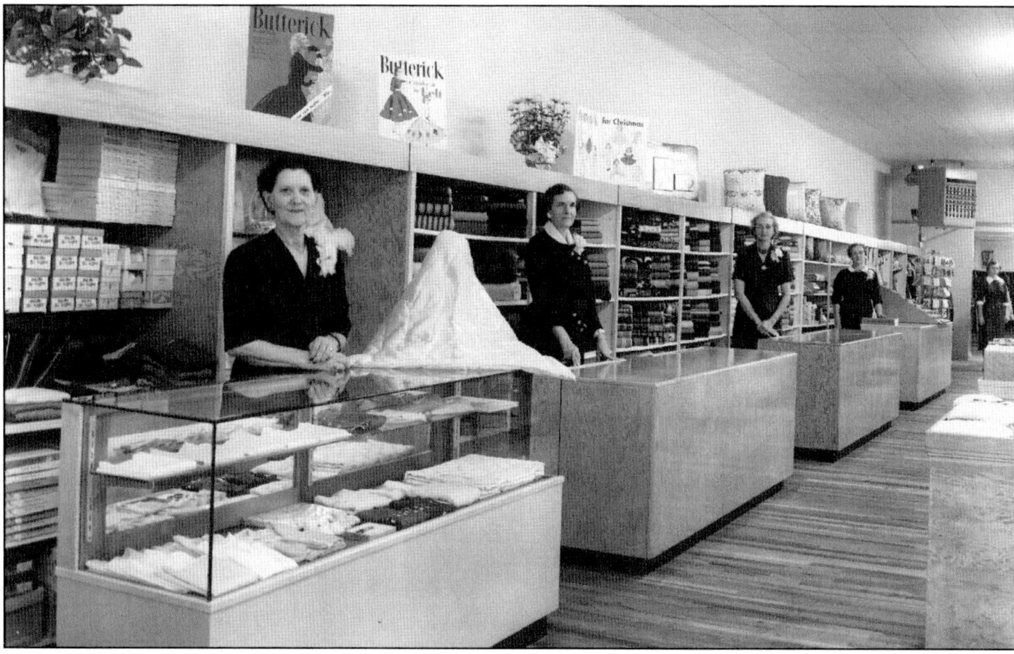

Lipscomb's Department store was located on Clay Street. It carried everything a woman of the 1940s and 1950s could need. Lula Cardwell is the saleswoman standing behind the second counter. In the first display case, there are baby booties and blankets. In the shelves are bolts of fabric. Along the top of the shelving are dress pattern advertisements from Butterick. (Steve Bishop.)

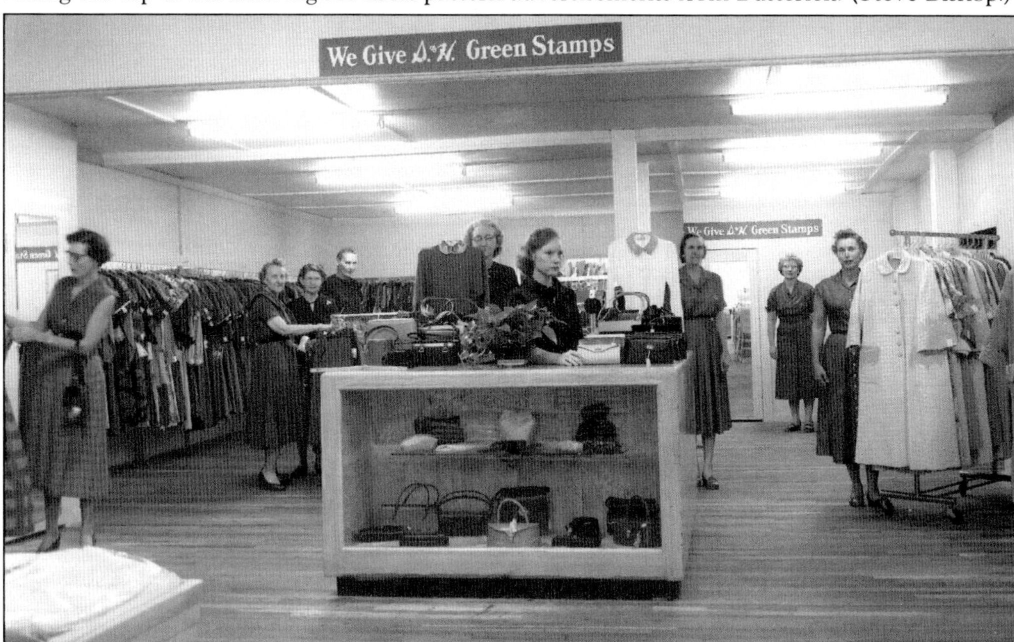

Lipscomb's Department store had an extensive line of women's clothing and accessories. The display in this photograph is full of handbags. Dresses are seen on the racks to the left, and housecoats are hanging on the racks to the right. Lula Cardwell is the saleswoman standing next to the pole behind the white sweater. (Steve Bishop.)

Jack Miller managed the Foxworth Galbraith lumberyard in Nocona. In 1923, Foxworth Galbraith bought 20 lumberyards from the Lyon Gray Lumber Company. Most of these lumberyards were along the Missouri, Kansas, and Texas railroad, including the one in Nocona. (Montague County Historical Commission.)

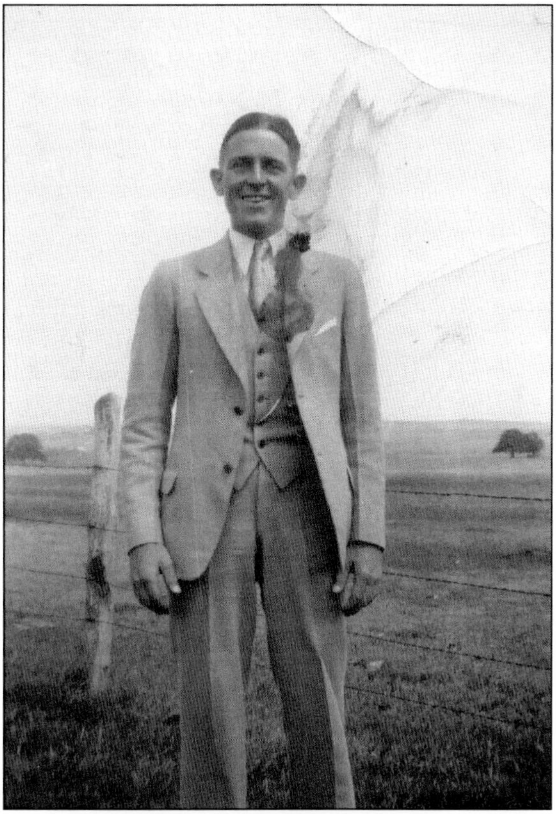

In conjunction with his hardware business, J.H. Cone (left) operated a funeral home. Here, he is proudly watching the first motorized funeral car in Nocona roll off the showroom floor. (Wanda Billings.)

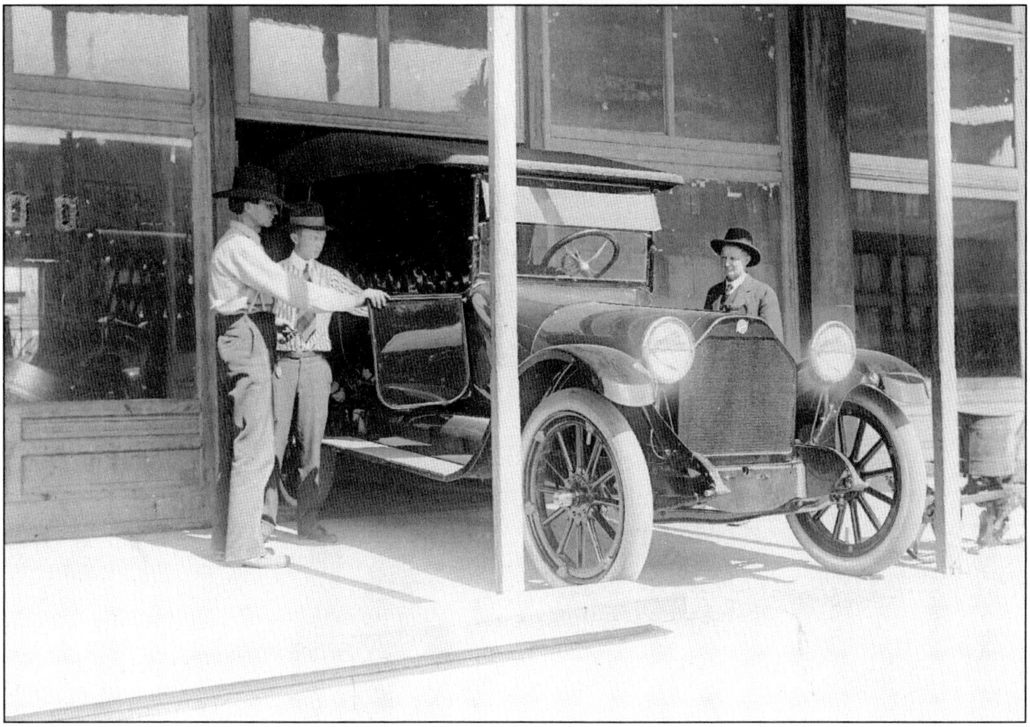

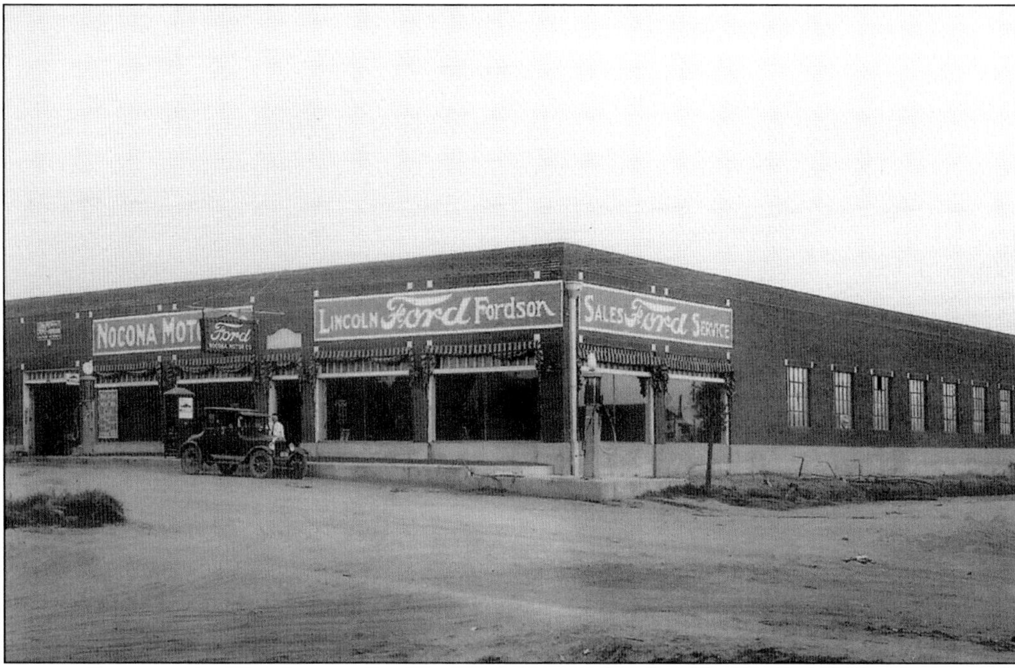

The Lincoln Ford dealership was located on the corner of West Walnut and Main Streets. This building later became a Buick dealership, and eventually it was used for the Piggly Wiggly grocery store. It was owned and operated by L.Z. Cone. (TNT.)

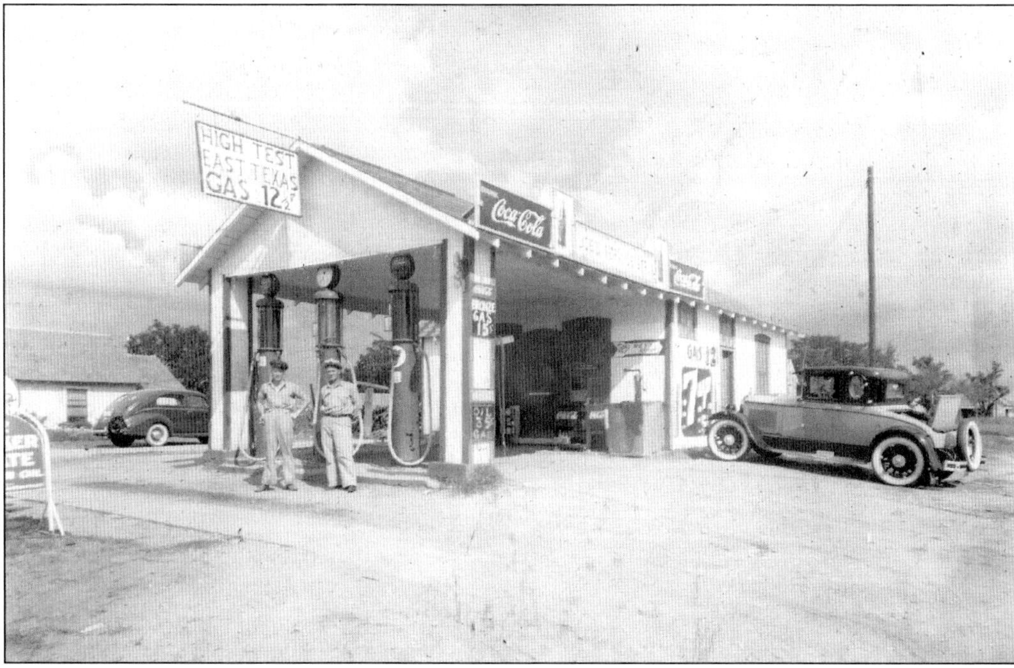

Joe's Service Station was owned and operated by Joe Jackson (right). Jackson operated the station from 1937 until his death in 1976. It was located in 400 block of Clay Street. Jack Arrington is the other gentleman in front of the station. At the time this photograph was taken in the late 1930s, gasoline was 12.5¢ a gallon. (Wanda Wood.)

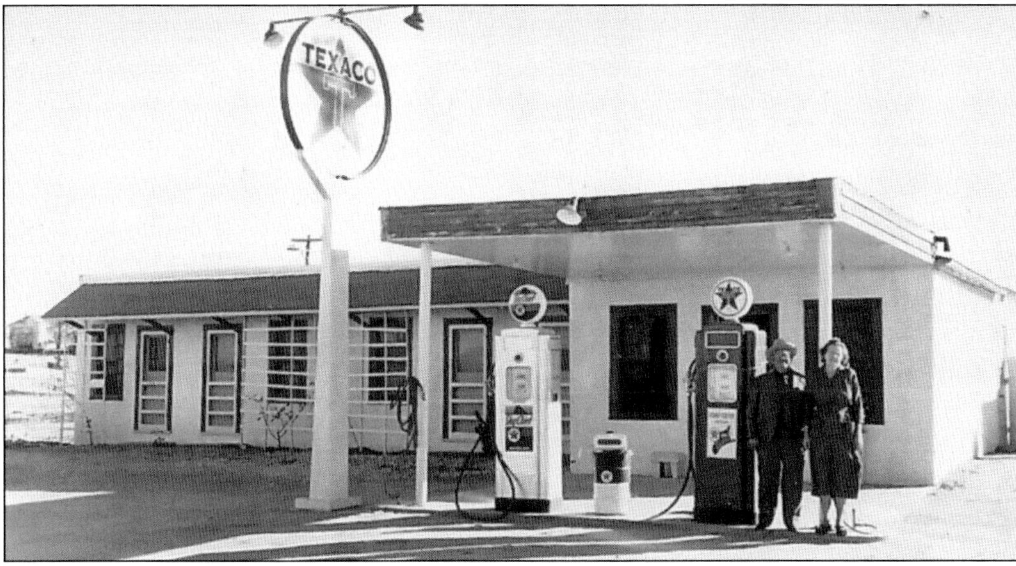

This Texaco was one of many gas stations located in Nocona during the 1940s. The owners not only operated the station but also lived in back section of the building as well. This station was located on East Highway 82. It was owned and operated by W.E. and Ellie Walton. (TNT.)

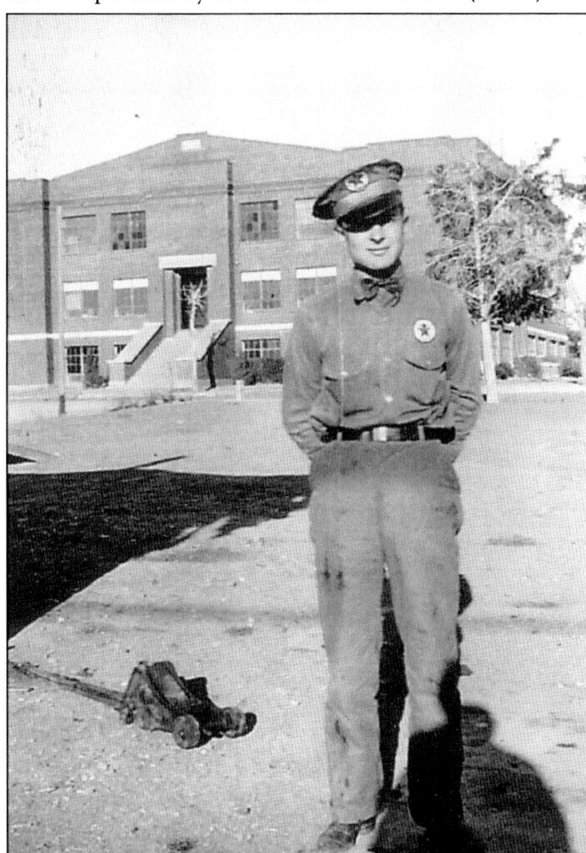

Glenn Stouder went to work at Floyd Nelson's Texaco station right out of high school in the early 1930s. The station was across the street from the North Ward School Building on the southeast corner of Clay and Willow Streets. Stouder later worked at the Nocona Truck and Tractor Company selling farm implements. (TNT.)

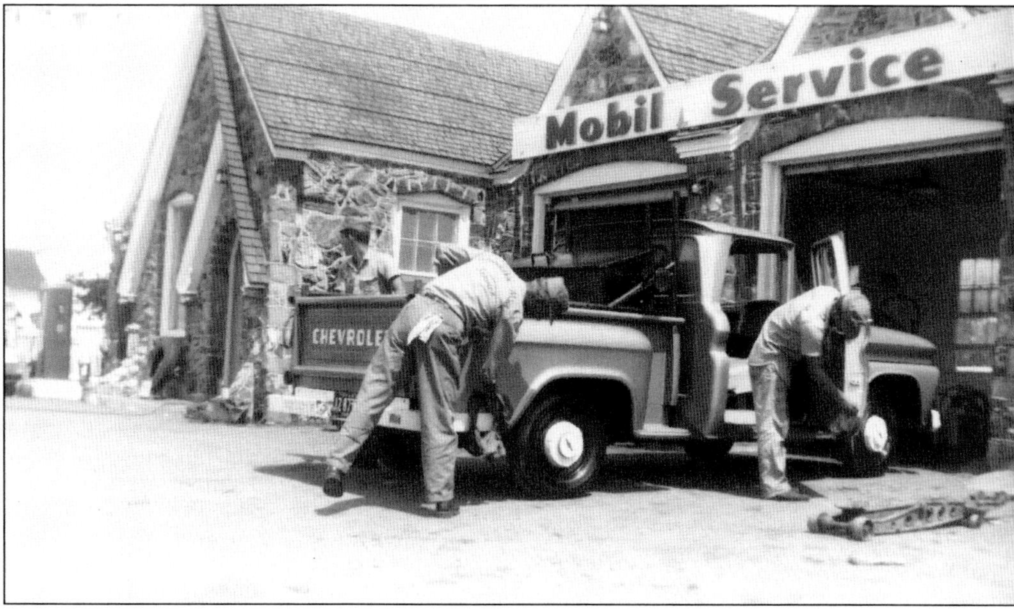

Womack's Mobil service station was owned and operated by Floyd Womack. He opened the business in 1961, but the rock building was built in 1930. Displayed on the wall inside the building was an unusual collection of cattle brands. The station was located at 310 East Highway 82. The building was destroyed when a truck careened off the highway into the stone structure. (Floyd Womack.)

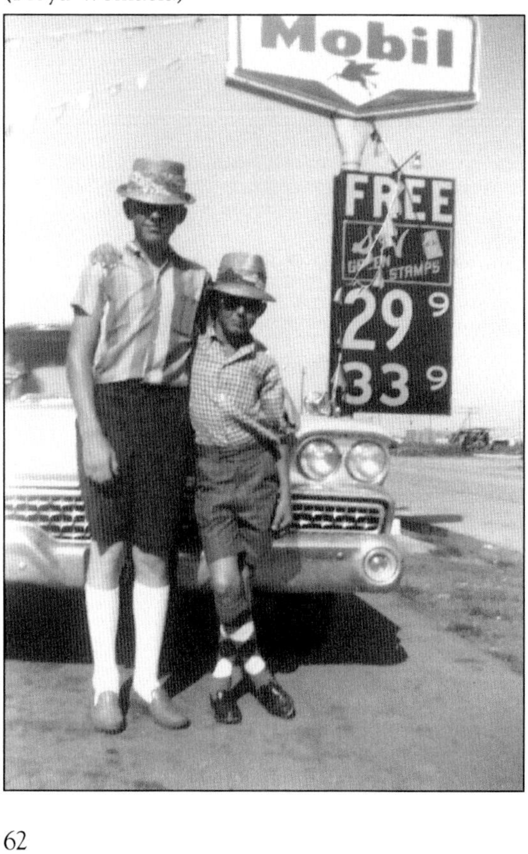

In the early 1960s, gasoline was less than 30¢ a gallon at Womack's Mobil service station. Womack's son Roger (right) and Bob Sutton are shown standing in front of the Mobil price placard that also states that the station rewarded patrons with S&H Green Stamps. Housewives collected these trading stamps to redeem for a variety of household objects ranging from dishes to furniture. (Floyd Womack.)

In the summer of 1911, about 100 Nocona families received electricity for the first time. This revelation was provided by the Nocona Ice and Power plant. H.D. Weathers was the original owner. The company exchanged hands several times before it became the Community Public Service Company in 1935. (TNT.)

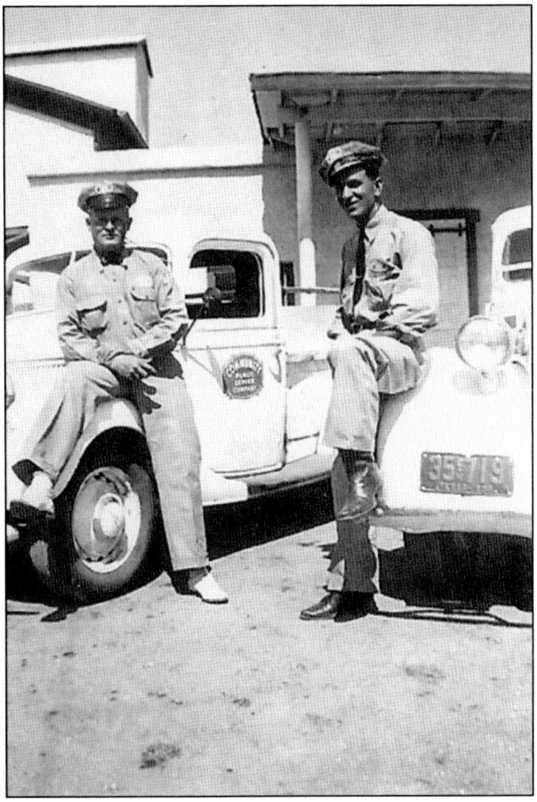

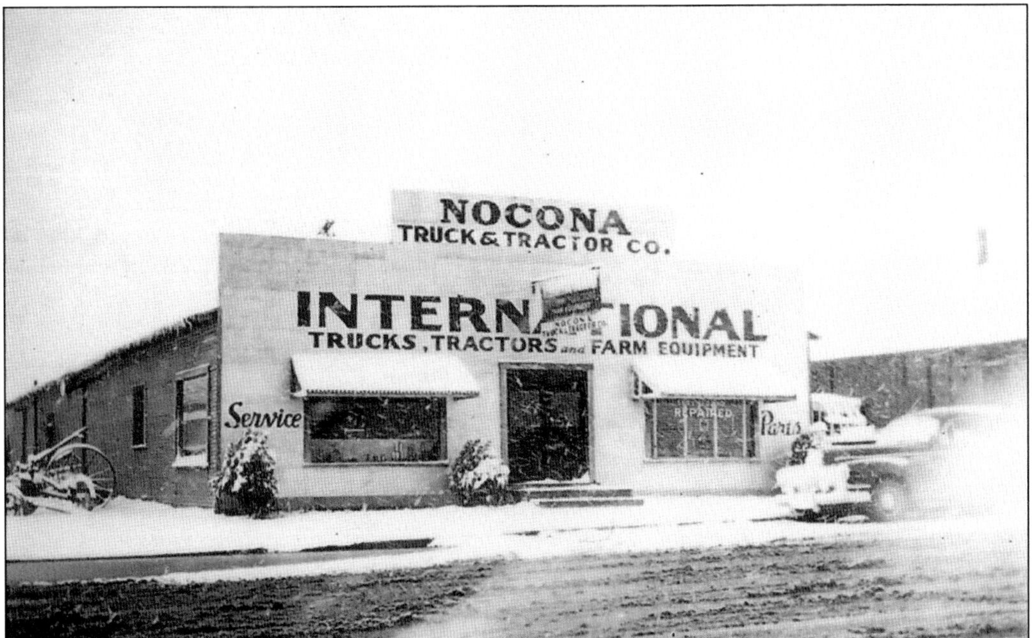

The Nocona Truck and Tractor Company was located across from McNabb's feed store. The company dealt in large equipment and farm implements. Glenn Stouder was a longtime employee. The company was in business during the 1940s and 1950s. (TNT.)

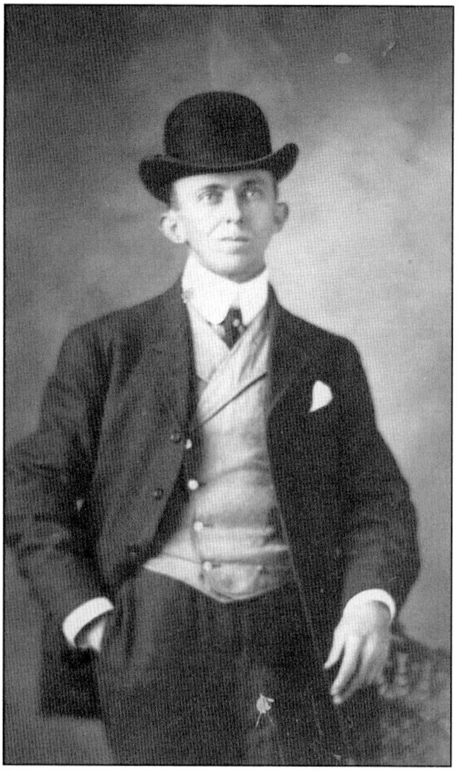

Several newspapers were published in the early years of Nocona. The *Nocona Argus* and the *Nocona Leader* merged as the *Nocona Times*. Another early newspaper was the *Nocona Post*. Henry Burns, shown here, purchased both the *Times* and the *Post* in 1900 and combined them as the *Times Post*, which he published until his death in 1946. (TNT.)

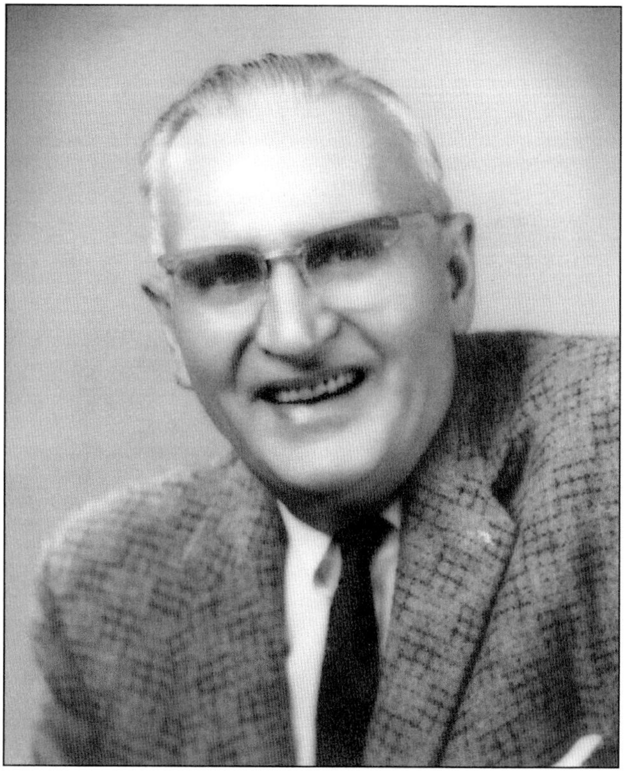

Rowland Peters purchased the *Nocona News* on March 1, 1952, from the Perry brothers, Franklin and Francis. The Perrys had been publishing the newspaper since 1936. Peters started his newspaper career in the late 1920s as a telegraph operator for the Associated Press in Pittsburgh. (Montague County Historical Commission.)

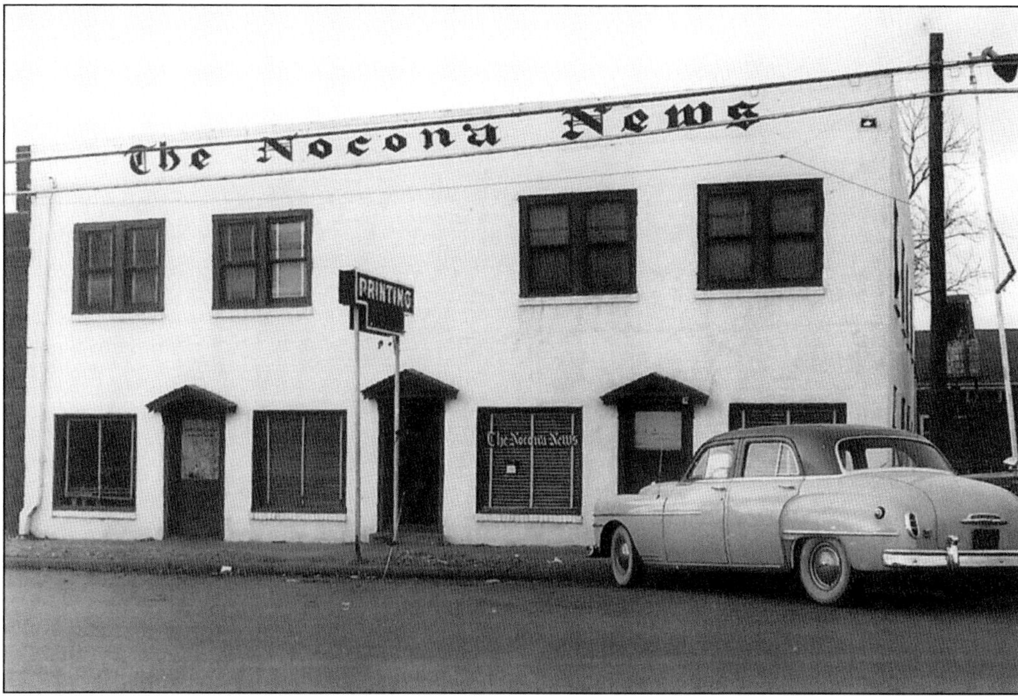

The *Nocona News* has had several owners and locations throughout Nocona since the first printing on June 6, 1905. The Nocona News Building in this photograph was located on Oak Street. The newspaper is still in publication today under the ownership of Tracy and Linda Mesler. (Montague County Historical Society.)

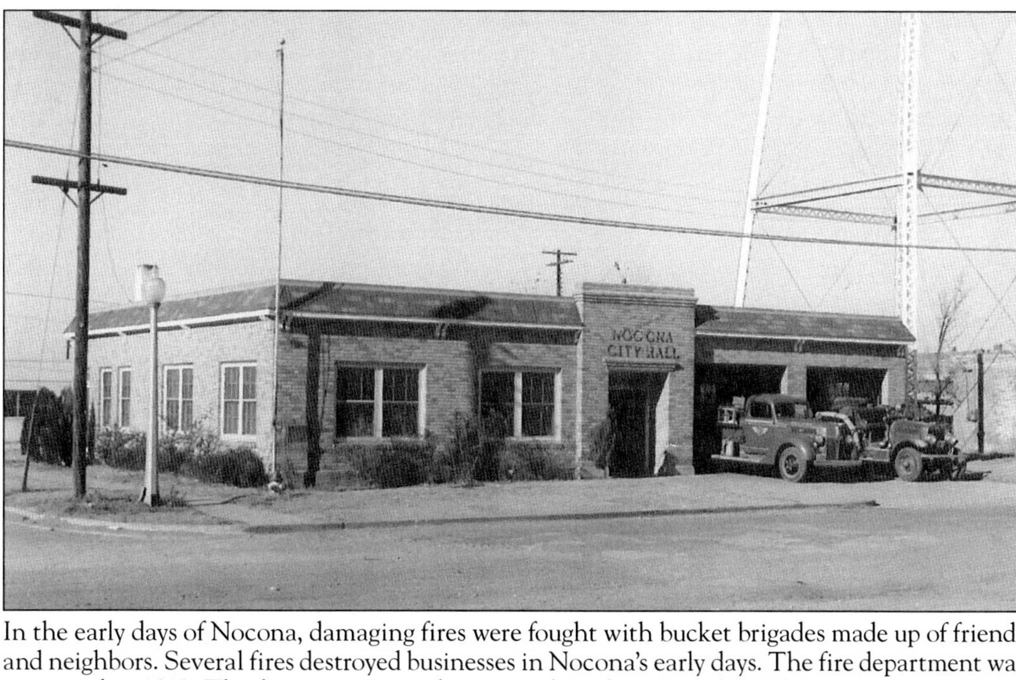

In the early days of Nocona, damaging fires were fought with bucket brigades made up of friends and neighbors. Several fires destroyed businesses in Nocona's early days. The fire department was organized in 1912. The first pumper truck was purchased in 1948. (TNT.)

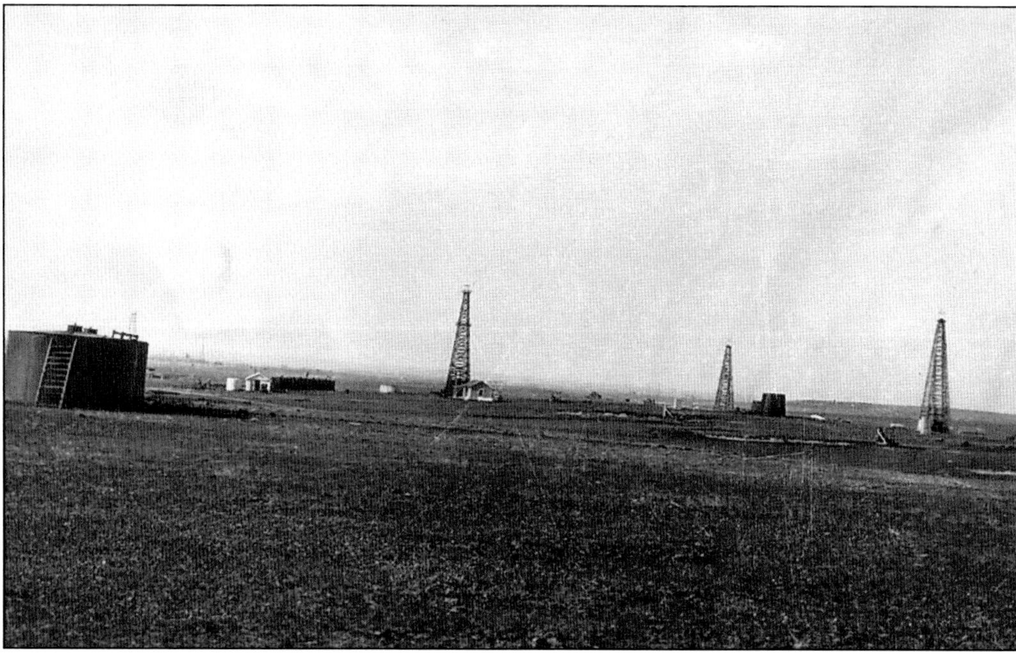

By 1922, Montague County had become a significant oil producing county. The most prolific oil field in the county was known as Nocona's North Field. In 1972, a historical marker was placed at the location commemorating the 50th anniversary of Nocona's big oil boom. (TNT.)

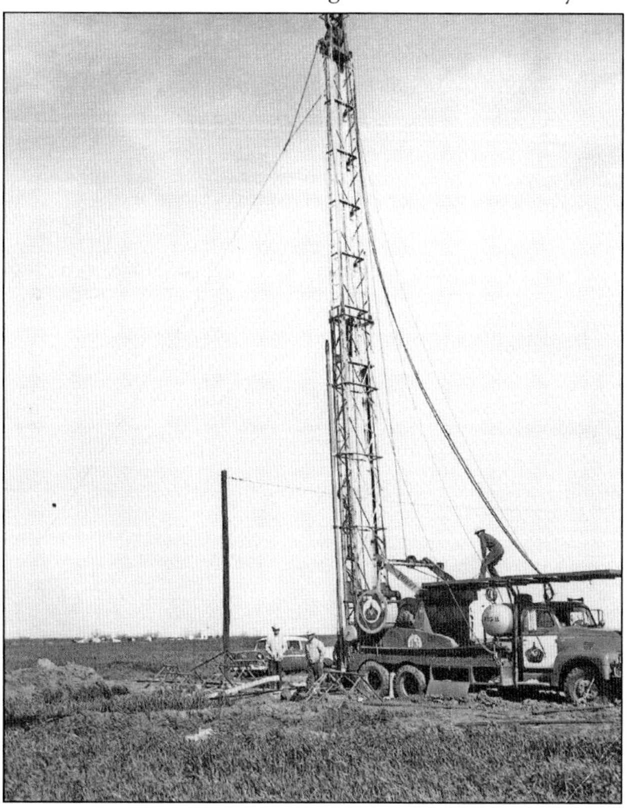

One of the first oil sites in the Nocona area was discovered quite by accident. In 1924, Cadmus McCall hired J.A.W. McGrew to drill a water well on one of the McCall farms. Instead of water, McGrew struck oil. McCall called in experts from Pennsylvania to confirm the discovery. (Mary Viola McGrew.)

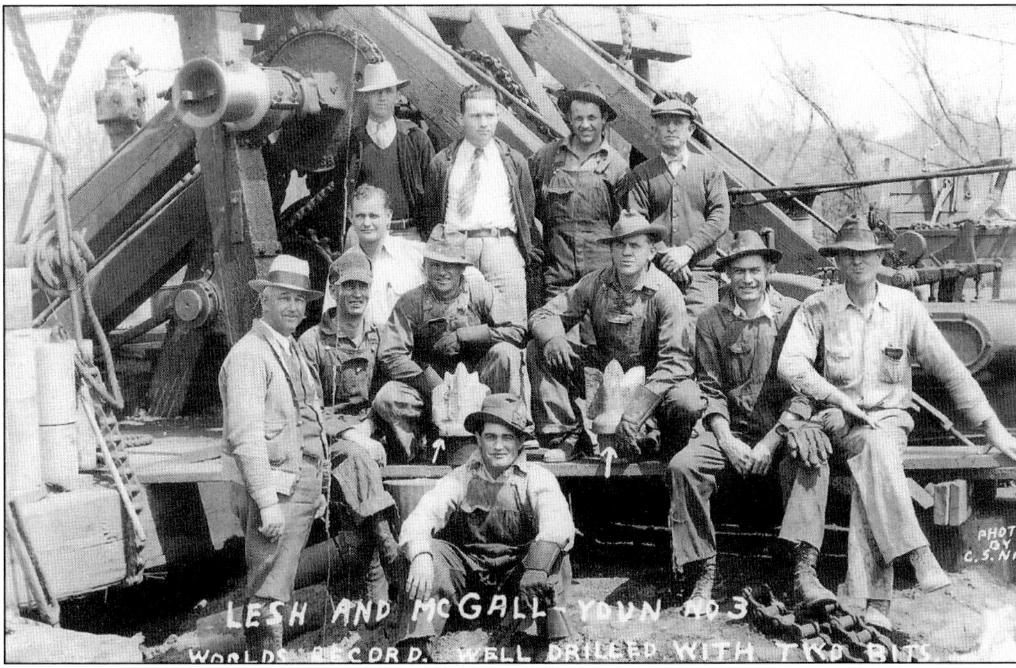

This photograph shows one of the oil field crews of the Lesh and McCall Company. Phil Lesh and Cadmus McCall formed a business partnership in 1925. They were drilling contractors and oil producers in Nocona's North Field. Both Lesh and McCall died in 1953. (TNT.)

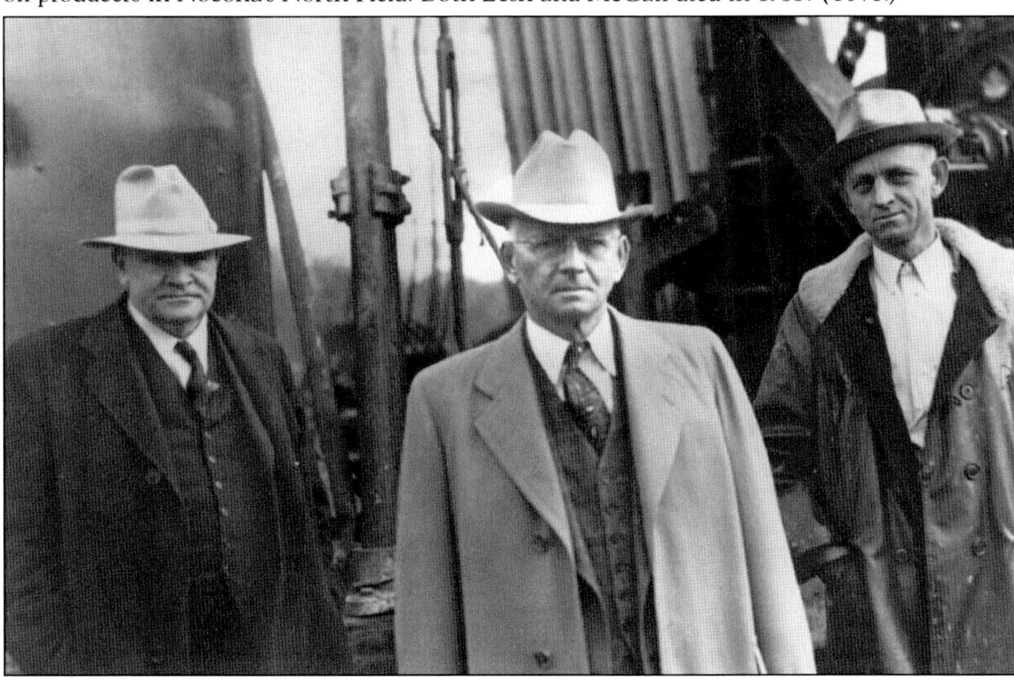

Joe Benton (left) and John W. Holmes (center) formed an oil drilling partnership in 1932. They brought in their first well in April 1933. As their business succeeded, they hired Holmes's son Chester (right) as the lease and drilling superintendent. Benton and Holmes remained business partners until Benton's death in 1958. (TNT.)

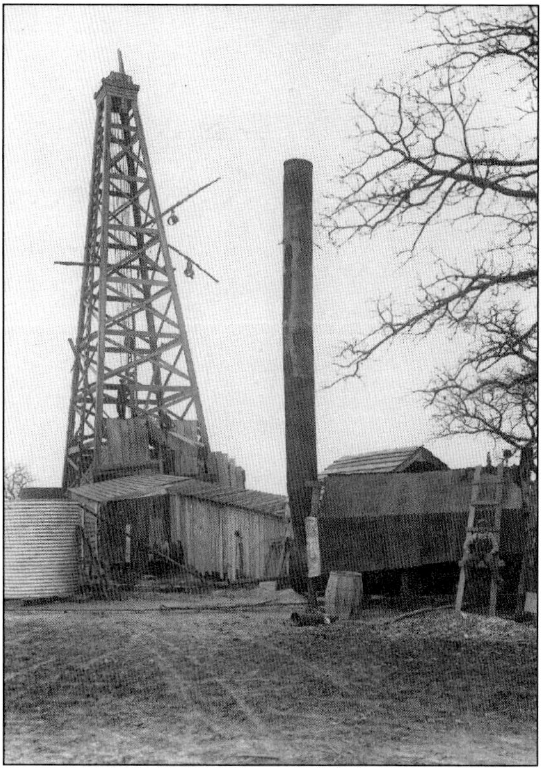

The Nocona Oil Company was one of the many businesses that formed after the discovery of oil in the Nocona area. The stock shares were valued at $10 each when the company was formed. The original officers were W.T. Russell, president; Cadmus McCall, vice president; J.G. Clark, vice president; S.T. Humphries, vice president; R.W. Leach, secretary-treasurer; and T.B. Wilkes, assistant secretary. (TNT.)

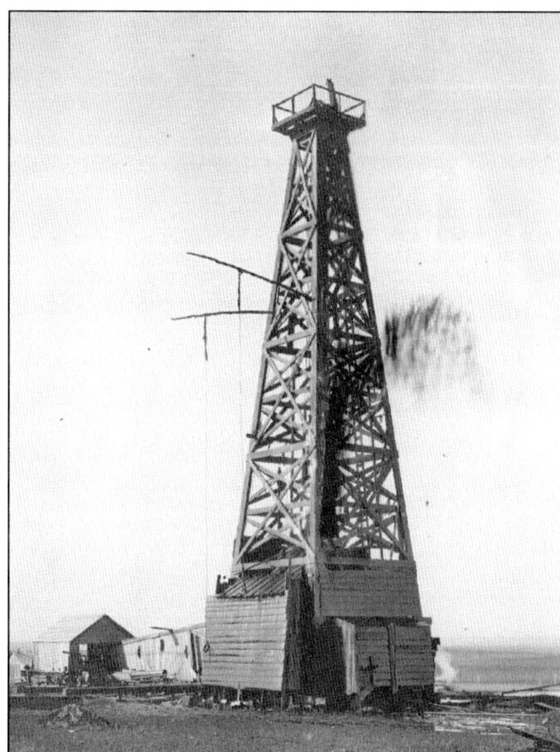

This rig, located in Nocona's North Field in the 1920s, was built in the typical fashion of the period. The derrick has an all wood construction, and the derrick platform is fully enclosed. There were few if any safety precautions in place to protect the drillers and roughnecks in the early boom years. Oil field work could be extremely dangerous and even deadly. (TNT.)

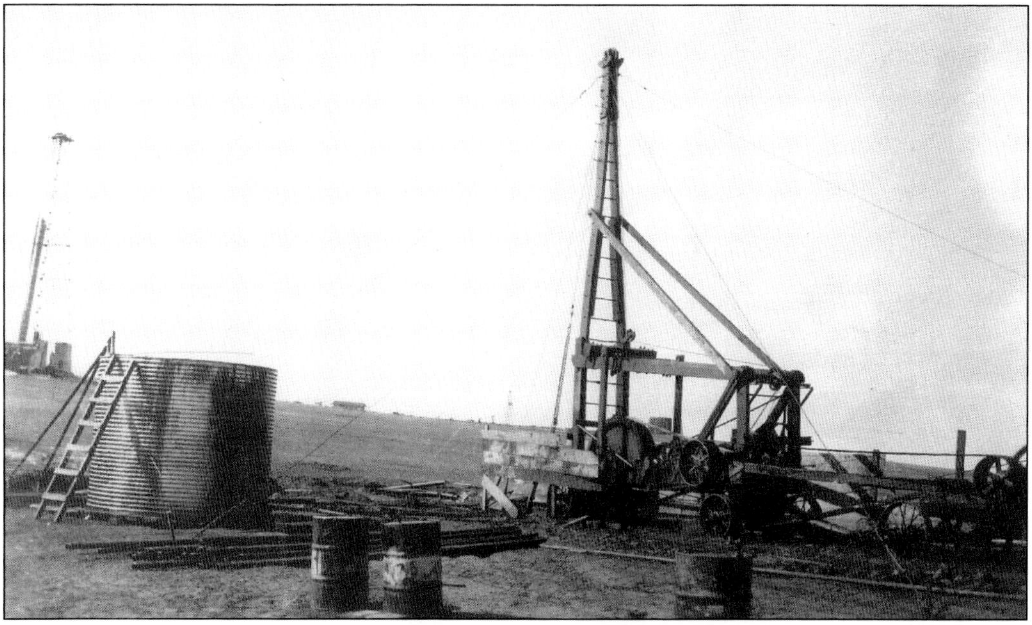

As the oil boom continued, more and more companies drilled for oil in Nocona's North Field. In 1925, the field produced 107,135 barrels of oil. Production rose to 1,963,088 barrels in 1926 and jumped even higher in 1927 to 4,241,242 barrels. (TNT.)

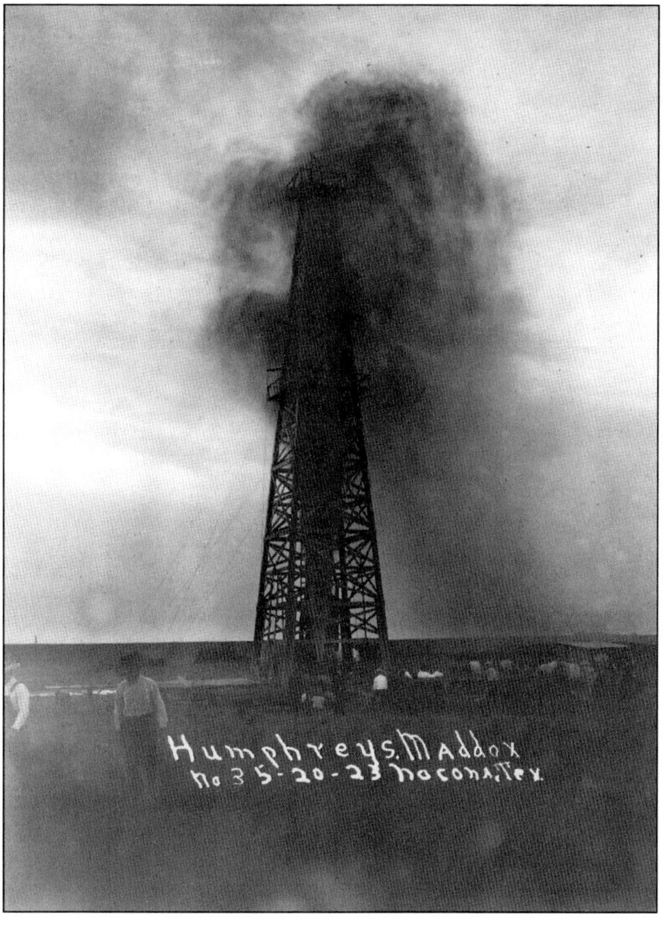

One of the first successful wells drilled in Nocona's North Field was the Humphrey's Maddox No. 3. John Maddox can be seen in the foreground of the photograph. The well hit on May 20, 1923. (TNT.)

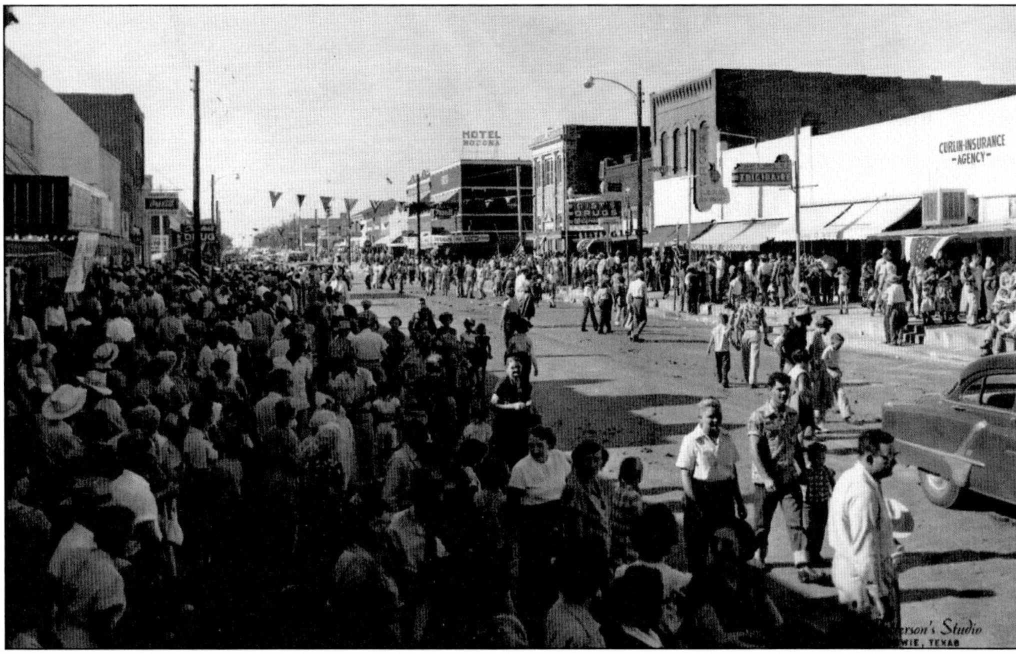

Looking north up Clay Street during a parade, many businesses can be spotted. On the left, Brownie's Grill and Chandler's Drugstore are visible. On the right, Curlin Insurance Agency, John D. White Appliances, Popular Dry Goods, Gist Drugstore, the Hotel Nocona, and the Cona Theater can all be identified. (TNT.)

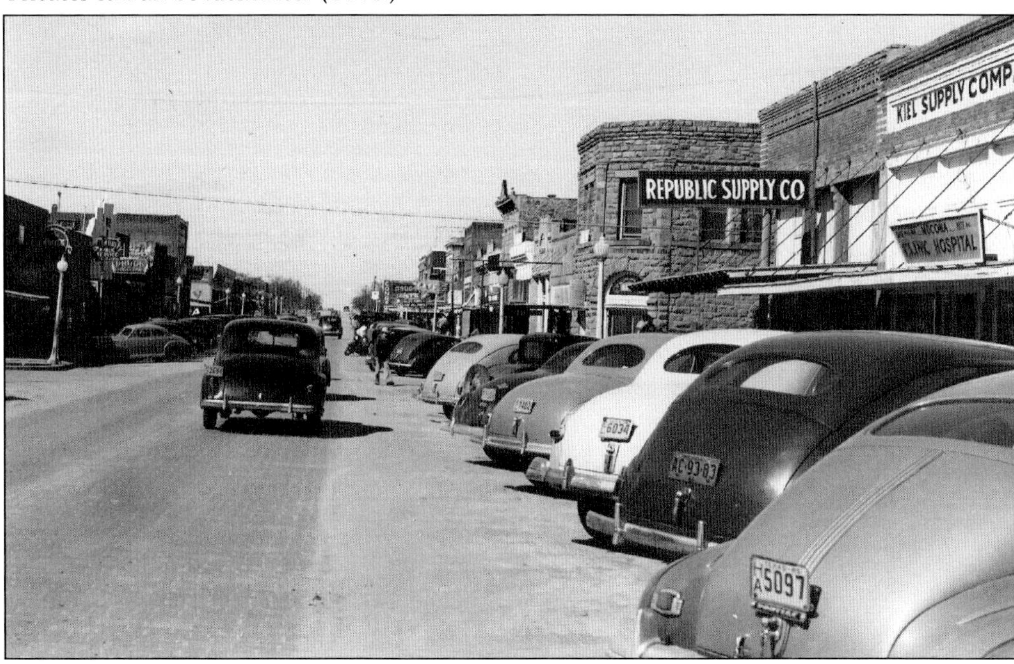

This photograph was taken looking up Clay Street in the mid-1940s. The businesses that can be identified on the left side of the street are Community Public Service and the Ritz Theater. Those on the right side of the street are Republic Supply, a café, Gist Drugstore, and the Cona Theater. (R. Storey.)

Parades have always been an enjoyed event in Nocona. People are lined all the way up and down the street to watch the horses, bands, and floats pass by. Due to the glare of the sun, no business signage on the left hand side of the street can be identified. The photograph was taken looking south down Clay Street. (Ken Coop.)

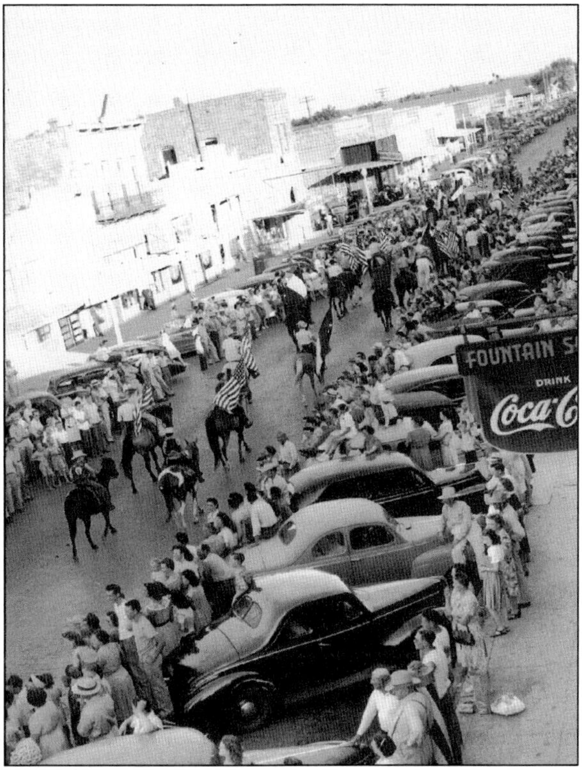

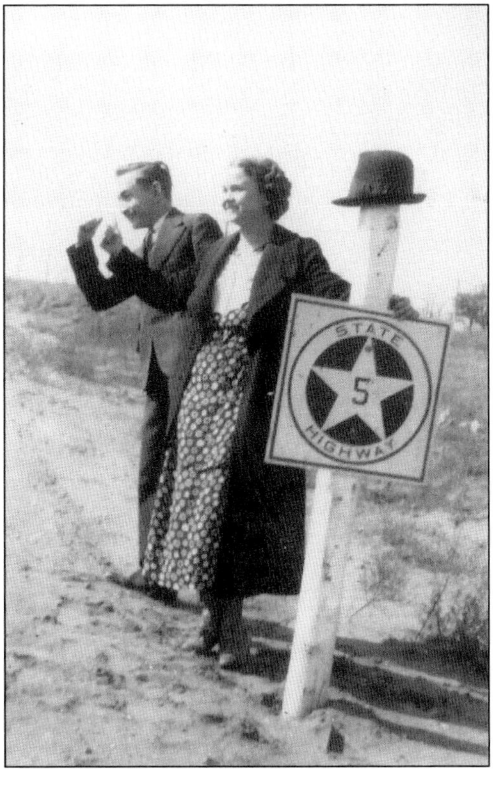

In 1931, the Texas State Highway Department adopted a plan to route State Highway 5 from Gainesville to Henrietta through Nocona. On June 6, 1938, people flocked to Nocona to witness East Texas meeting West Texas as the last section of the highway was completed. Soon afterward, the new highway was designated as Highway 82. (TNT.)

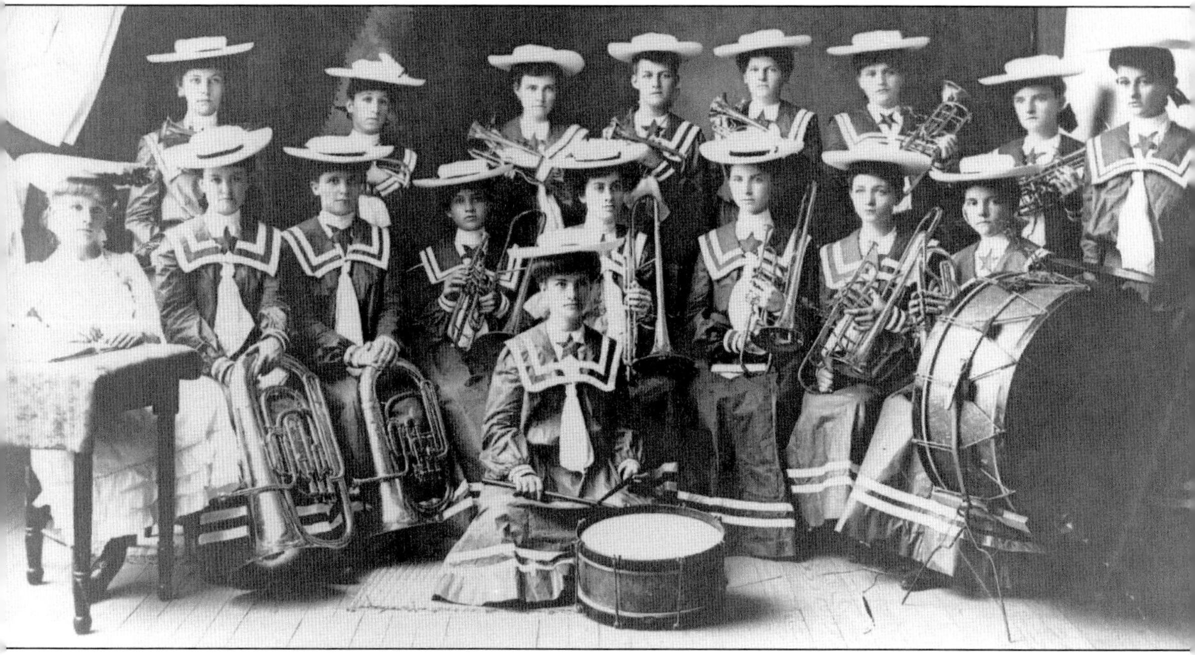

Members of the Lone Star Band shown in this photograph are, from left to right, (first row) Eva Matlock; (second row) Obie Fatheree, Grace Wilson, Hattie Carson, Winnie Horton, Jennie Lee Cochran, Laura Womack, Eula Moore, and Sally McIntire; (third row) Mattie McIntire, Mabel March, Hattie Horton, Lena Matlock, Nell Berry, Fay Horton, Alma Russell, and Haughty Utt. (Montague County Historical Commission.)

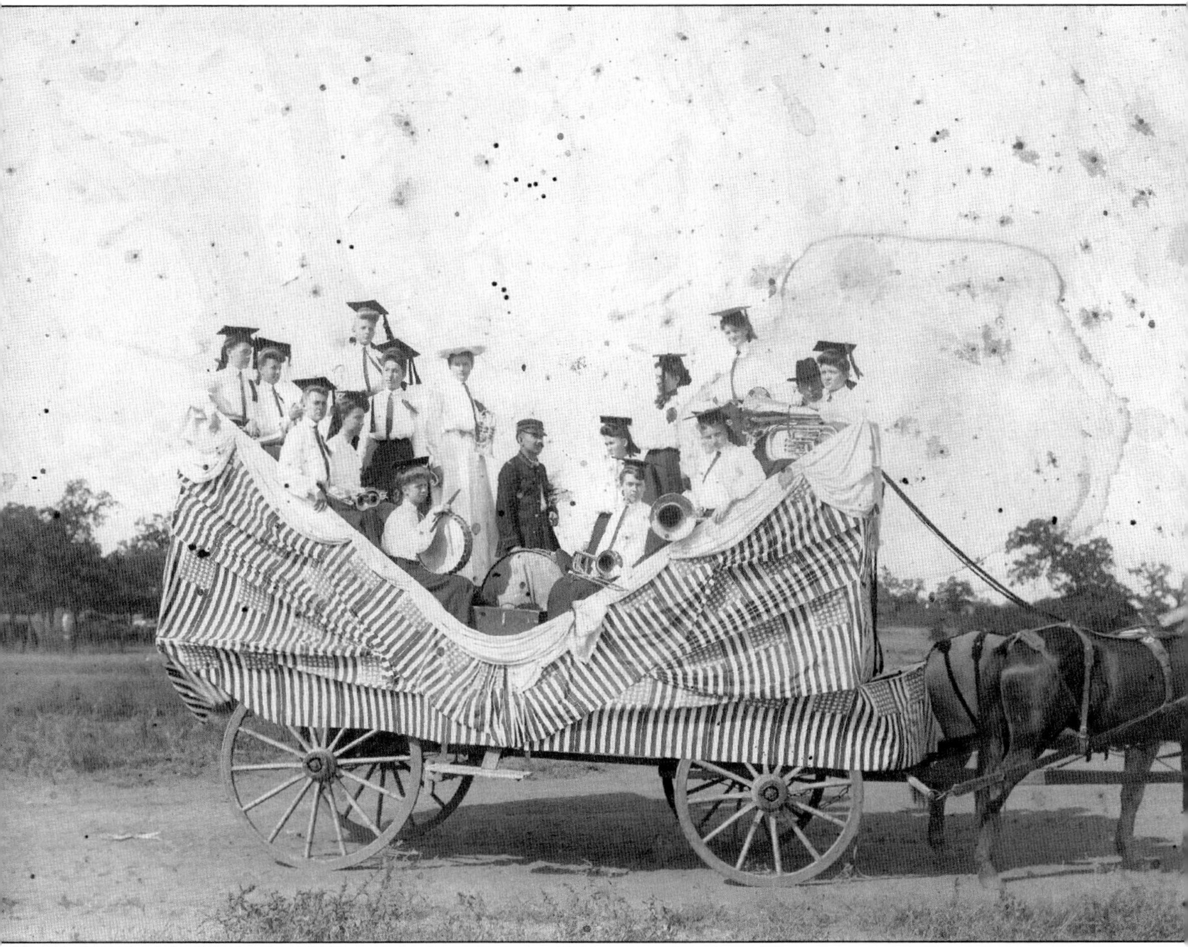

Postmaster W.M. Merritt formed the all-girl Lone Star Band on May 4, 1908. They traveled throughout Texas to perform, including to the Texas State Fair and the Fort Worth Stock Show. Their buggy was decorated with red, white, and blue bunting. They were invited to perform at the World's Fair in St. Louis, but their parents would not allow them to make the long trip. (TNT.)

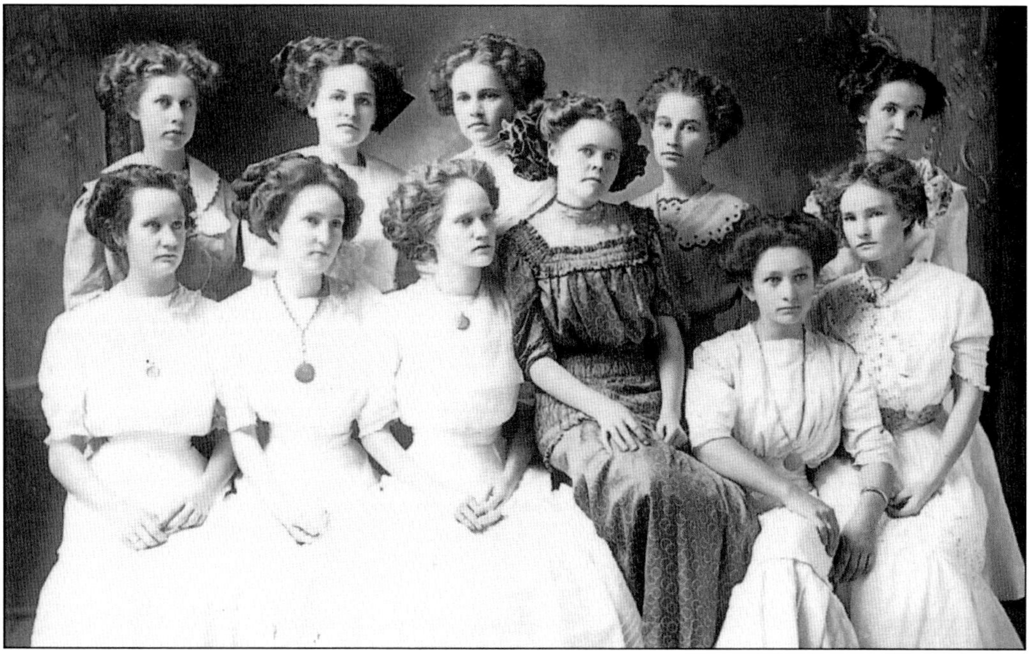

This girls' social club was known as Just Us Ten. It was to have only 10 members, but by the time the group was formed, there were 11 members. The 1905 members were, from left to right, (first row) Enid Justin, Cloe March, Fern Justin, Lillie Baynham, Una Flowerney, and Gladys Russell; (second row) Nell Jordan, Ruby March, Hortense LaForce, Mattie Antrum, and unidentified. (TNT.)

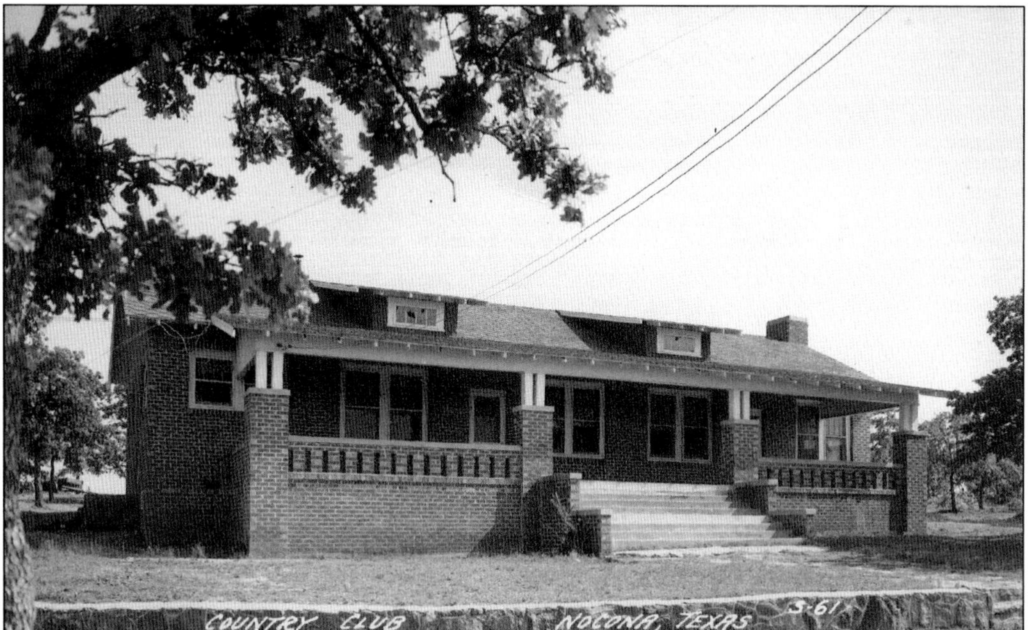

Nocona's elite formed the Nocona Country Club in 1926. Some of the founding families included the Storeys, McCalls, Fooshees, Cones, Leshes, and Justins. The original building burned in December 1927 and was replaced with this brick structure in 1928. The country club had a nine-hole golf course and a small lake. (TNT.)

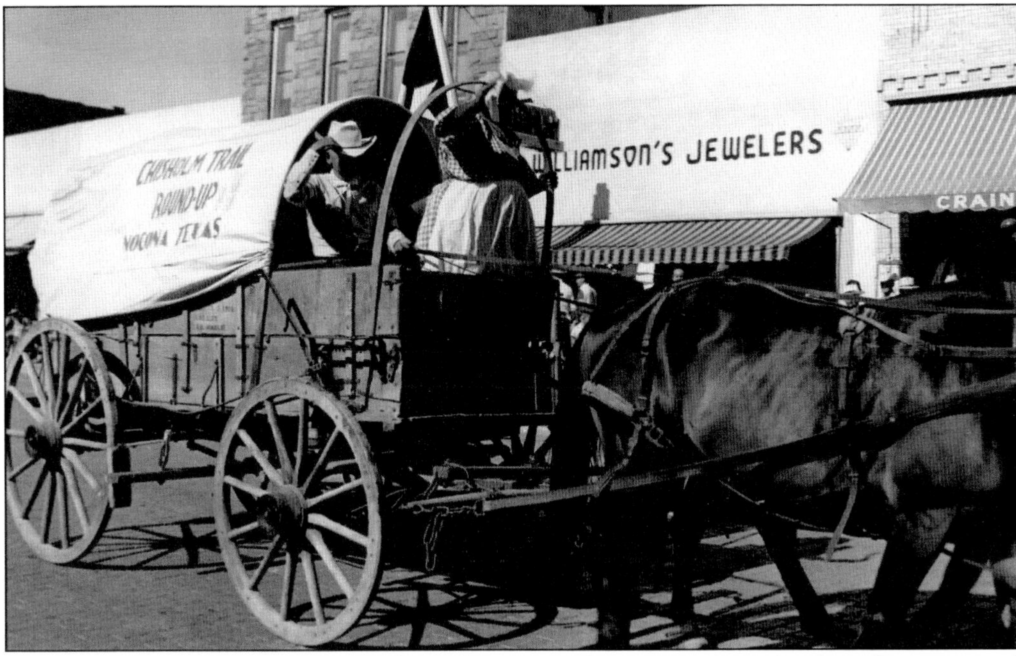

The Chisholm Trail Riding Club was formed in 1953 with an original membership of approximately 120 horse and rodeo enthusiasts. The club performed in area parades and rodeo grand entries. In 1958, the riding club appeared in the annual Rose Parade in Tyler, Texas. During parades, the riding club carried a flag from each of state of the union. This was an impressive sight. (TNT.)

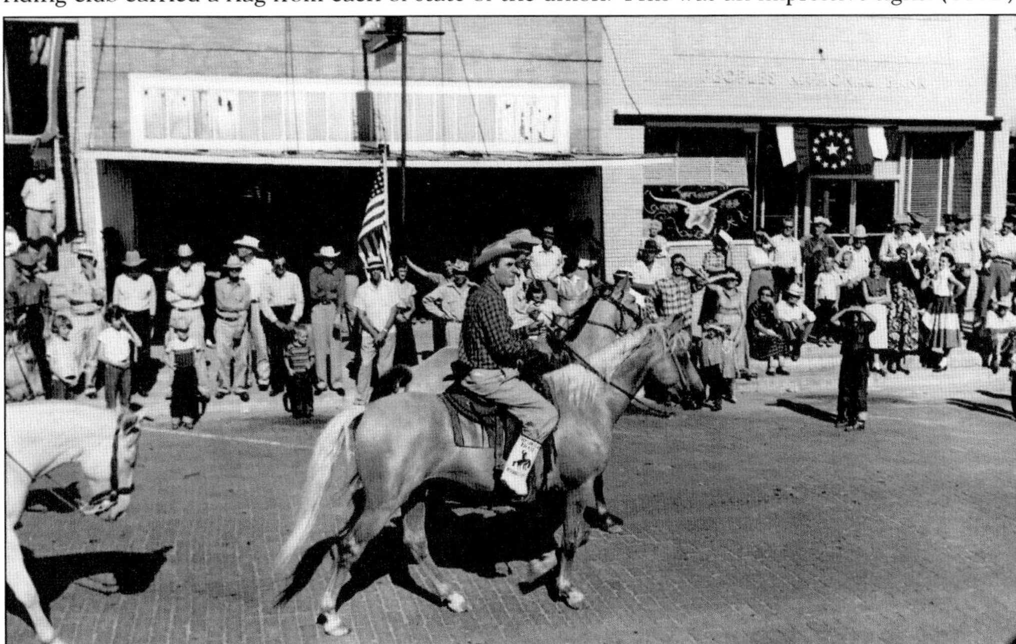

The Chisholm Trail Riding Club wore flashy green and gold costumes, which made them immediately recognizable. They all had matching chaps and boots that were manufactured by the Nocona Boot Company. Enid Justin, president of Nocona Boots, was a member and a big supporter of the riding club. (TNT.)

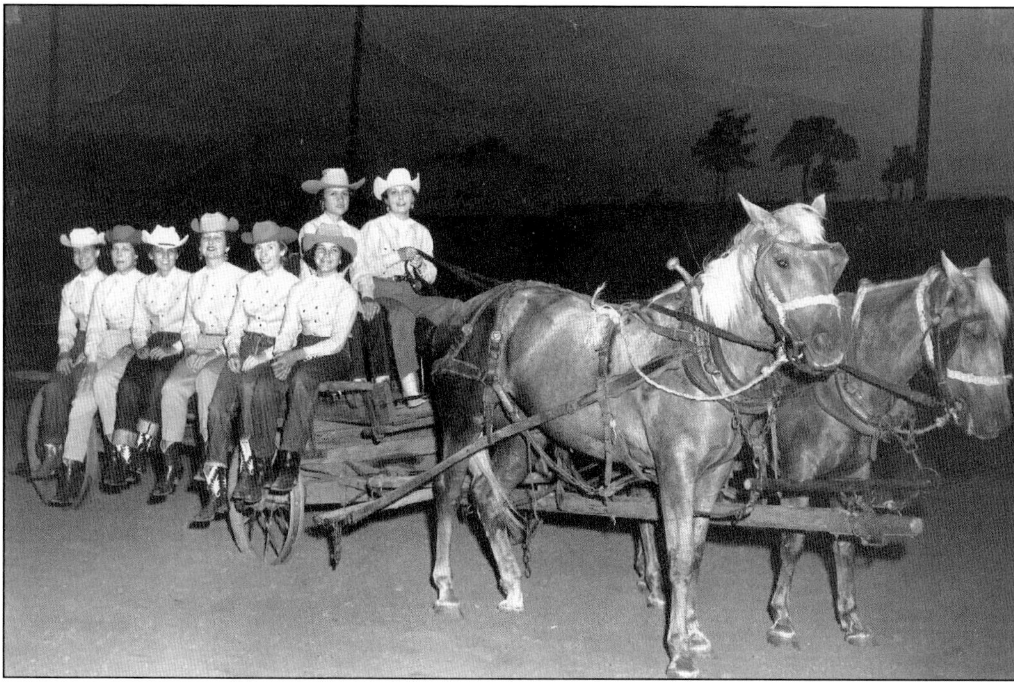

These young ladies are, from left to right, Joann Wolfe, Anita White, Peggy Wyler, Nettie Ann Buck, Shirley Lowrie, and Sandra Henderson. Sitting in the driver's seat is Bonne Seay Rich (left). The girls belonged to a quadrille club, which was a square dancing on horseback activity. (TNT.)

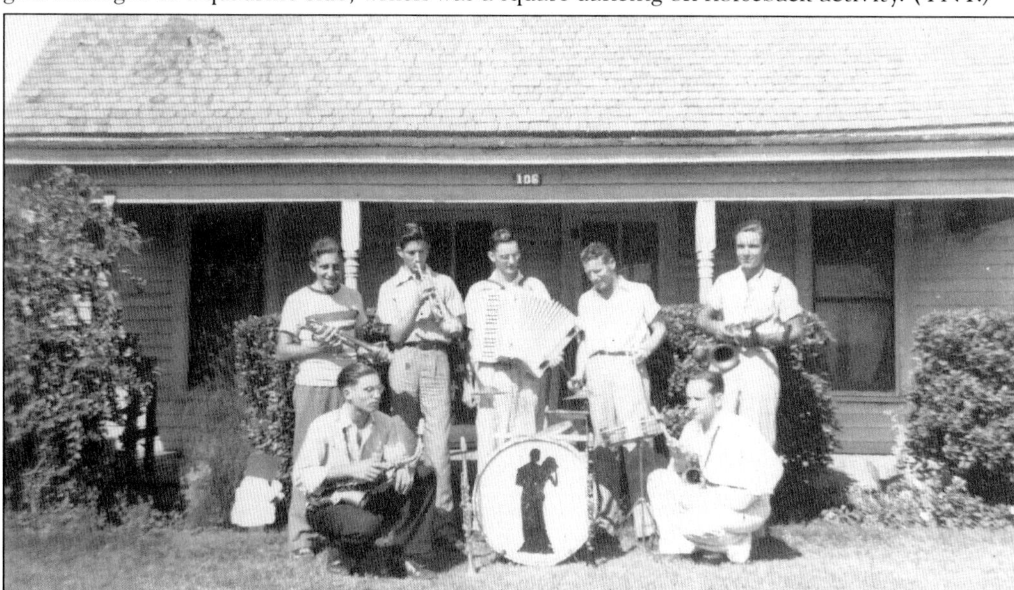

A group of young men and one young lady formed a small club, the Norris McGrew Orchestra. The orchestra consisted of nine pieces. The members shown in this photograph have not been identified, but a list of members indicated the following young people were involved: Norvan Bourland, Allen Cribbs, J.C. Chandler, Billy John Hill, Ralph Strong, Bernard Rosen, C.W. Freeman, and Gladlys Duggan. (TNT.)

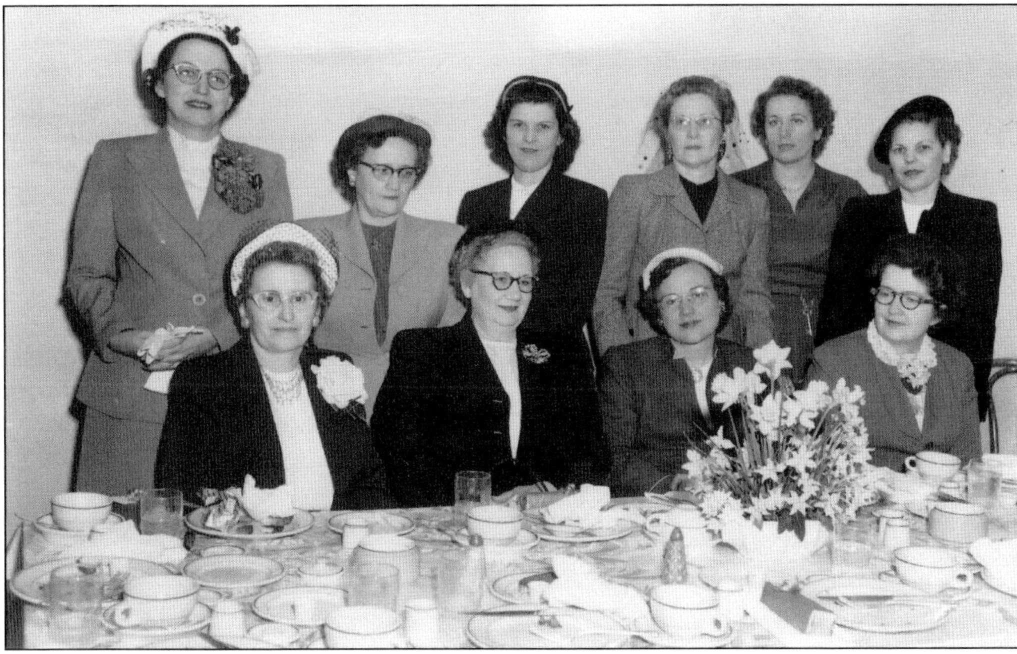

These women belonged to the Business and Professional Women Organization. They are, from left to right, (first row) Kate Gilbert, Enid Justin, Ruth Henry, and Ruth Davis; (second row) Louise Addington, Aubery Mitchell, Ruth Hamilton, Katie MeElhannon, unidentified, and Genelle Miles. (TNT.)

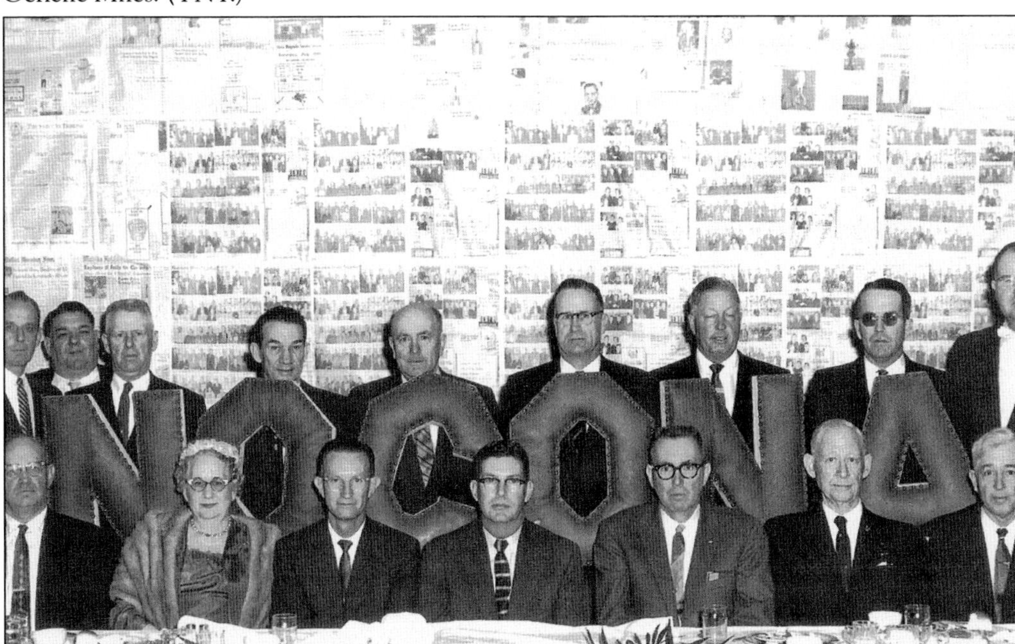

Nocona Chamber of Commerce members shown here are, from left to right, (first row) unidentified, Enid Justin, Dr. Wallace, Grant Hoover, Bas Gist, G.W. Humphreys, and W.L. Scott; (second row) ? Gardner, Jeff Henderson, S.D. Howard, James McCall, Glenn Wilson, Hinds Clark, W.J. Stone, Jack Lest, and W.R. Robb. (TNT.)

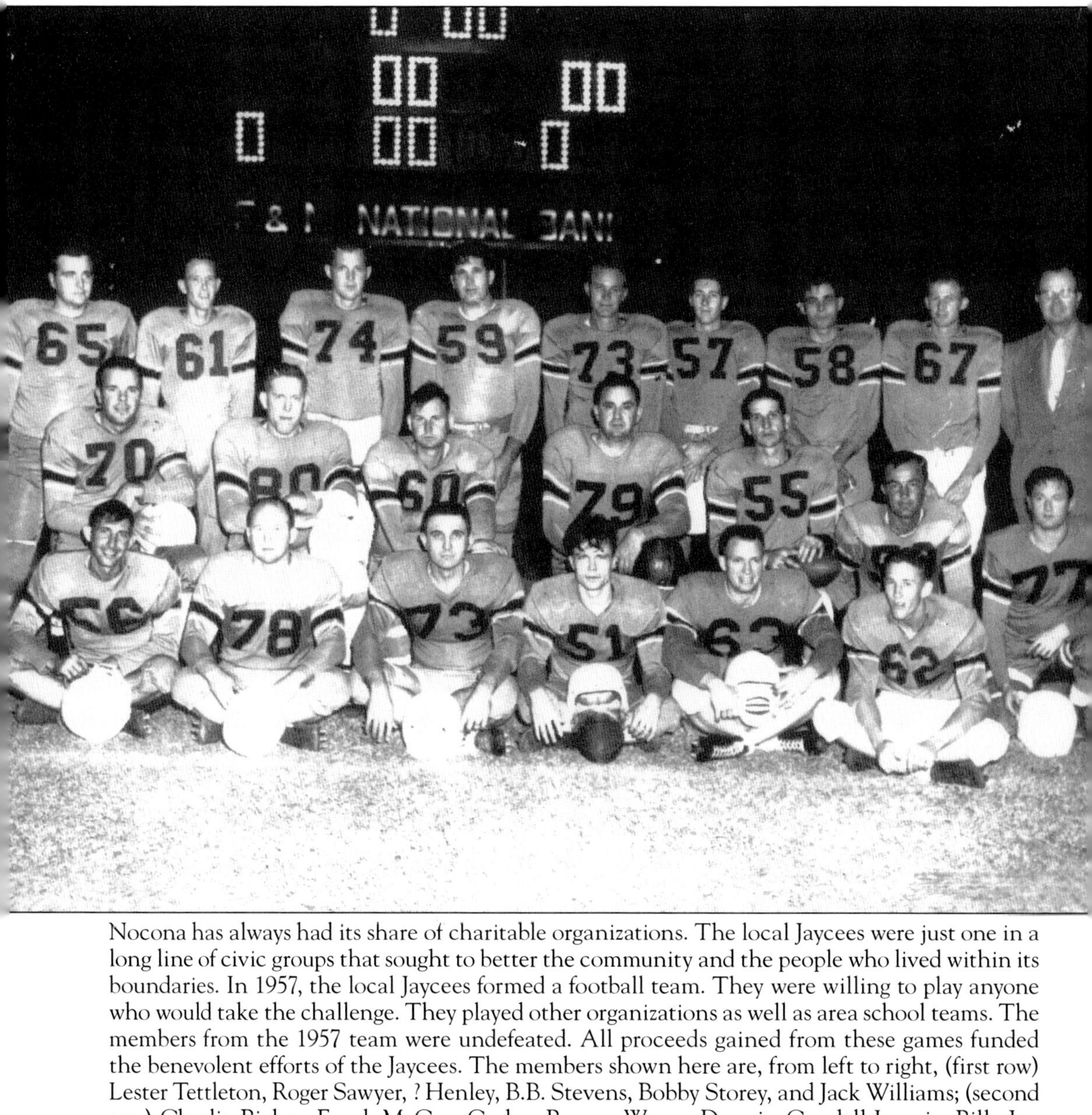

Nocona has always had its share of charitable organizations. The local Jaycees were just one in a long line of civic groups that sought to better the community and the people who lived within its boundaries. In 1957, the local Jaycees formed a football team. They were willing to play anyone who would take the challenge. They played other organizations as well as area school teams. The members from the 1957 team were undefeated. All proceeds gained from these games funded the benevolent efforts of the Jaycees. The members shown here are, from left to right, (first row) Lester Tettleton, Roger Sawyer, ? Henley, B.B. Stevens, Bobby Storey, and Jack Williams; (second row) Charlie Bigbey, Frank McCoy, Corkey Breeze, Wayne Dennis, Condell Lowrie, Billy Joe Greer, and Calvin Duckworth; (third row) Linton Campbell, Westall Williams, Don Russell, Donnie Orrel, Bill Murphy, David Rodawalt, Gene Pollard, Earl Yarbrough, and Weldon Robb. (Condell Lowrie.)

Three

Schools and Churches

Education, both academic and religious, was important to the early settlers of Nocona. Establishing schools and churches was among the first endeavors completed by the residents of the newly formed township.

When David Crockett Jordan donated land for the town, he included land specifically designated for a schoolhouse. The school district was formed by consolidating many one-room schools from the outlying communities. The first graduating class was the class of 1899. The original school burned. It was replaced with a large stone structure in 1900 that served as the school for all grade levels until 1923. At that time, a new three-story facility was built in the same location. In the early 1920s, the building underwent a major overhaul. The top floor was removed, as were the exterior staircases. A new high school was built in 1957. Lower grades continued attending North Ward for several more years.

Although the schools' main focus was education, the district also supported many athletic activities. Nocona had football, baseball, and basketball teams. For a few years, there was also a boys' volleyball team. Unlike some school districts, the girls were able to participate in sports as well. There were girls' basketball and volleyball teams.

Religious endeavors were also well attended in Nocona. Churches of several denominations were established early on, including Presbyterian, Catholic, Methodist, and Baptist. Many are still active today. Many met in members' homes or businesses until they could raise the funds to construct a building.

Nocona residents had a firm foundation in all areas. Their social, educational, and theological needs were met from the first days of the town's settlement.

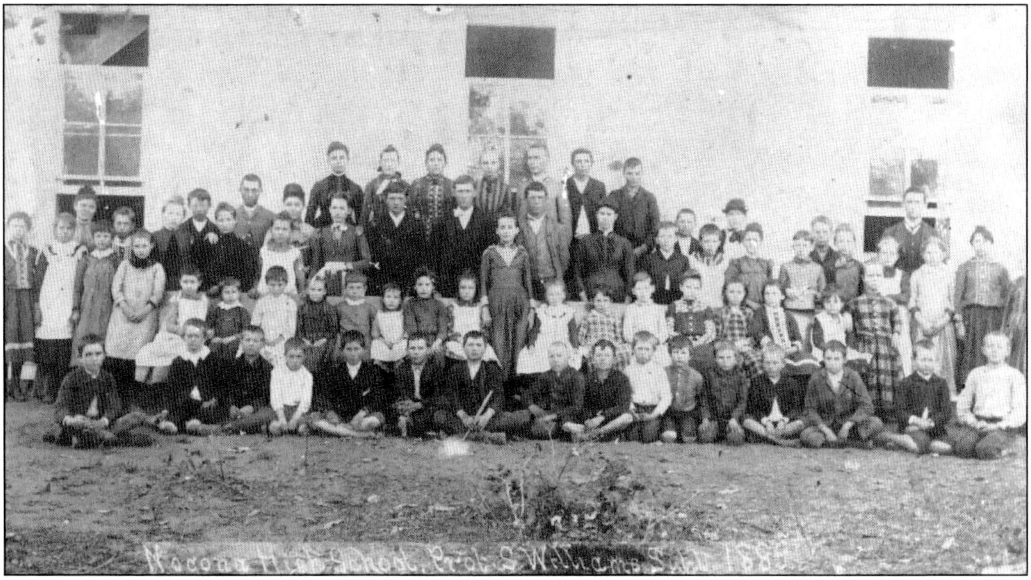

This 1889 photograph is believed to be one of the oldest pictures of Nocona still in existence. The photograph was taken in front of the first school building in Nocona. The gentleman on the right in the back row is Prof. S. Williams, the school's superintendent at the time. (TNT.)

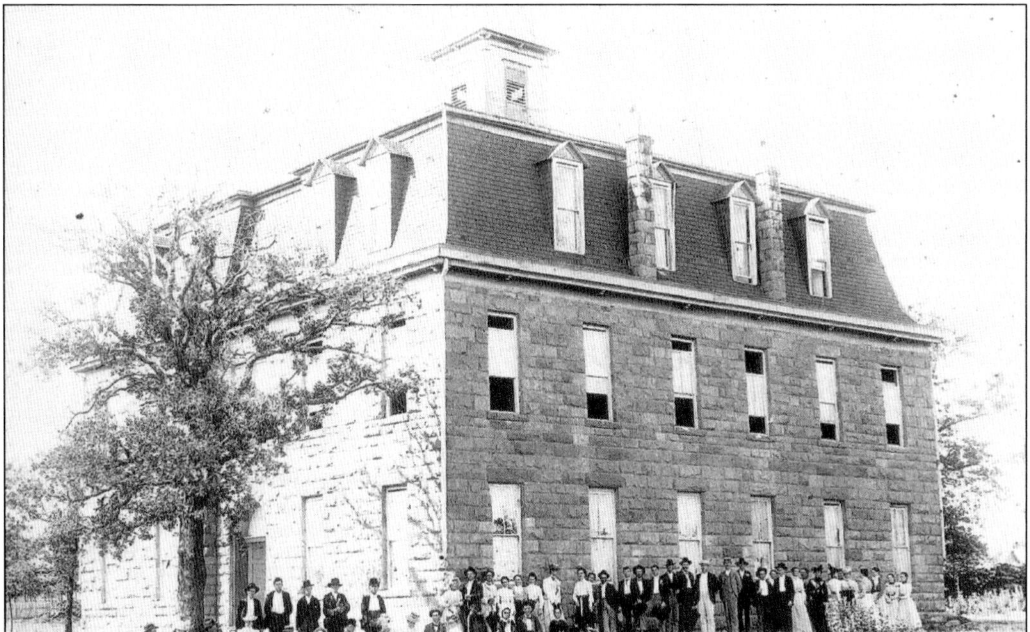

When the original school was destroyed by fire, this building was erected in 1900. It was known as North Ward. Several smaller community schools consolidated to form the Nocona School District. These included Barrel Springs, Dixie, Sandy Mound, Farmers Creek, Belcherville, Green Briar, Long Branch, Eureka, and Lone Prairie. (TNT.)

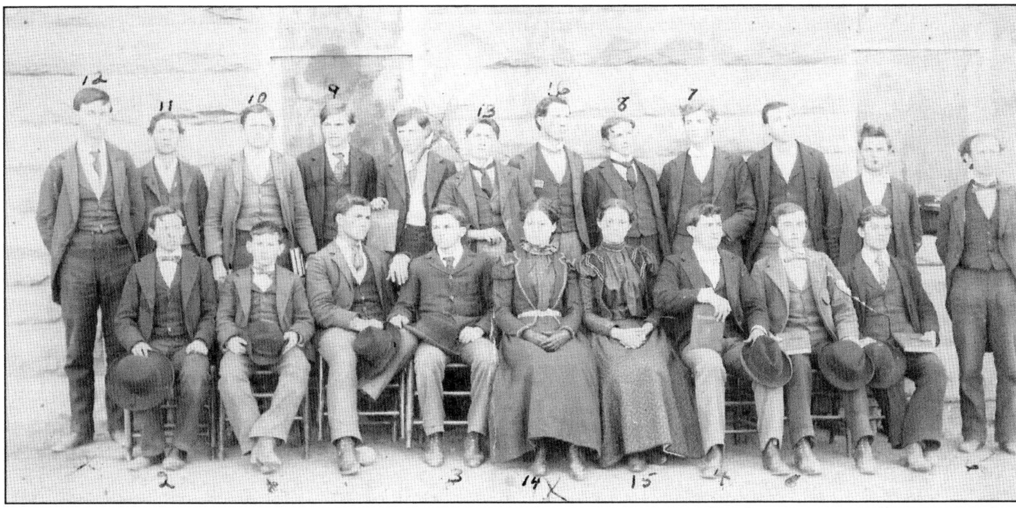

The members of the class of 1902 are, from left to right, (first row) Charles Gentry, Thomas Jordan, unidentified, Hezz Howell, Ada Hill, Sudie Pucket, Tom Shaw, and two unidentified; (second row) unidentified, ? Fox, ? Reed, Joe Benton, unidentified, Horace Carter, Ford Frey, Edd Howell, Will Click, two unidentified, and the teacher, Mr. Dunbar. (TNT.)

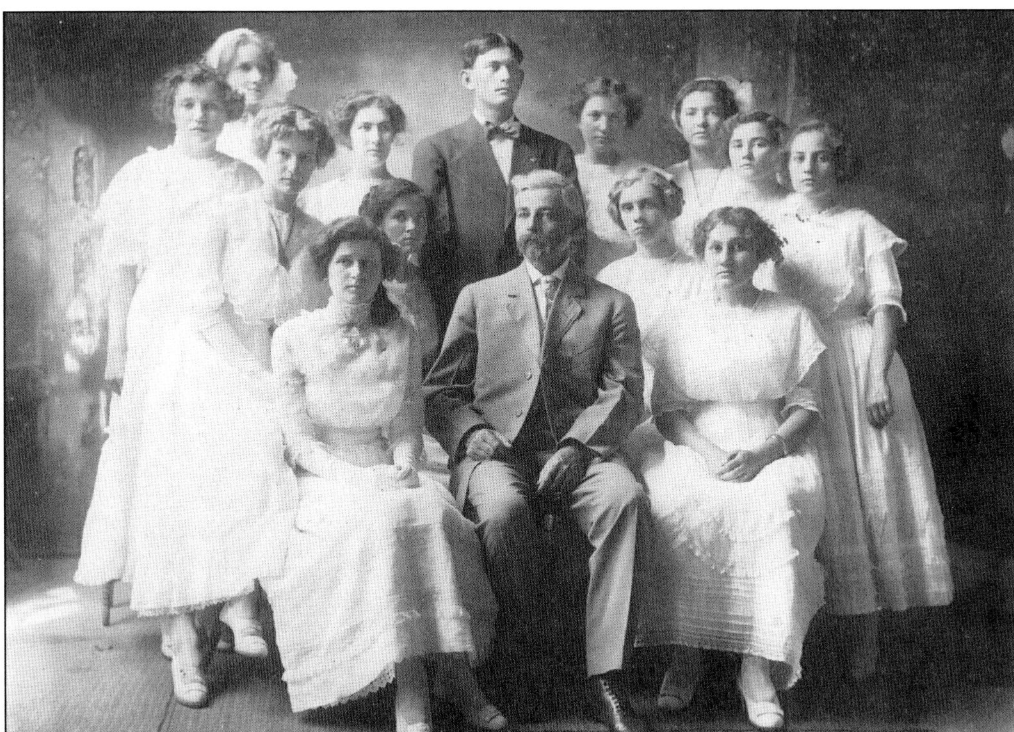

Those pictured are, from left to right, (standing) Iris Clark, Hilda Clark, Vern Flynt Priestly, Edna Howard, Ross McMahan, Mamie Hill Beal, Linda Peters Estes, Lillie Henley, and Bess Barry Berry; (seated) Connie Alverson, Kate Davis, Mr. Mace, Evelyn Powers, and Florence Humphrey Justin. (TNT.)

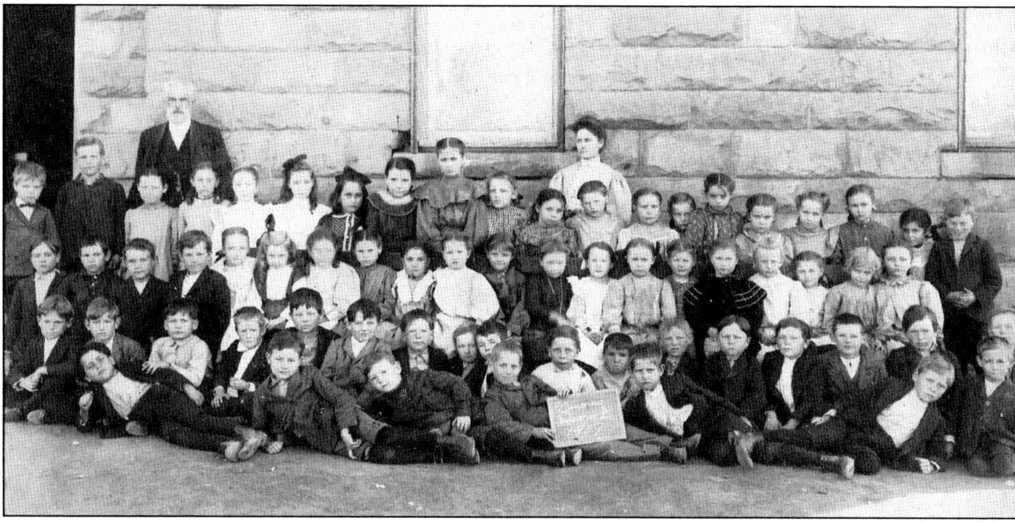

This 1907 school photograph is of a group of young school children. The young men are posed reclined onto their sides in order for the photographer to fit such a large group into the photograph. Those pictured in the 1921 fourth-grade photograph below are, from left to right, (first row) Cyrena Wilkes, Lora Dell Van Dyke, Josephine Stump, unidentified, Helen Skinner, Helen Hill, two unidentified, Cleo Nelson, Ruth Lee, and unidentified; (second row) Miss Carmichael, Clark Hood, Grace Priddy, two unidentified, Robert Wilson, Roy McCarley, J.N . Cardwell, Bill Pribble, two unidentified, Albert Harrell, unidentified, and Frances Beck; (third row) Foye Wood, Rowland Bratcher, Lois Emery, Helen Miller, Helen Cone, unidentified, Perry Patterson, and unidentified; (fourth row) A.C. Wood, unidentified, Bertha McNew, L.C. Addington, Mary Clark, unidentified, and Rankin Underwood. (Above, Cecil Fenoglio; below, TNT.)

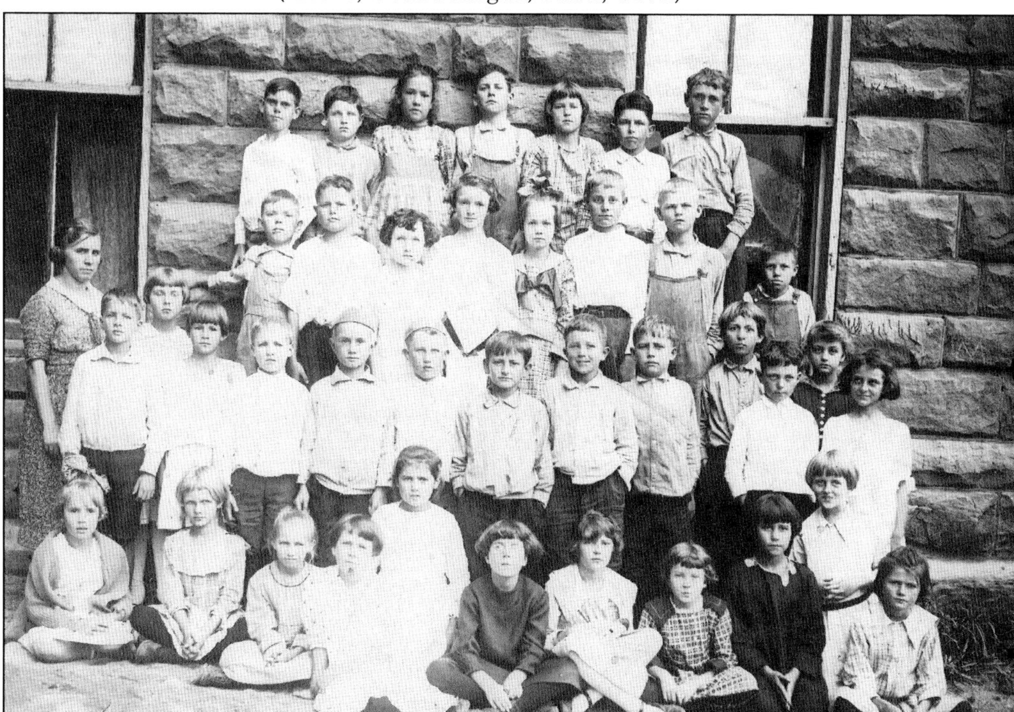

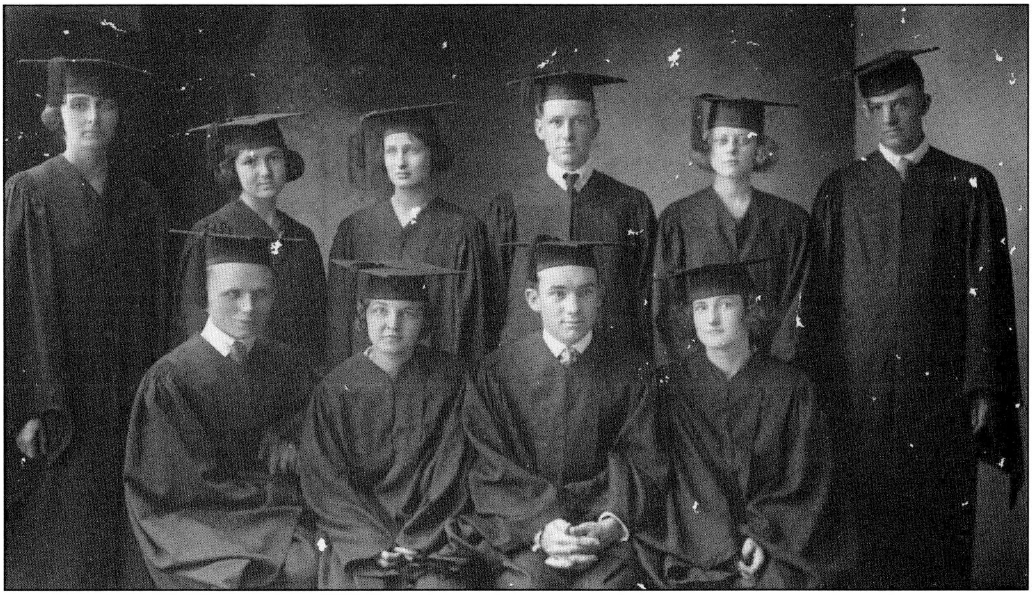

Members of the class of 1921 are, from left to right, (first row) Arthur Tripp, Frances Flandos, James McCall, and unidentified; (second row) Ruth Priddy, Eula Priddy, Lona Atkins, Bob Flynt, Cyril Martin, and Rich Modrell. (Montague County Historical Commission.)

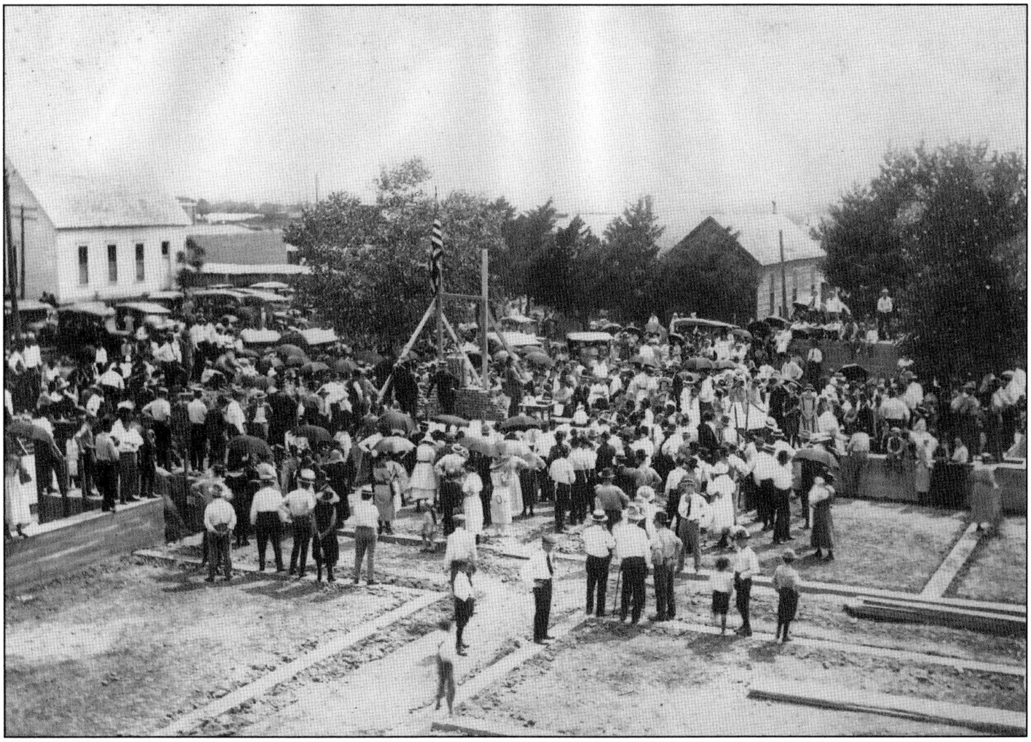

The construction of the North Ward School was important to the community. During the dedication of the school, everyone came to witness the laying of the cornerstone in the new building. Everyone was dressed in his or her best attire. Most of the women are holding parasols for protection from the summer sun. (Montague County Historical Commission.)

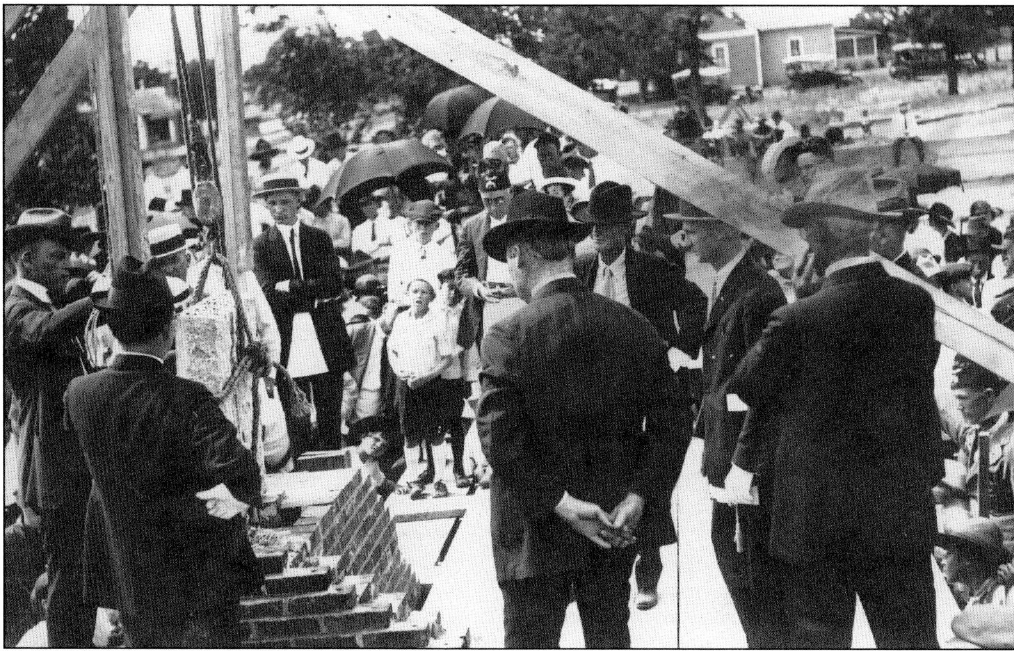

Many of Nocona's prominent citizens were involved in the dedication of the new North Ward School. The gentleman placing the cornerstone is Bob Collins. The three men with their backs to the camera are, from left to right, Dr. S.T. Humphreys, Sam Fleming, and John Miller. The two men under the support beam are John Maddox (left) and Earl Justin. (Montague County Historical Society.)

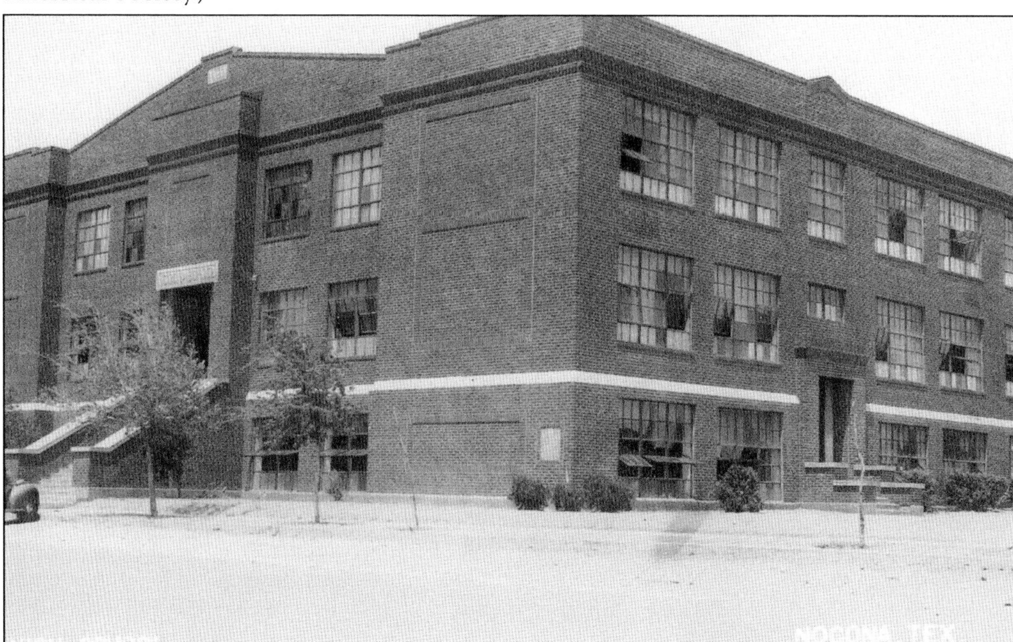

The new North Ward School was used from 1923 until the new high school was built in 1957. During that time, the school underwent an extensive overhaul. The upper floor and exterior stairs were removed. The building has been turned into apartments and is still in use today. (TNT.)

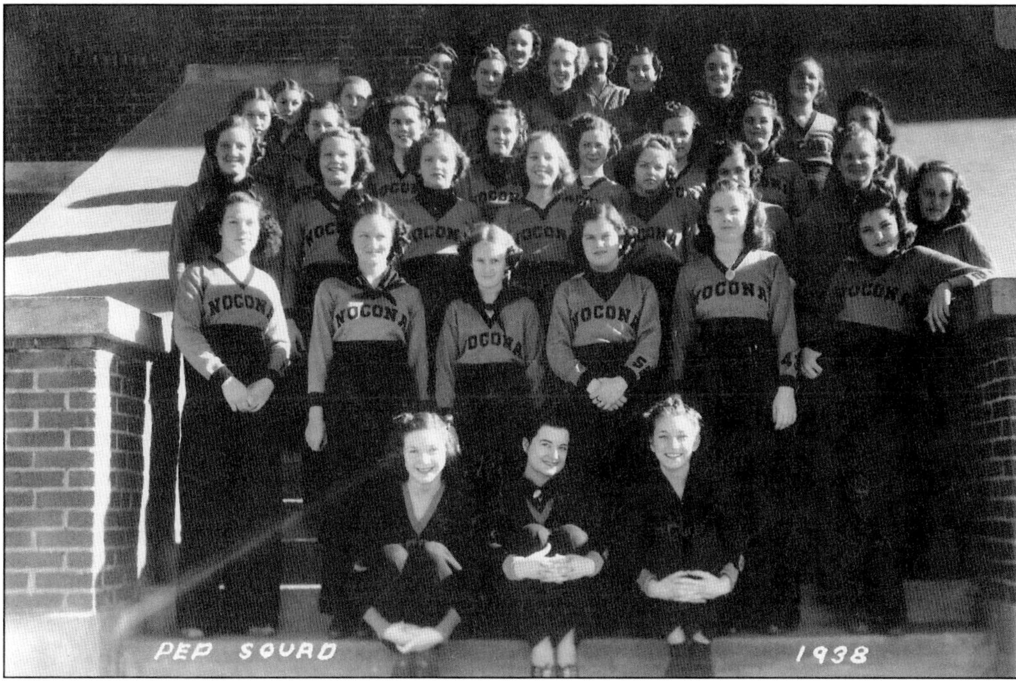

The 1938 pep squad poses for a photograph on the steps of the North Ward School. The pep squad attended all of the athletic activities to cheer the school teams on to victory. (Mary Viola McGrew.)

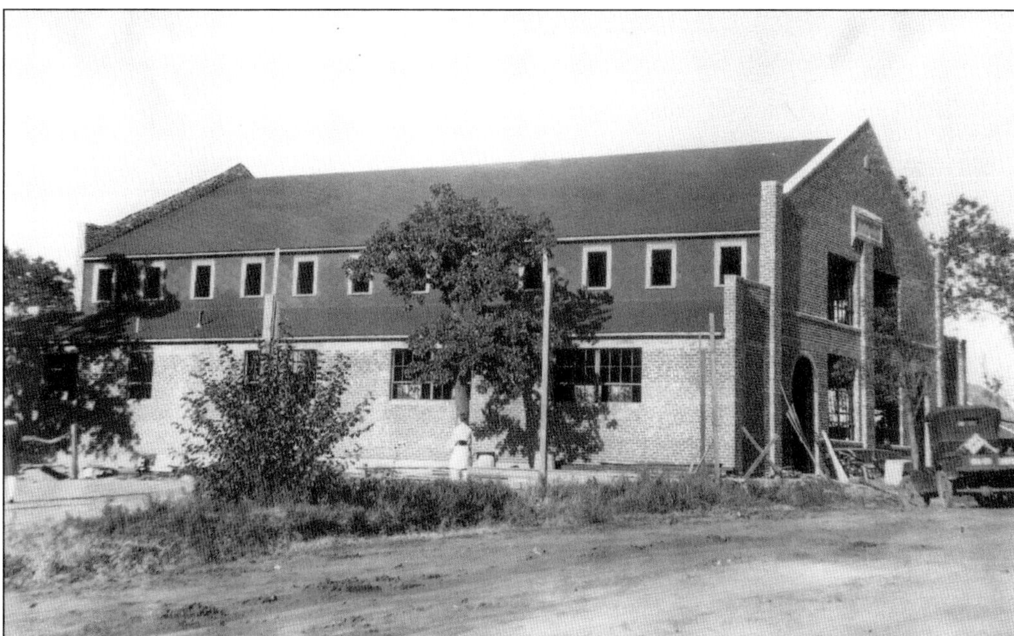

The gymnasium was added a few years after the North Ward School was built. The large facility provided much needed space to hold athletic competitions as well as other school activities, such as banquets and dances. (TNT.)

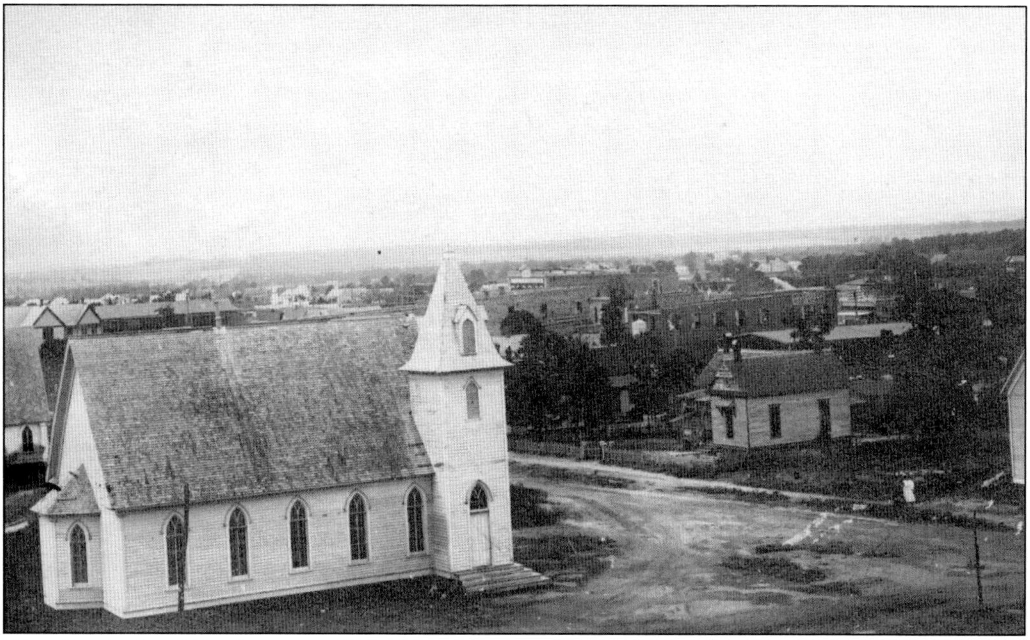

The Cumberland Presbyterian Church was built in the early 1880s. The Methodist and Baptist congregations helped erect the structure. It was located on Cooke Street. The church was destroyed by a fire on Wednesday, October 12, 1938. The congregation chose not to rebuild after the fire. (TNT.)

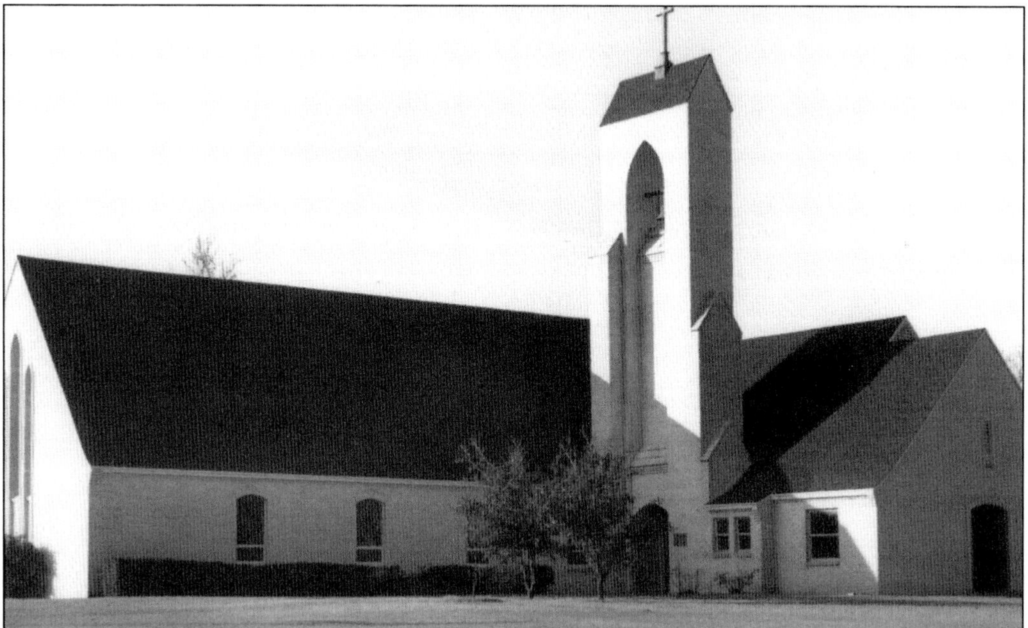

Prior to 1952, members of the First Presbyterian Church met in homes or in W.L. Scott's hardware store. Joe and Geneva Benton donated the building site for the church that was located on Eleventh Street. A total of 32 members signed the original petition to organize the church. (TNT.)

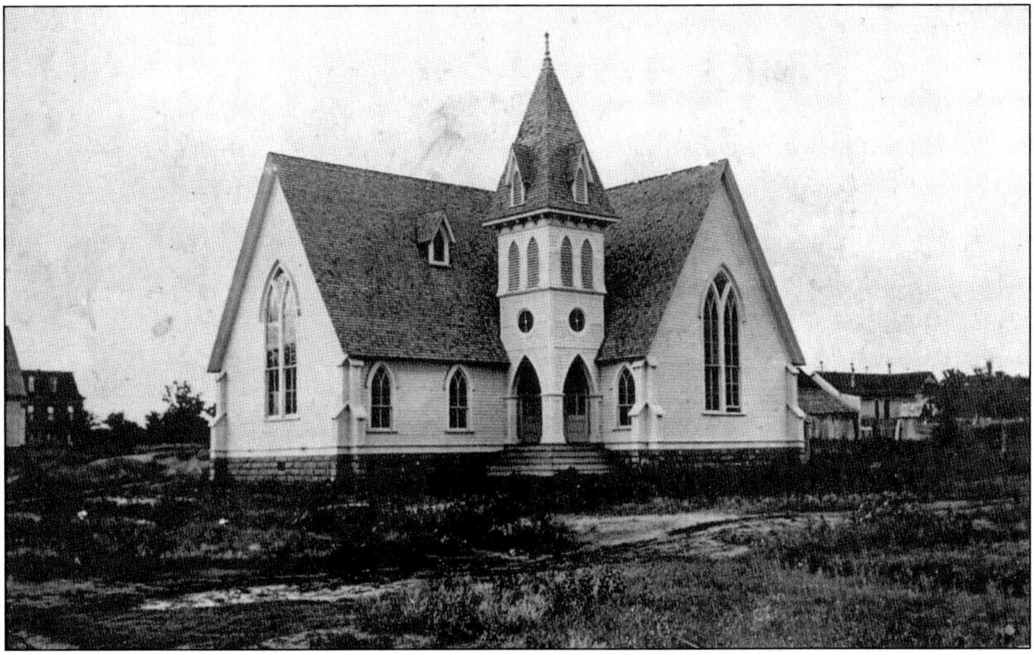

This building of the Central Christian Church was built in 1894. It was built by the Roger brothers and R. Chenowith and dedicated by A.J. Bush. The church was organized by the first minister, M.F. Smith, in 1888. Until this permanent structure was erected, members met in homes and other buildings. (TNT.)

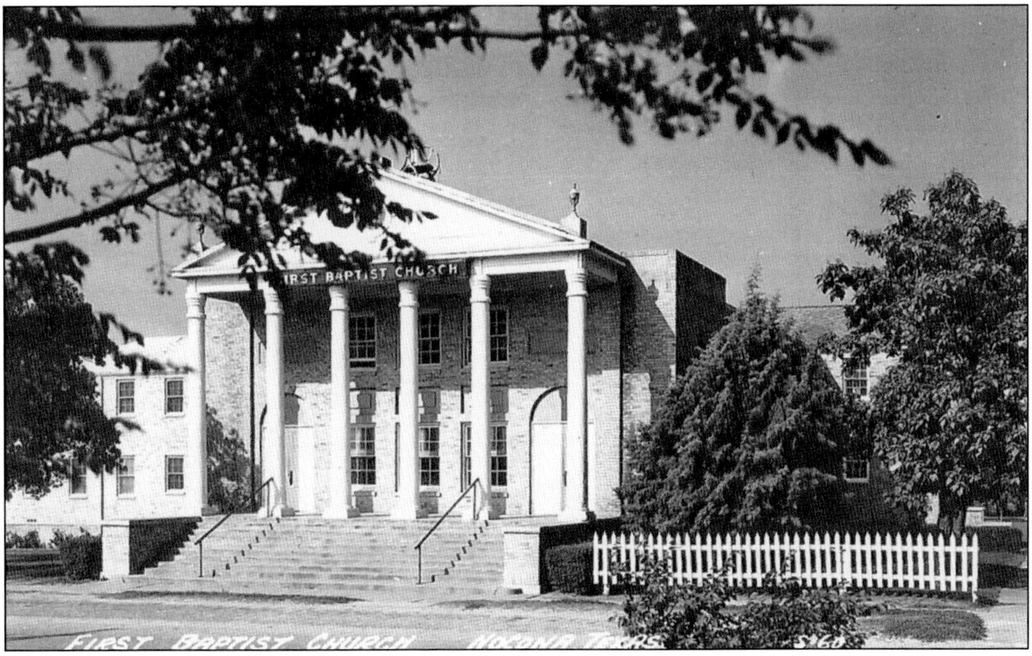

The Nocona Baptist Church was organized on August 22, 1889. The original church building was constructed in 1896. In 1904, the name was changed to First Baptist Church. The original structure was torn down in 1927 and replaced with this more modern facility. (TNT.)

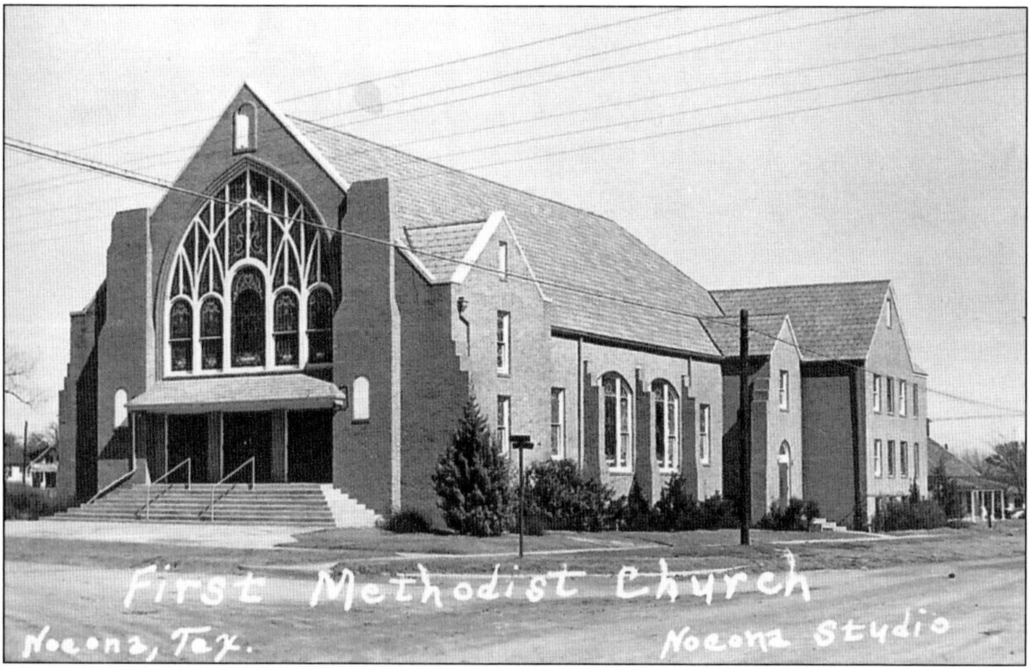

This is the third building to be constructed and used as the Methodist church in Nocona. The first was erected in 1895 and the second in 1912. This building was constructed in 1943, after the previous building was torn down in 1937 to make room for a larger facility. (TNT.)

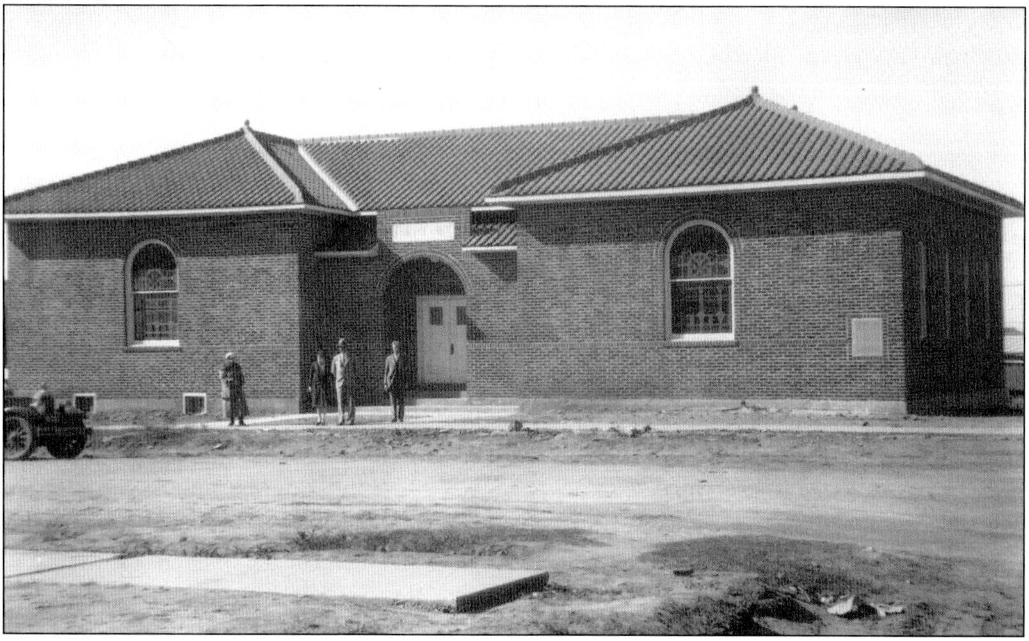

The Church of Christ is located at 311 Cooke Street. The first service was conducted on November 22, 1904, in a small wood-framed building. By 1920, the congregation had outgrown the facility, and a new building was required. The construction was almost completed when this photograph was taken. (TNT.)

Four

Leather Center of the Southwest

In the fall of 1879, Herman Joseph Justin hitched a ride with a wagon train driver from Gainesville to Spanish Fort, Texas. When the 20-year-old, road-worn Justin arrived in Spanish Fort, he set out looking for a job. Before the end of the day, he had acquired the job of sweeping up at Frank See's barbershop. While these wages supplied room and board, it did not fulfill his ultimate goal. His dream was to open a cobbler shop and make boots for the Chisholm Trail cowboys. After a few months, See agreed to front Justin $35 for a good leather hide. From that moment on, Justin was in the boot-making business. When the railroad bypassed Spanish Fort in favor of nearby Nocona, Justin moved his operation to take advantage of the railway service. The Justin Boot Company was the first in a long tradition of leather crafters in Nocona.

The Justin Boot Company continued to thrive in Nocona until H.J. Justin's death in 1918. Soon afterward, his sons decided to relocate the business to Fort Worth, Texas. In 1919, Earl Justin and G.W. Humphreys established Justin Leather Goods Company, which manufactured handbags, wallets, and belts. Enid Justin, daughter of H.J. Justin, disagreed with her brothers' plans to relocate the boot company and, in 1925, opened the Nocona Boot Company. Although the Justin family played a large role in establishing Nocona as a major contender in the leather industry, several other companies and individuals helped along the way.

The Nocona Leather Goods Company began in 1926. The name was eventually changed to Nocona Athletic Goods Company. Among other quality athletic items, they manufacture the world-famous Nokona baseball glove. The company has survived two devastating fires, one in 1927 and the other in 2006. They rebuilt each time and have been a leader in Nocona's leather industry for over 75 years.

The quality work produced by these companies, along with several individual saddle makers and leather artists, put Nocona on the map as the Leather Center of the Southwest.

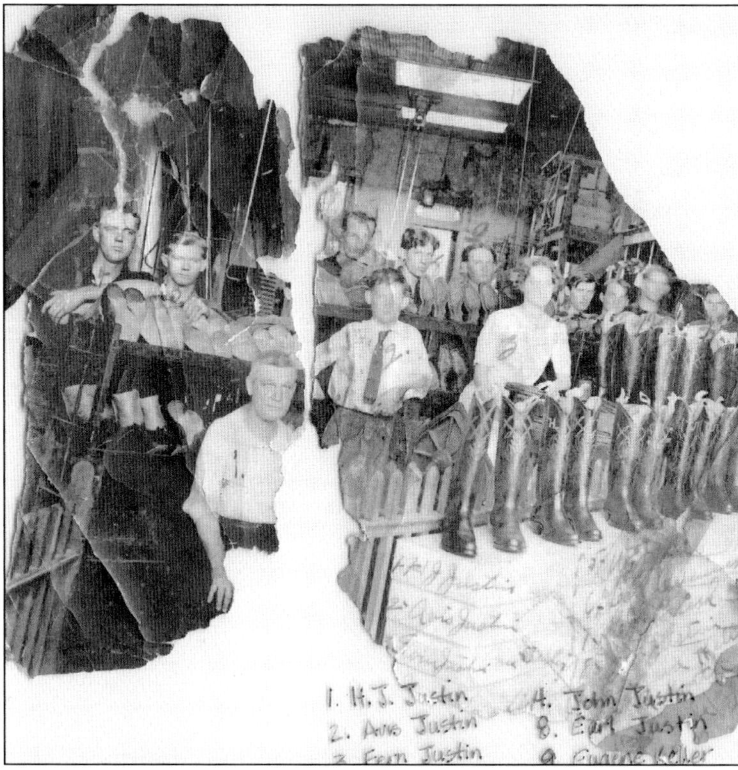

While damaged, this photograph represents a time in Nocona's history that was too important not to include. H.J. Justin moved his boot making business to Nocona in 1887, starting the leather industry for which Nocona became known. Shown here are, from left to right, (first row) H.J. Justin, Avis Justin, and Fern Justin; (second row) John Justin, Earl Justin, and Eugene Keller. The others are not identified. (TNT.)

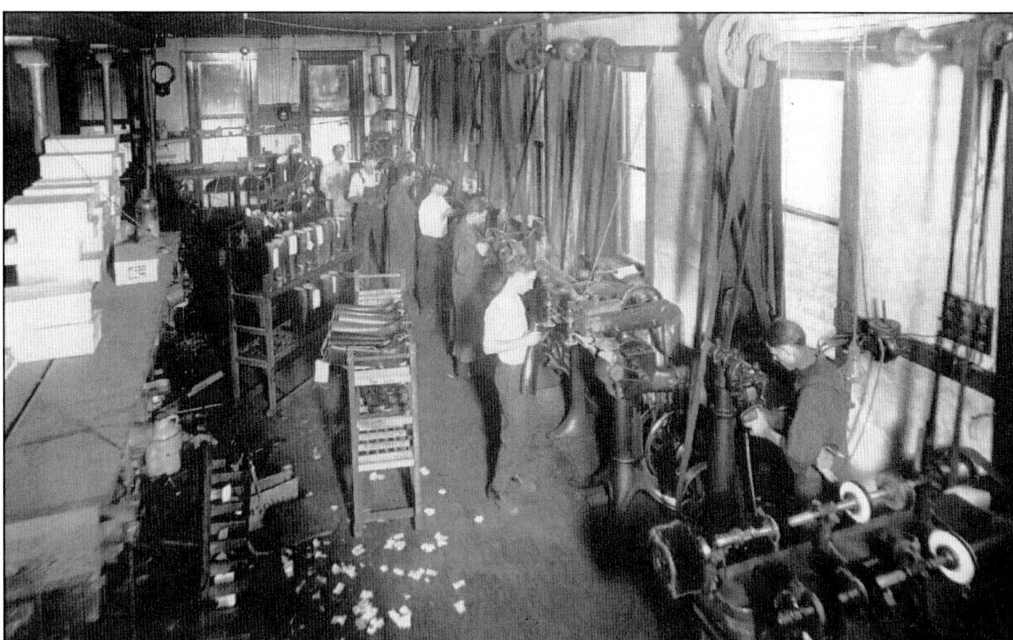

This is an early photograph of the interior of H.J. Justin's factory. The machinery used in the boot-making process worked on a large belt-and-pulley system. The boots on the rack have 18-inch tops, which was customary of the time period. The factory was originally located on the east side of Clay Street and later moved to the west side. (TNT.)

H.J. Justin Boot Company began in Spanish Fort in 1879 and moved to Nocona in 1887. Justin continued to run the company, along with his sons, until his death in 1918. The sons continued the business after his death. In the early 1920s, the sons moved the operation to Fort Worth, against their sister Enid's wishes. Enid continued with her own offshoot of the company in Nocona, which is still in operation today. (TNT.)

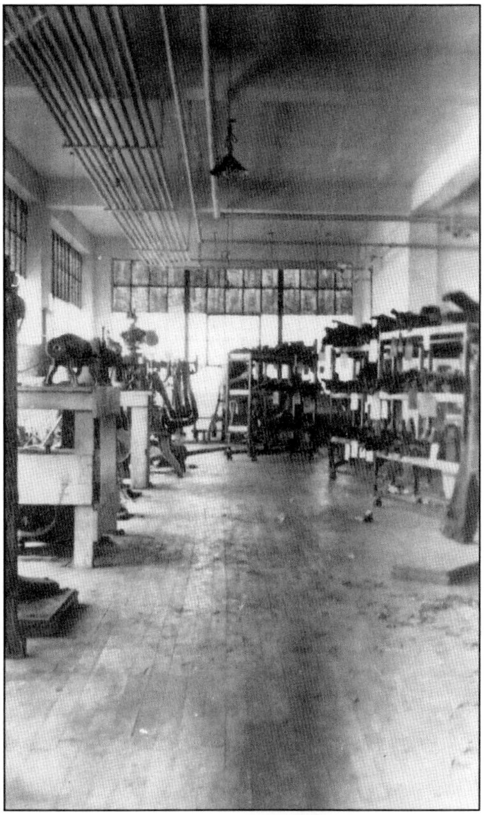

This early photograph, taken in approximately 1915, shows the employees of the H.J. Justin Boot Company. When the company moved to Fort Worth, a handful of these employees chose to stay and work for Enid Justin in the new Nocona Boot Company. (TNT.)

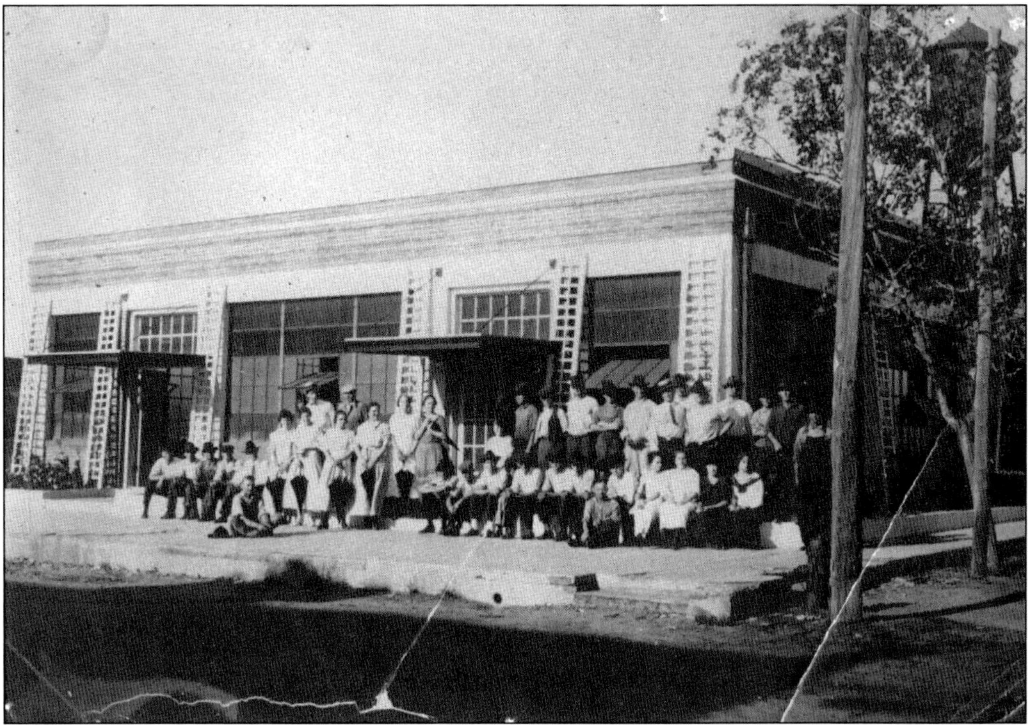

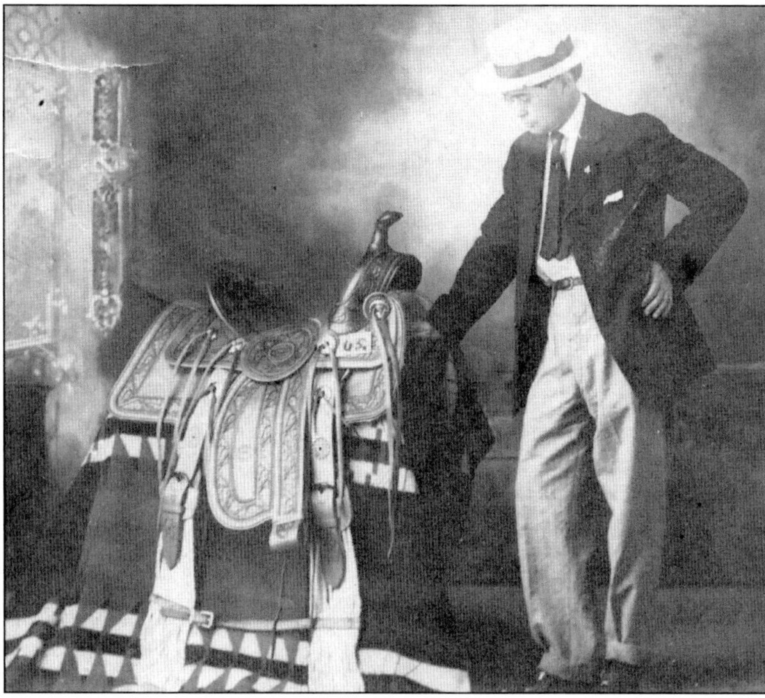

John M. Drake came to Nocona in the early 1900s. He first worked as a clerk at Thurston's Hardware. Thurston allowed him to set up a small saddle making shop at the store. By 1908, Drake opened his own saddle shop on Clay Street, south of the Farmers and Merchants Bank. Drake's hobby was constructing miniature saddles that were as detailed as the life-sized models. (TNT.)

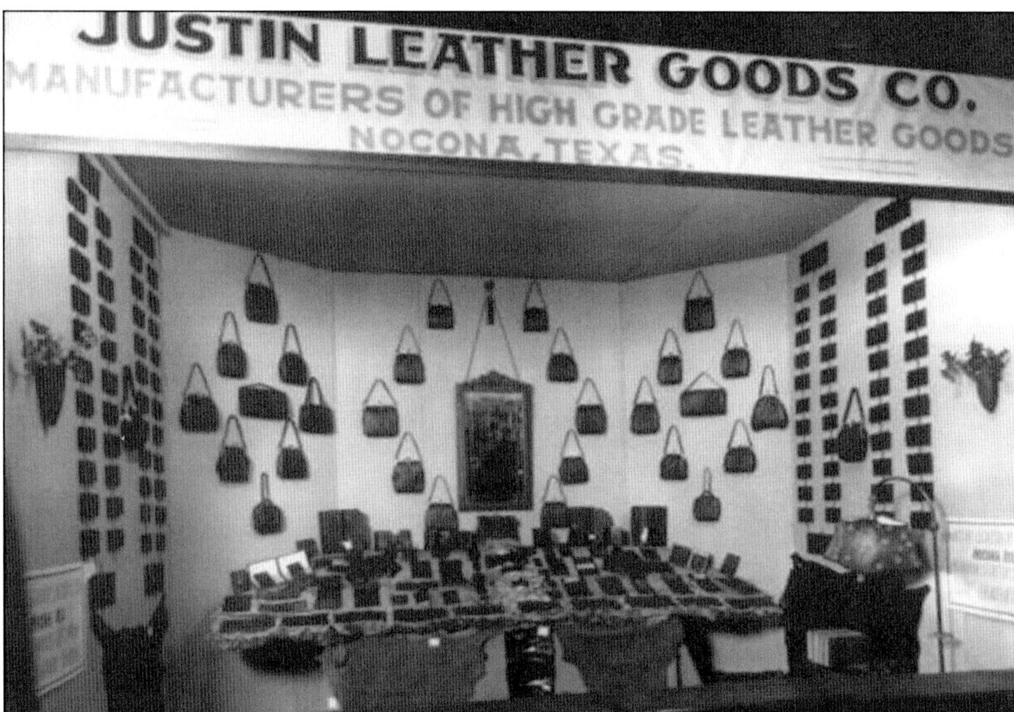

During Justin Leather Goods' peak, the company employed between 80 and 100 people, including outside salesmen. The salesmen worked on commission. Justin Leather Goods set up display booths at all of the major markets, like the one in this picture. H.J. Justin and Sons purchased controlling interest in the business and moved the factory to Fort Worth. (TNT.)

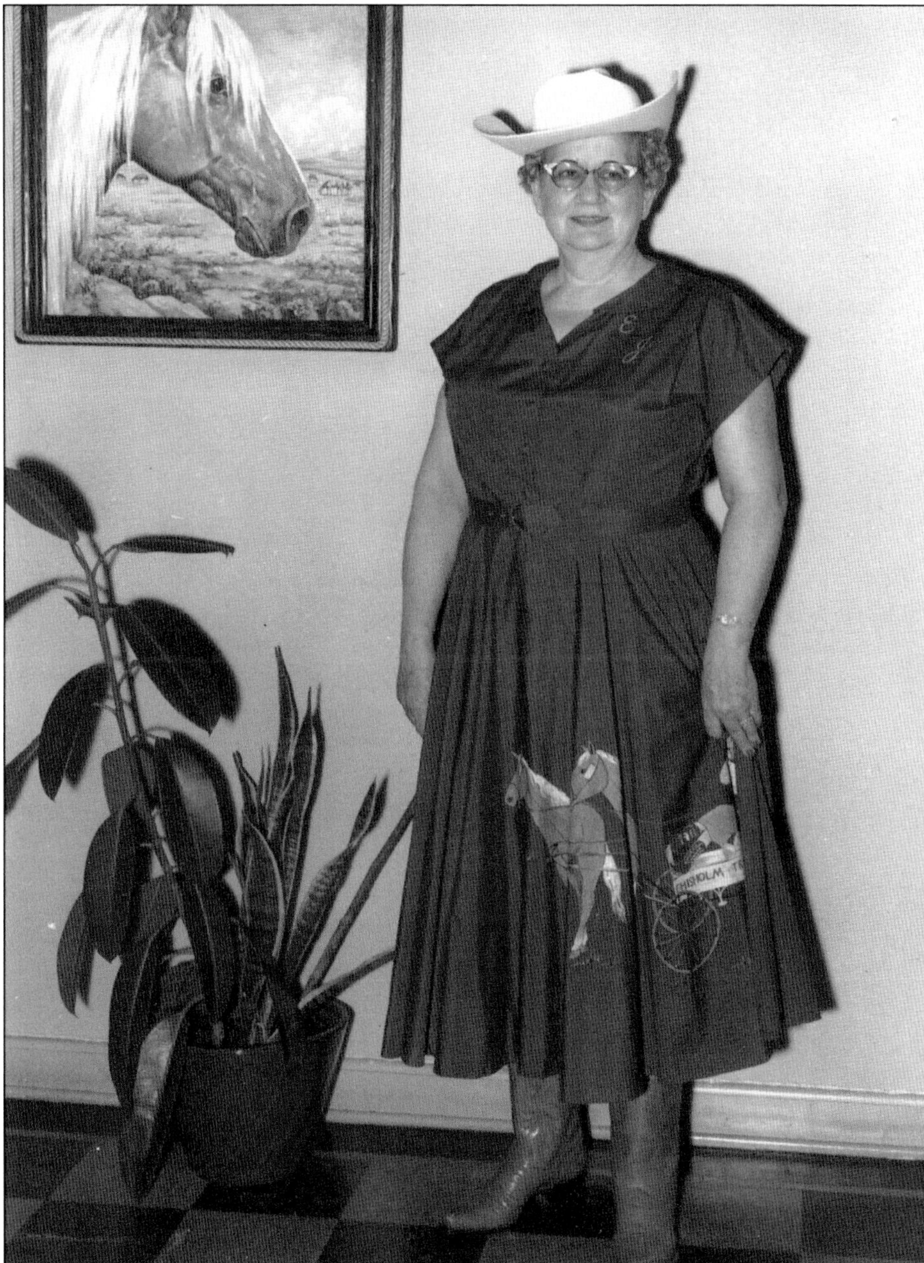

Enid Justin was the daughter of boot maker H.J. Justin. She was opposed to her brothers' decision to move the H.J. Justin Boot Company to Fort Worth. In 1925, with $5,000 borrowed from the bank, Miss Enid established the Nocona Boot Company. She was the first female owner of a cowboy boot manufacturing business. Even though cowboy boots were her livelihood, she was seldom seen wearing boots. On special occasions or promotional events, Miss Enid would don a pair of her famous boots. In 1981, Nocona Boot Company merged with Justin Industries. Miss Enid retired as the president and chief executive officer of the company in September 1982 at the age of 88. She continued to serve as honorary chairman of the board and as a consultant until her death in 1990. (TNT.)

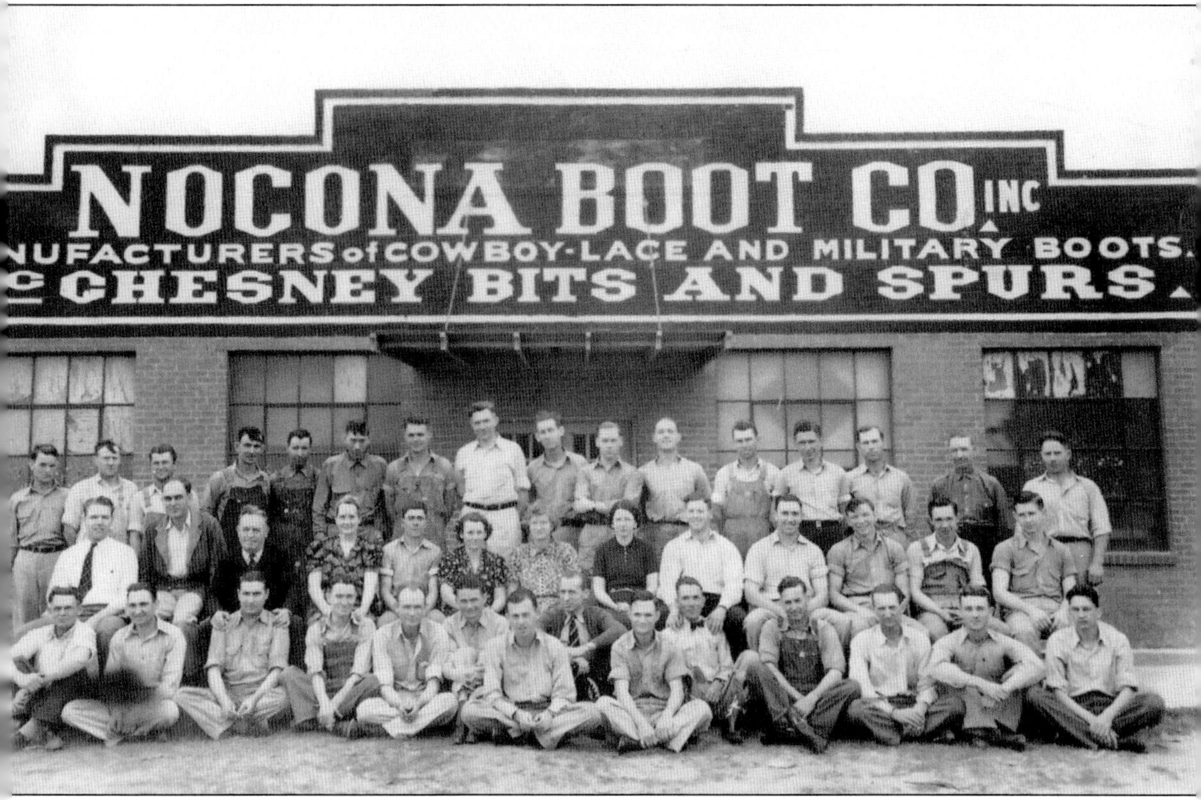

The Nocona Boot Company purchased the McChesney Bit and Spur Company in 1929 and added McChesney to its product line. McChesney was famous for its gal leg spurs, which are very collectible today. Posed in front of the original factory facing Willow Street in 1938 are, from left to right, (first row) N.J. Dunaway, Loyd Winningham, H.D. Croxton, Ted Hewitt, Ben Walker, Johnny Coleman, Thurston Drake, Jesse Thompson, Paul Haggerton, E.B. Vice, Fred McGrew, Walter Cooper, Tom Yancy, and Winstead Cooper; (second row) Dean Taylor, R.S. Lemon, Roy Berry, Enid Justin, Bill Hewitt, Rosa Redman, Mrs. Bill Hagler, Mrs. Tony McGrady, Wayne Jackson, Elmer Adkins, Pete Rice, Cal Benton, and Jack Goodspeed; (third row) Tommy Cain, Bill Hagler, Roy Hillard, W.T. Ray, J.R. Welch, W.D. Barnett, Kent Garrison, S.B. Alexander, Frank Milson, Gene Keller, Horace Henry, Floyd Payne, Bill Stouder, Leon Henry, H.W. Payne, and Jim Richey. (TNT.)

At the Nocona Boot Company, Miss Enid proudly displayed some of her father's boot-making and leather-working tools. These were the tools with which H.J. Justin started the boot-making tradition that Miss Enid would spend her life following. Her nephew Joe is shown next to the tool display. (TNT.)

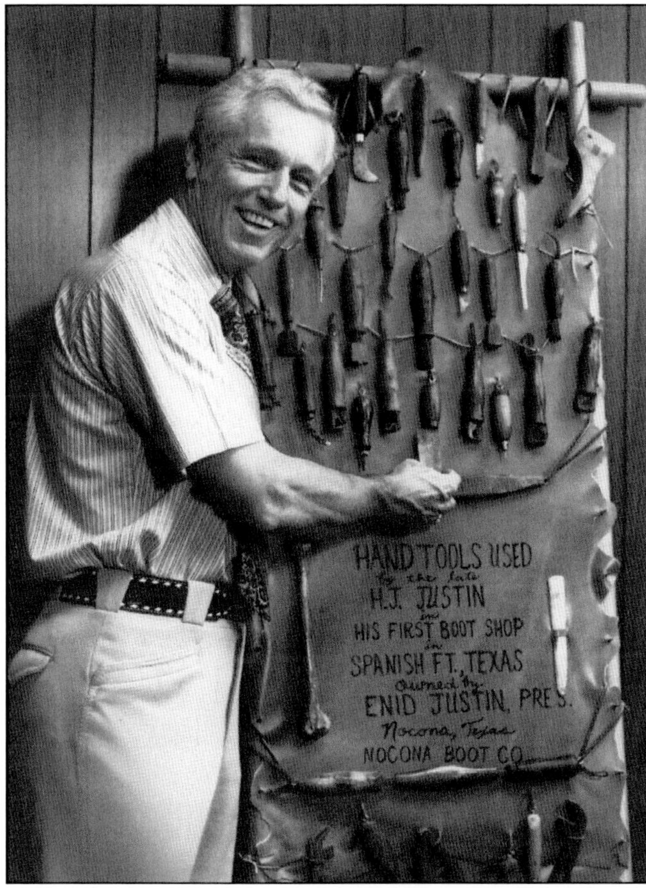

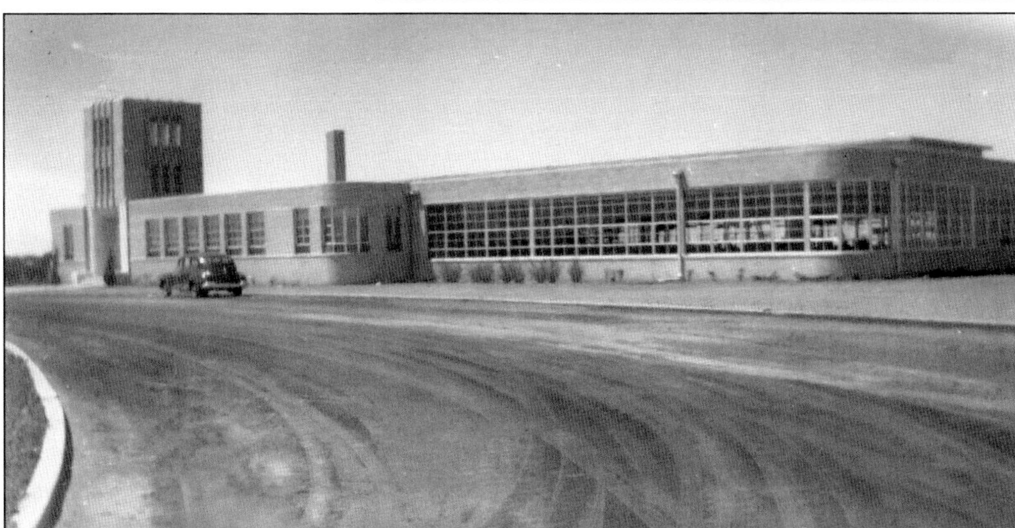

Miss Enid broke ground on this new factory building on June 29, 1947. The building was completed in June 1948. It was located on Highway 82, just east of Nocona proper. The structure originally was 53,000 square feet, but over the years, 125,000 square feet have been added. (TNT.)

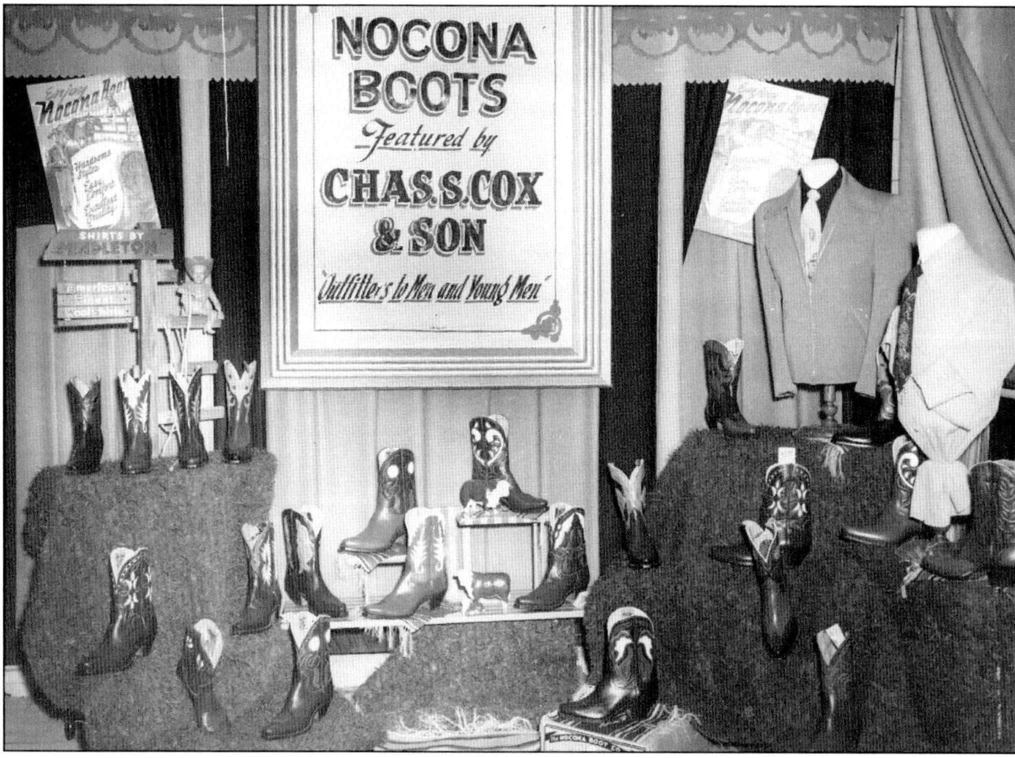

Miss Enid was an astute businesswoman. When she first opened her company, she did whatever it took to keep it afloat. She rented out rooms in her home for extra cash, worked in every department of the book company, and hired the best possible people. She knew she had to market her boots. She hired outside salesmen to travel across the country. Nocona boots were popular in all areas of the nation. Several retail stores throughout the country carried the Nocona Boot Company line. These photographs from the 1950s show the displays set up by the Charles S. Cox and Son and Dick Bardon stores featuring Nocona Boots. (Both, TNT.)

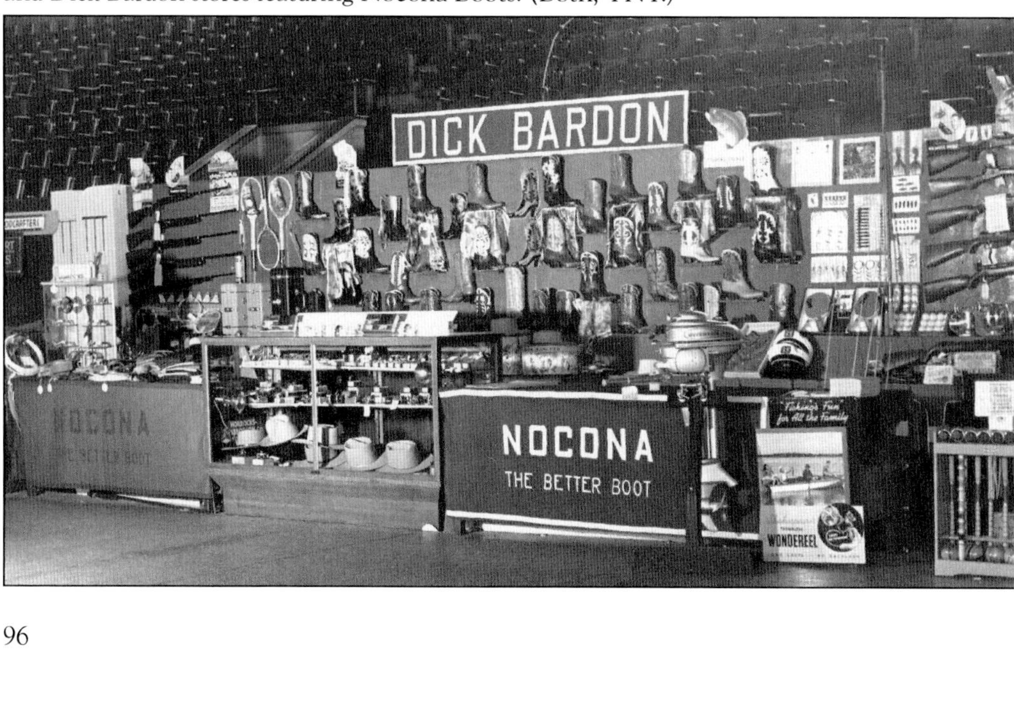

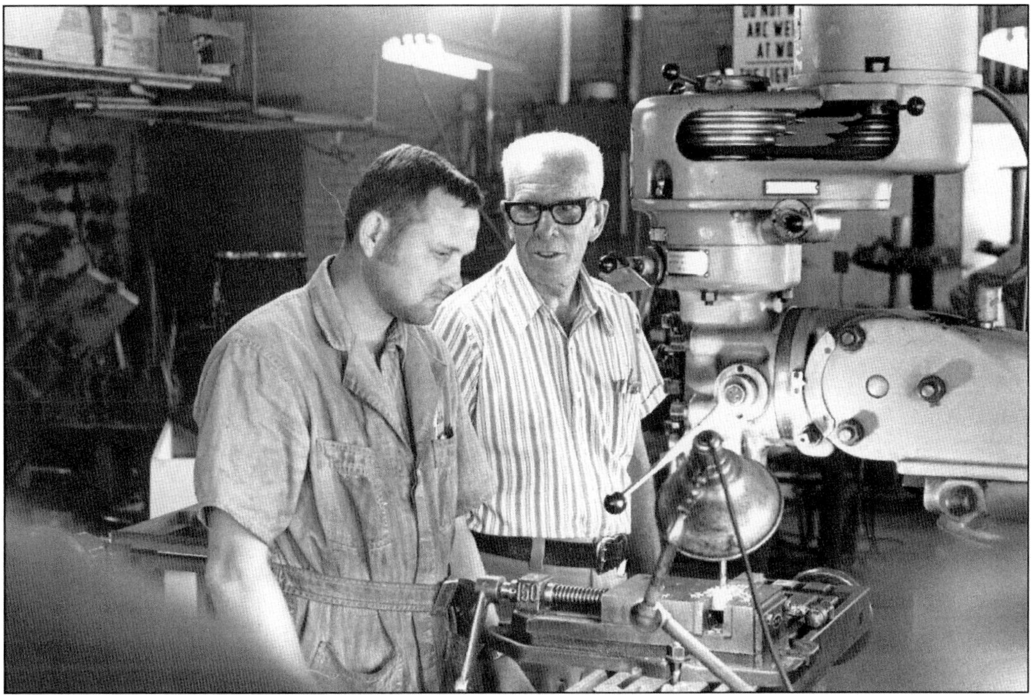

Arnold Dennis (left) and Al Ramsey inspect an endmill in the Nocona Boot Company maintenance department. Ramsey was responsible for starting the department in the early 1970s, and prior to its organization, each department foreman was accountable for the machines in his area. Creating a department solely for maintenance freed the foreman to attend to other matters and, in the long run, sped up the production line. (TNT.)

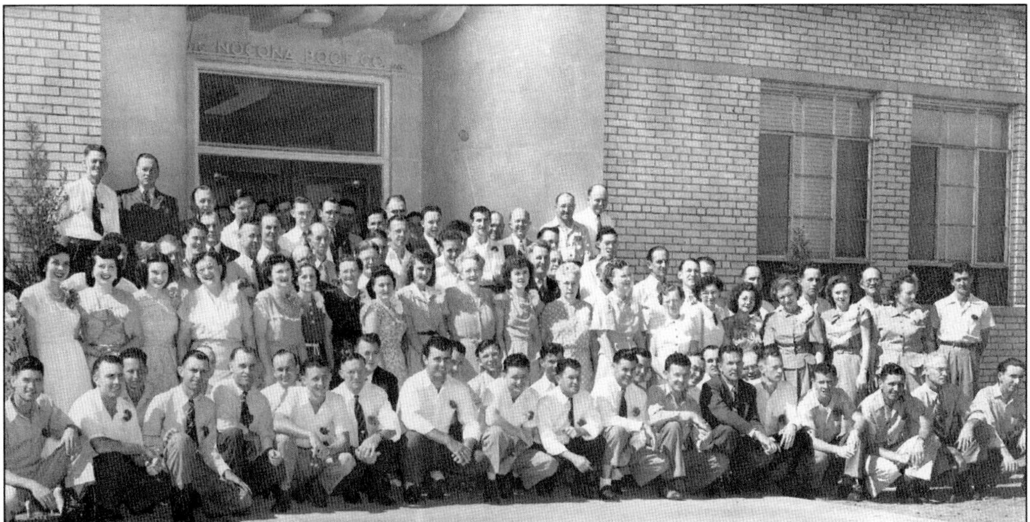

This photograph shows a group of Nocona Boot Company employees in the 1950s. The Nocona Boot Company was one of the largest sources of employment for Nocona residents for several years. Many employees spent their entire working career at the boot company. The company ceased manufacturing in August 1999. At the time it closed the doors forever, 183 people worked for the company. (TNT.)

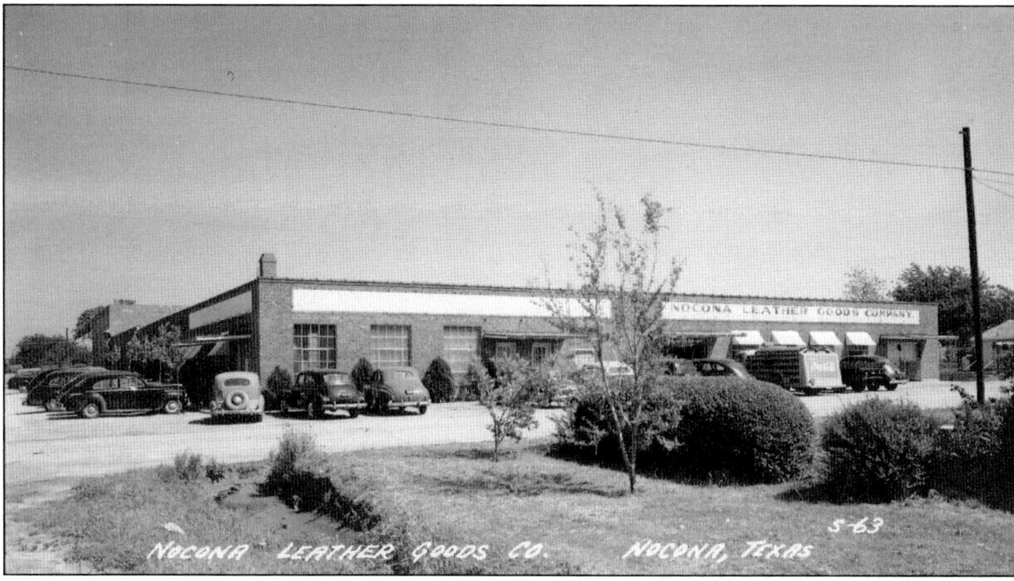

Cadmus McCall and T.B. Wilkes established Nocona Leather Goods in 1926. The first product produced by the new company was a lady's steer-hide purse. In order to stay in business during the Depression, the company turned its focus to manufacturing sporting equipment. The name of the company was eventually changed to Nocona Athletic Goods. (TNT.)

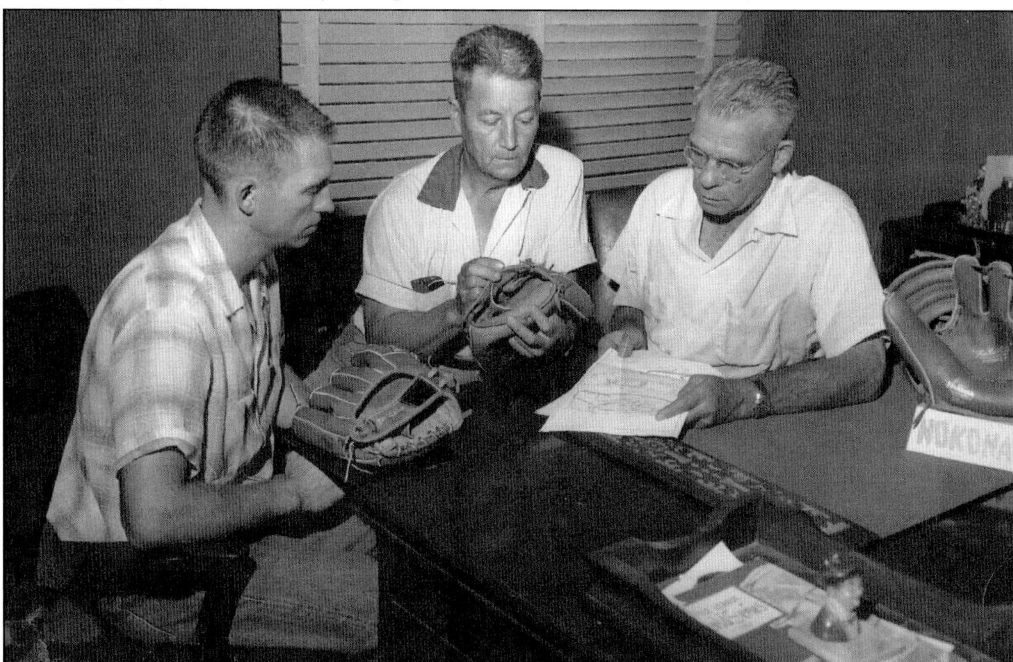

Cadmus McCall hired his son-in-law Roberts E. Storey (right) as the company's president in 1933. The company prospered under Storey's direction. The company began manufacturing children's sporting equipment, often to match school colors. The Storey family is still involved in the company today. Storey's son Roberts M. Storey (left) also worked at the company and eventually took over the presidency. (TNT.)

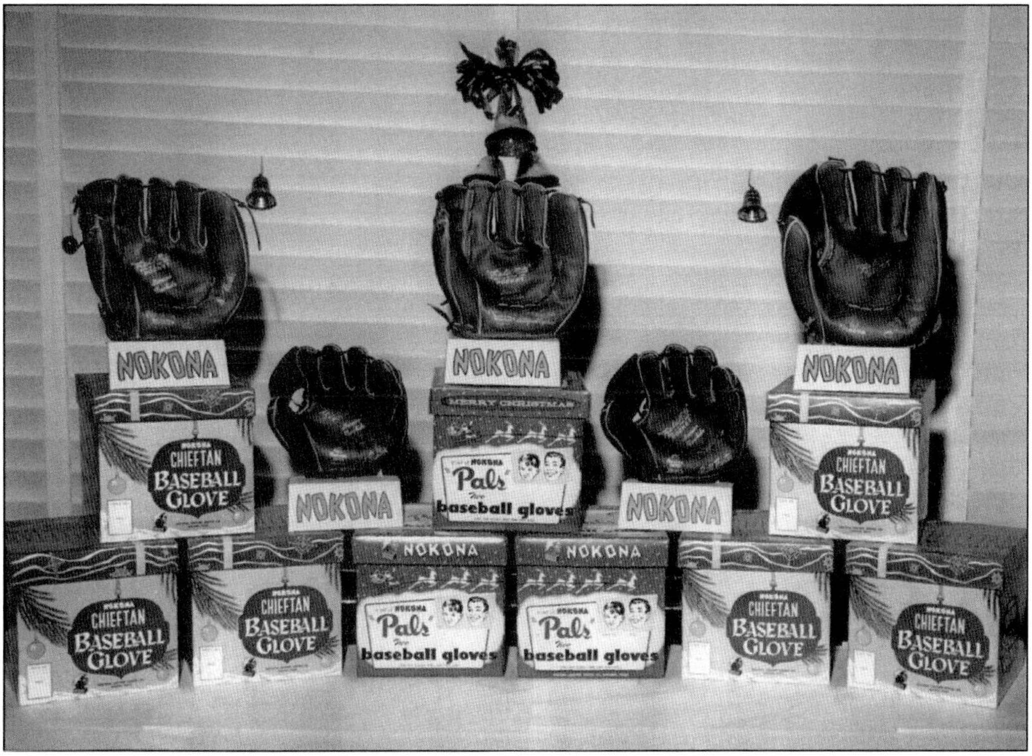

One of the most recognized products manufactured by the Nocona Athletic Company was the iconic Nokona baseball glove. There was discrepancy over copyright issues with the name Nocona, so the company chose to use a "k" in the spelling of its brand of gloves. These gloves were used by schools and professional athletes and are still manufactured in Nocona today. (TNT.)

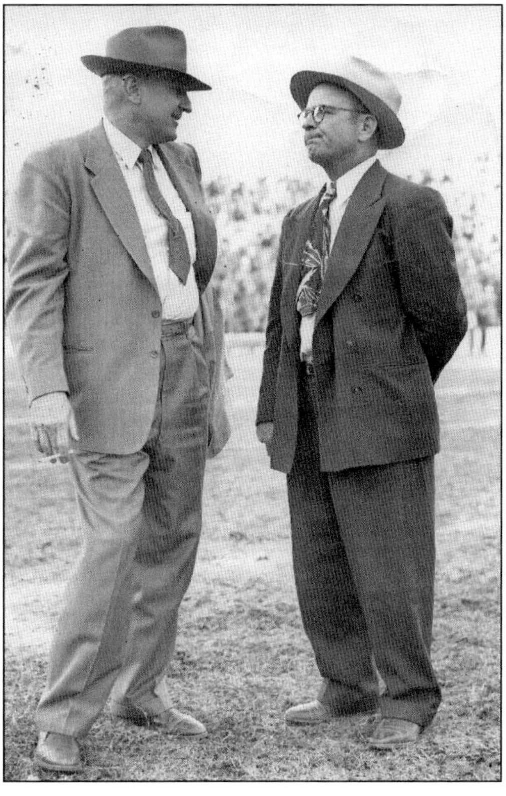

Nocona Athletic Goods was instrumental in changing football history. In 1934, Southern Methodist University coach Mattey Bell (left) and Texas Christian University coach Leo R. "Dutch" Meyer wanted a ball more conducive for a passing game. At this time, each team was responsible for providing the balls for each game. Nocona Athletic Goods designed and manufactured the pointed oblong-shaped football that is the standard of today. (TNT.)

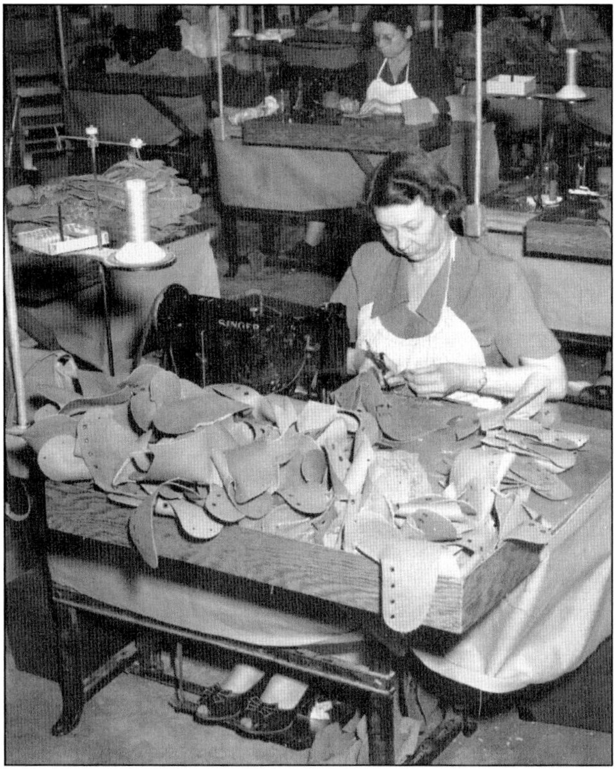

All of the sporting goods manufactured at the Nocona Athletic Company were created by hand. Hazel Fields is shown in this photograph stitching gloves together. She is using a pedal-style Singer sewing machine. Each of the workstations seen in the background is executing another step in the production process. (TNT.)

This 1950 photograph shows Pete Hanson working on a clicker machine in the Nocona Athletic Goods factory. This machine was used to cut out the various pieces of the baseball gloves. The die was laid on the leather, much like a cookie cutter, and the clicker machine pressed the die and cut the desired shape from the leather. (TNT.)

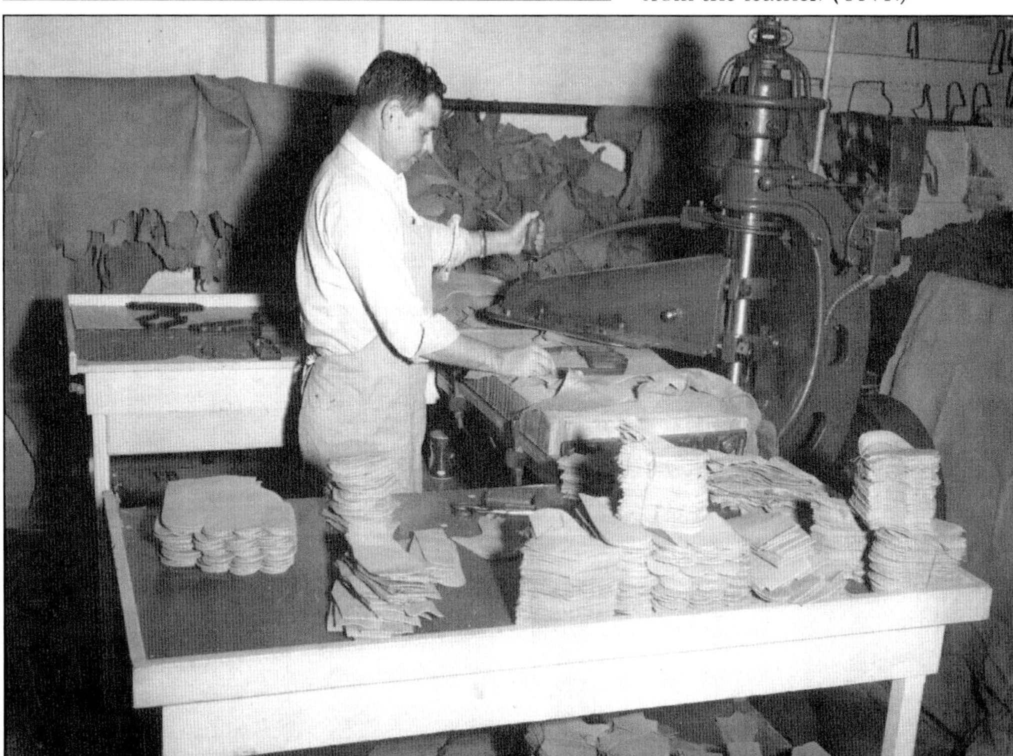

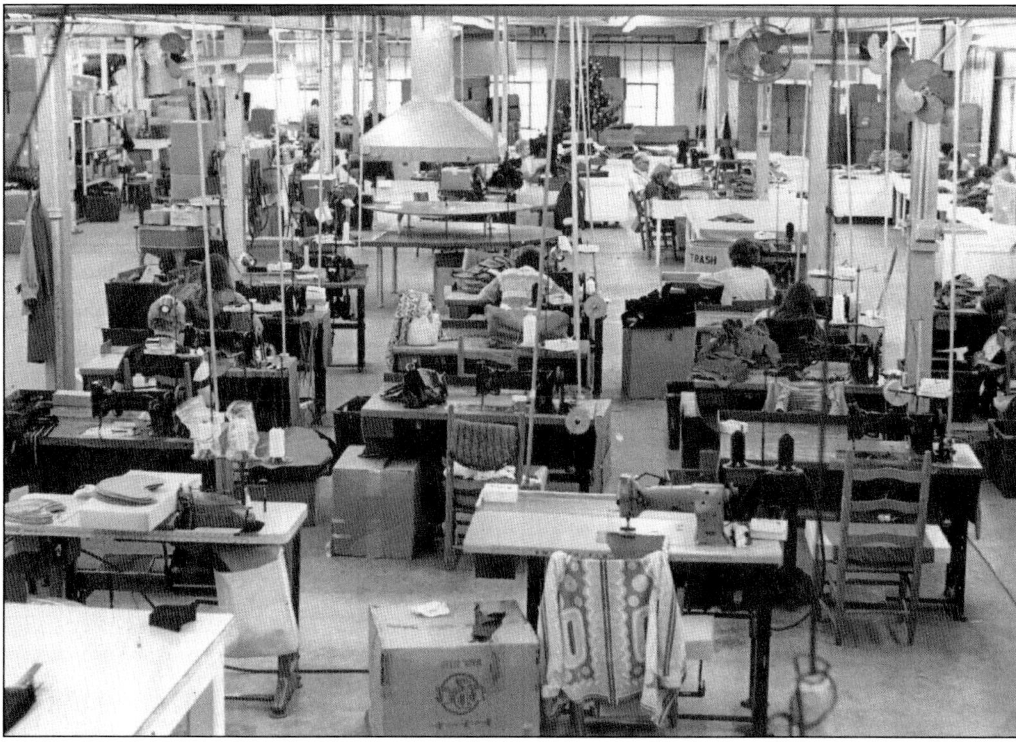

A great overview of the factory of the Nocona Athletic Goods Company is shown in this photograph. The ladies at the sewing machines each have a specific stitching task to complete. When their portion of the process is completed, the gloves move to the next stage in the production line. (TNT.)

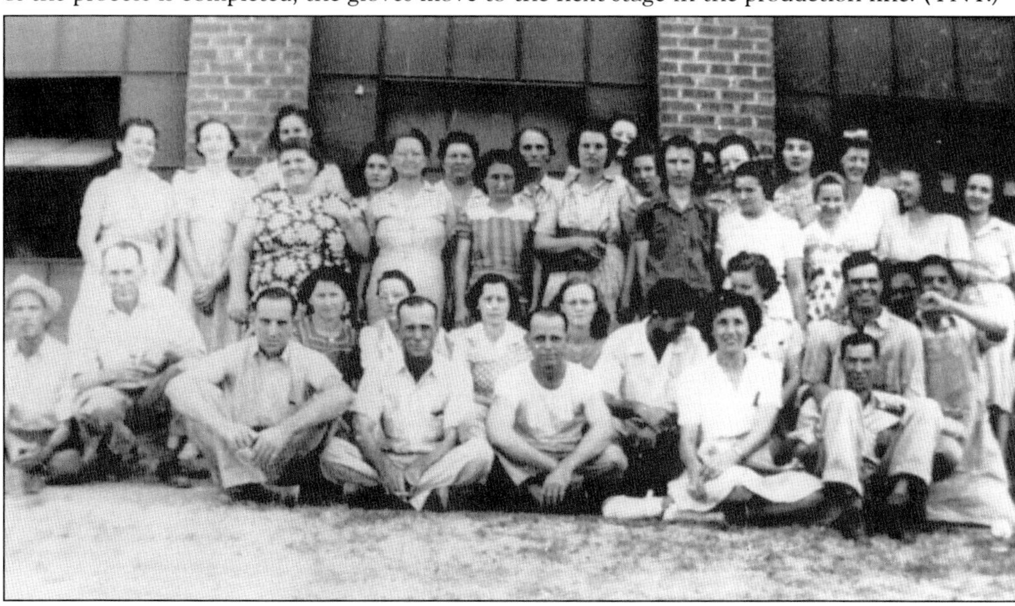

This group photograph of the employees of the Nocona Athletic Company was taken in front of the second building used by the company. This building was located at 208 West Walnut Street. It was completely destroyed by fire in July 2006. The company temporarily used the old Nocona Boot Company factory until it moved into its current location at 105 Clay Street. (TNT.)

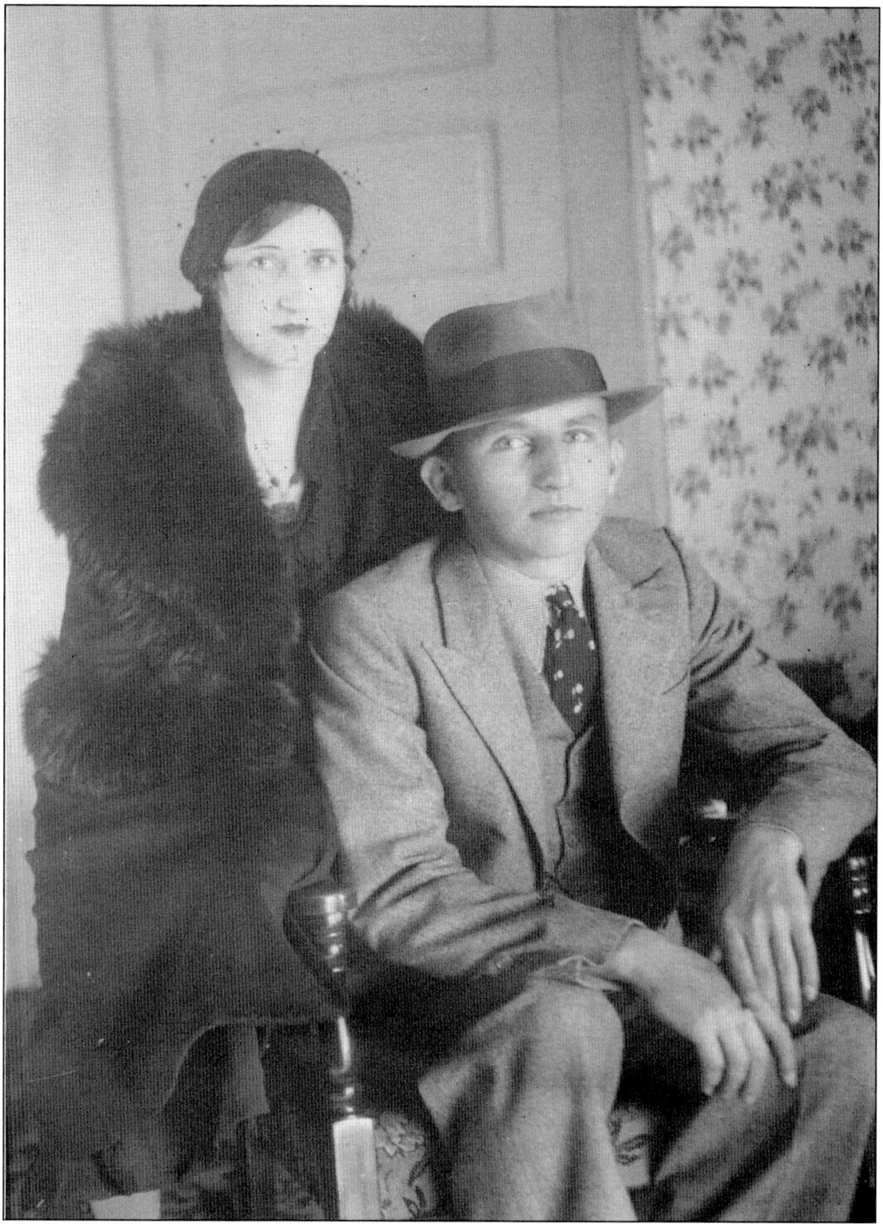

Floyd and Ethel Garner fell in love with each other—and with leather—while working together in 1927 at the Nocona Leather Goods Company. They worked at several different leather companies in Missouri and in Dallas, Fort Worth, and Wichita Falls. They also worked for a short time for Olsen Stelzer in Henrietta. On May 15, 1945, they opened their own leather goods shop in Nocona called F&E Leather. They manufactured a variety of small leather goods, including pillows and purses. The Garners used several types of leathers, including calf, lizard, alligator, ostrich, and emu. Their primary product was leather watch bands. These watch bands were specially treated to resist perspiration. These watch bands were very popular with servicemen due to the fact that they did not retain heat like the standard metal bands did. Floyd Garner had an unusual hobby. He belonged to the Clay County Rattlesnake Hunters Association and caught several hundred of the venomous reptiles for zoos across the country. (Sam and Robbie Mitchell.)

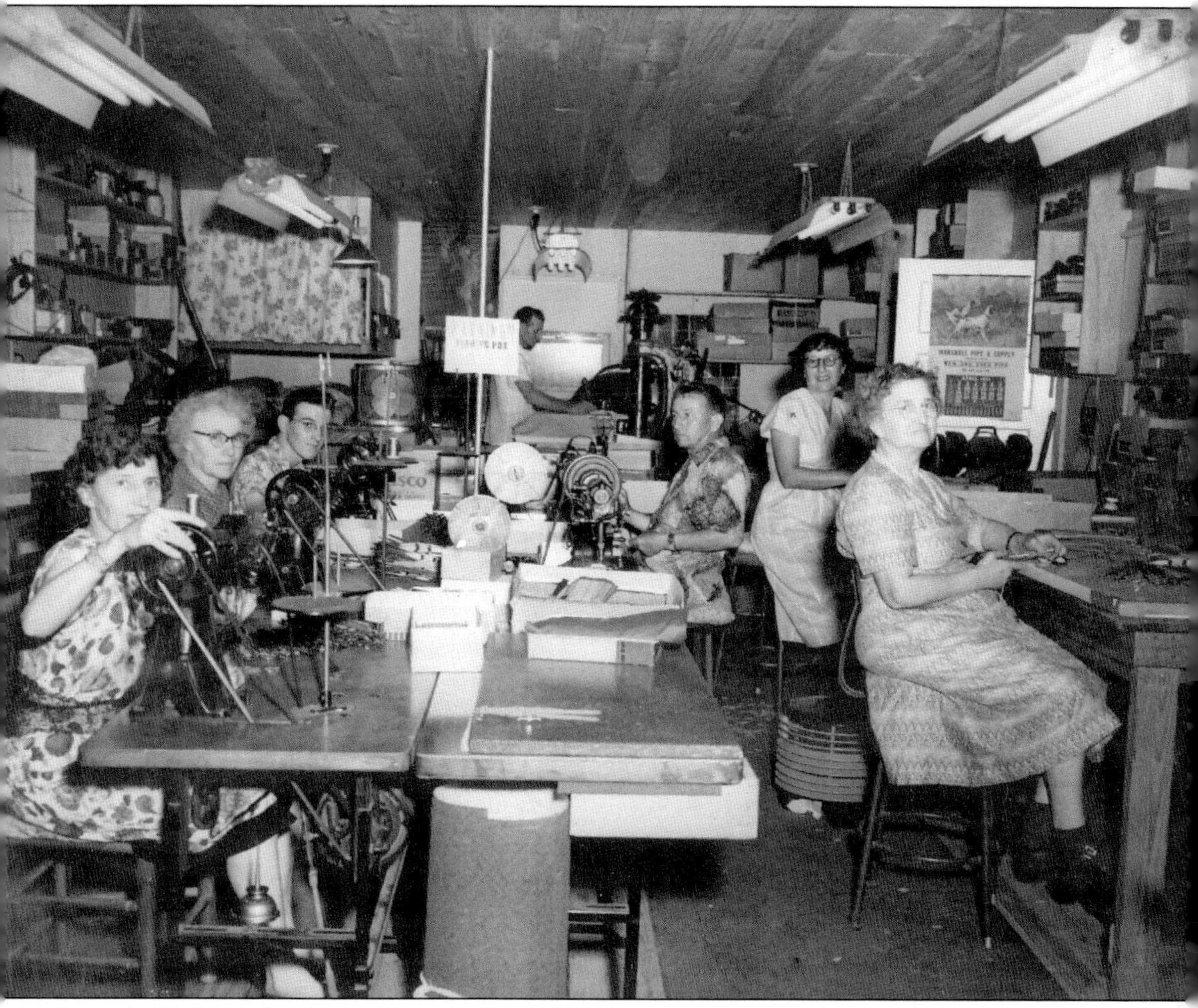

By 1951, F&E Leather had grown until it was necessary to build a small factory next to their home on the corner of Main and Elm Streets. The primary cause for the increase in business was a large contract with the Tandy Leather Company. F&E manufactured all of the leather craft kits for Tandy. These kits contained several small pieces. F&E purchased more than four dozen cutting dies in order to cut the various pieces needed. Tandy had recently undergone an ownership change. The company offered to pay the Garners in Tandy stock in order to keep its cash flow at a minimum. Floyd Garner graciously declined the offer, telling Tandy just to pay when it could. In hindsight, this was one decision that Ethel never let Floyd live down. Tandy became the leader in the leather craft business, and the stock prices soared. (Sam and Robbie Mitchell.)

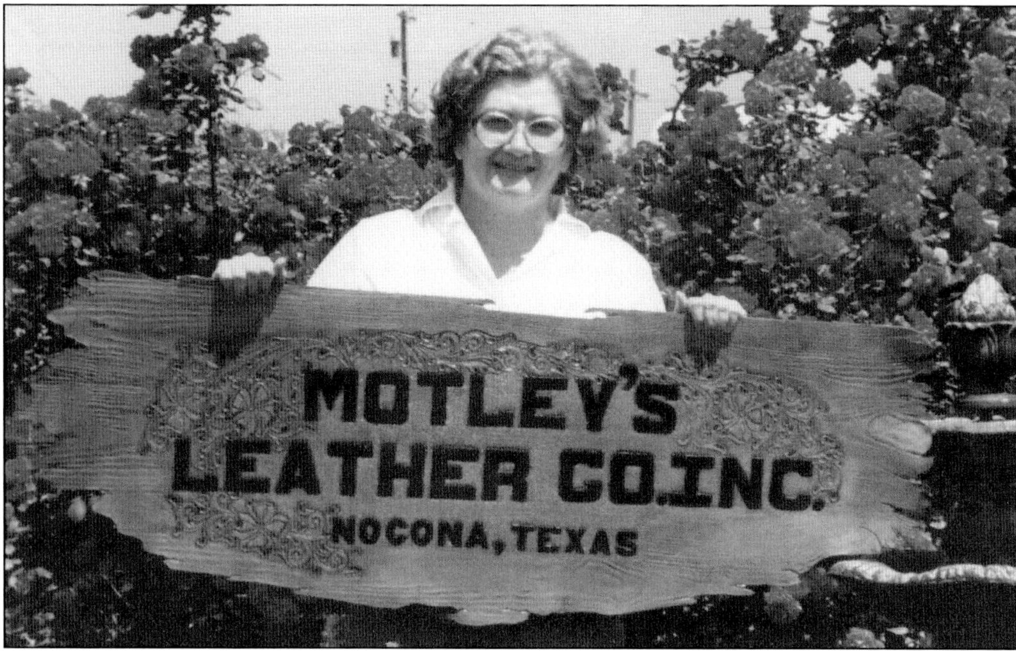

Dell Motley came from a family of leather workers. She began her leather-tooling career in 1949 at Joe Kirkpatrick's leather shop in Gainesville. She was hired as a designer by the Justin Leather Goods Company in 1953 and relocated to Nocona. She and her husband, Oliver, eventually opened their own leather goods store. (TNT.)

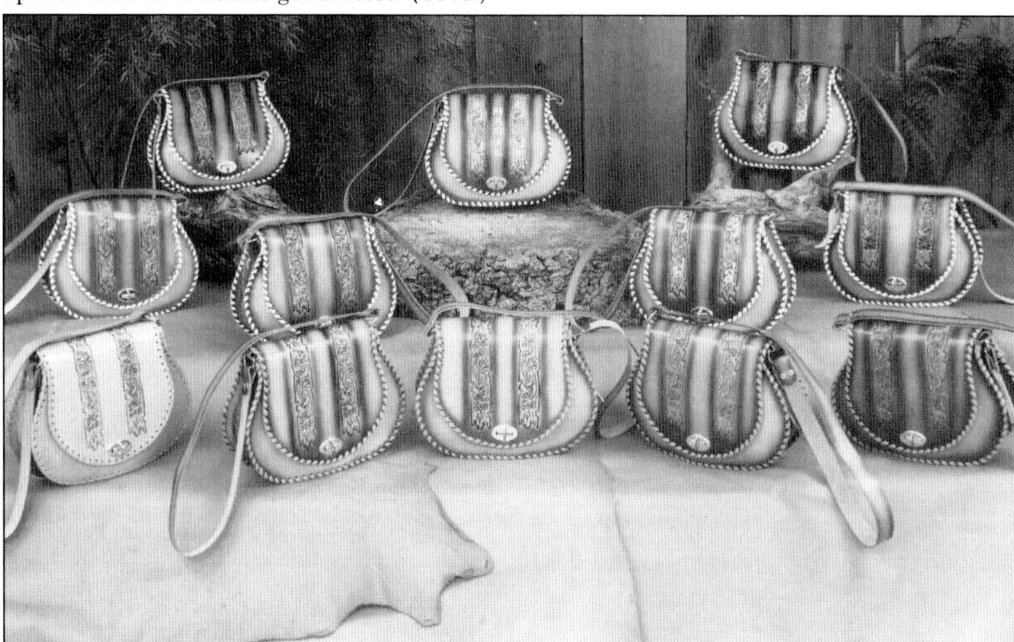

While working for Justin Leather Goods, Dell Motley designed and hand-tooled handbags, billfolds, and belts. Motley continued working for Justin Leather Goods after opening her own business with her husband. Justin Leather Goods sold seconds through the Motleys' new store to help boost business. (TNT.)

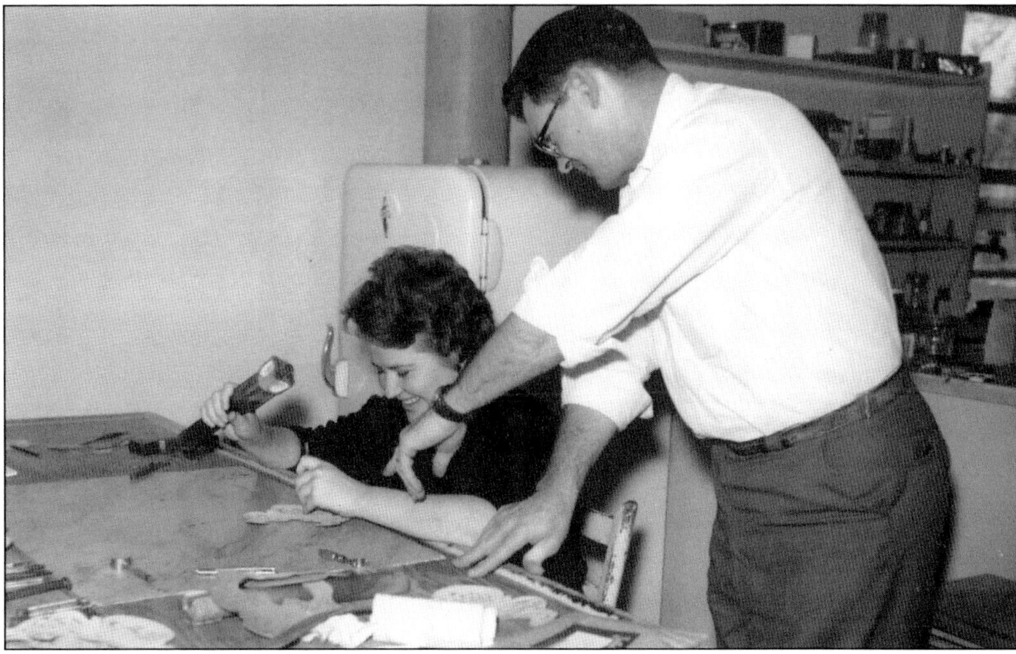

The Motleys hired Mary Edwards (left) shortly after opening their business. Edwards worked for the Motleys for 26 years until her death in 1991. Several of Edwards's family worked for the Motleys throughout the years. In this photograph, Oliver Motley watches as Edwards hand tools a product. (TNT.)

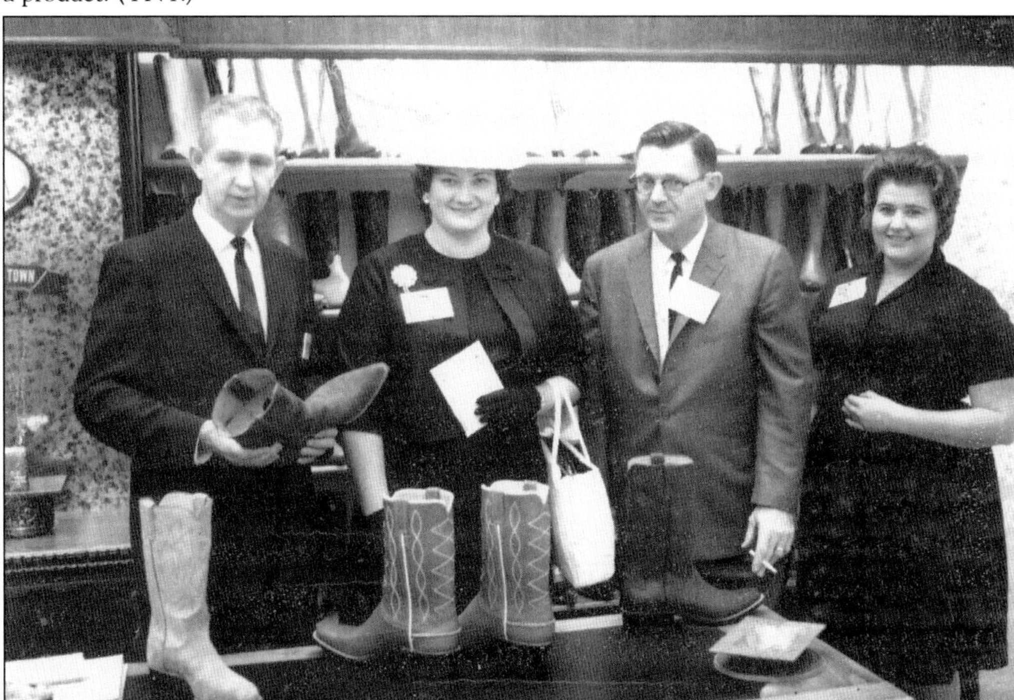

The Motley Leather Goods staff took time to shop while set up at market. Shown in this photograph are, from left to right, unidentified, Dell Motely, Oliver Motley, and Mary Edwards. (TNT.)

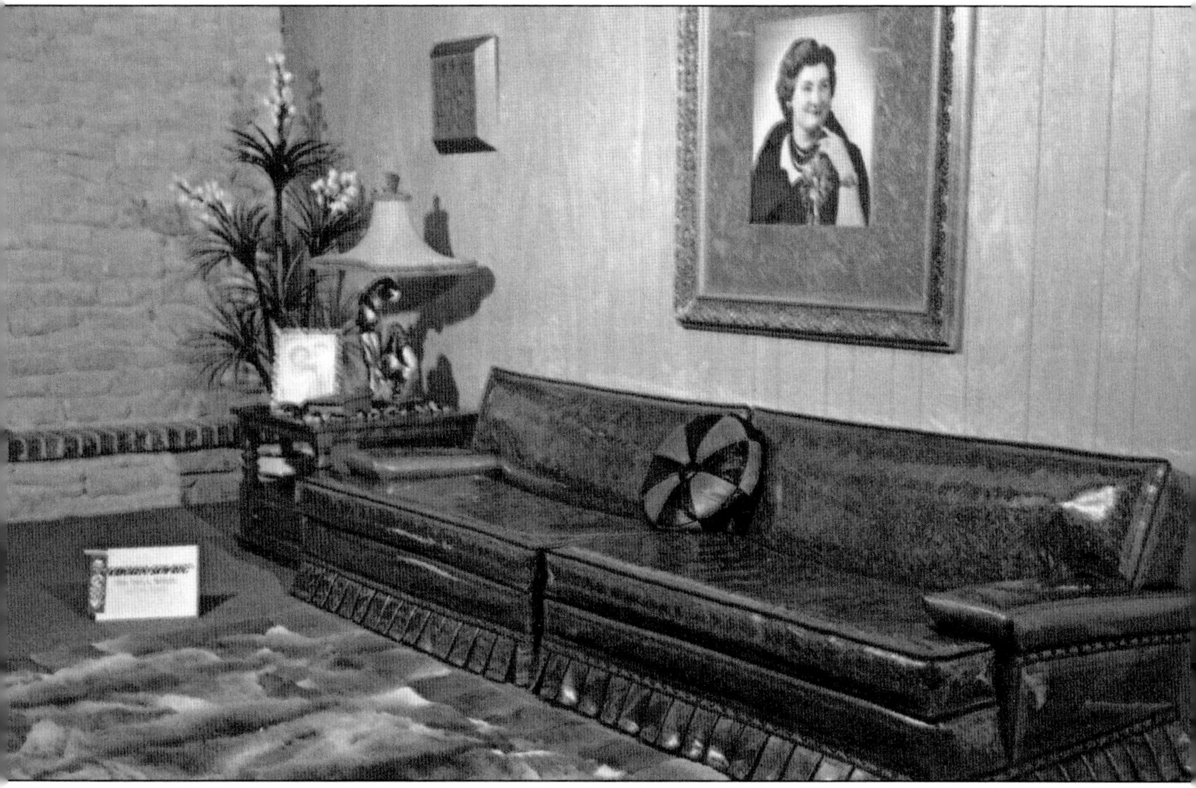

Dell Motley planned to buy a new sofa, but her husband, Oliver, suggested she recover their existing one in hand-tooled leather. The sofa was a 12-foot sectional. Motley began the tooling process in 1966 and completed the project in 1967. A local furniture maker, Elmer Adkins, offered Motley the use of his shop during the construction phase of the project. He had all of the necessary tools and clamps to hold the large sofa while doing this upholstery work. For months, she toiled in Adkins's shop. On a whim one night, she decided to take all the pieces home. Adkins Building burned to the ground that very night. As in all things, Motley felt God had a hand in saving her sofa. Once Adkins was able to resume business, Motley returned with the sofa pieces to have it assembled. (TNT.)

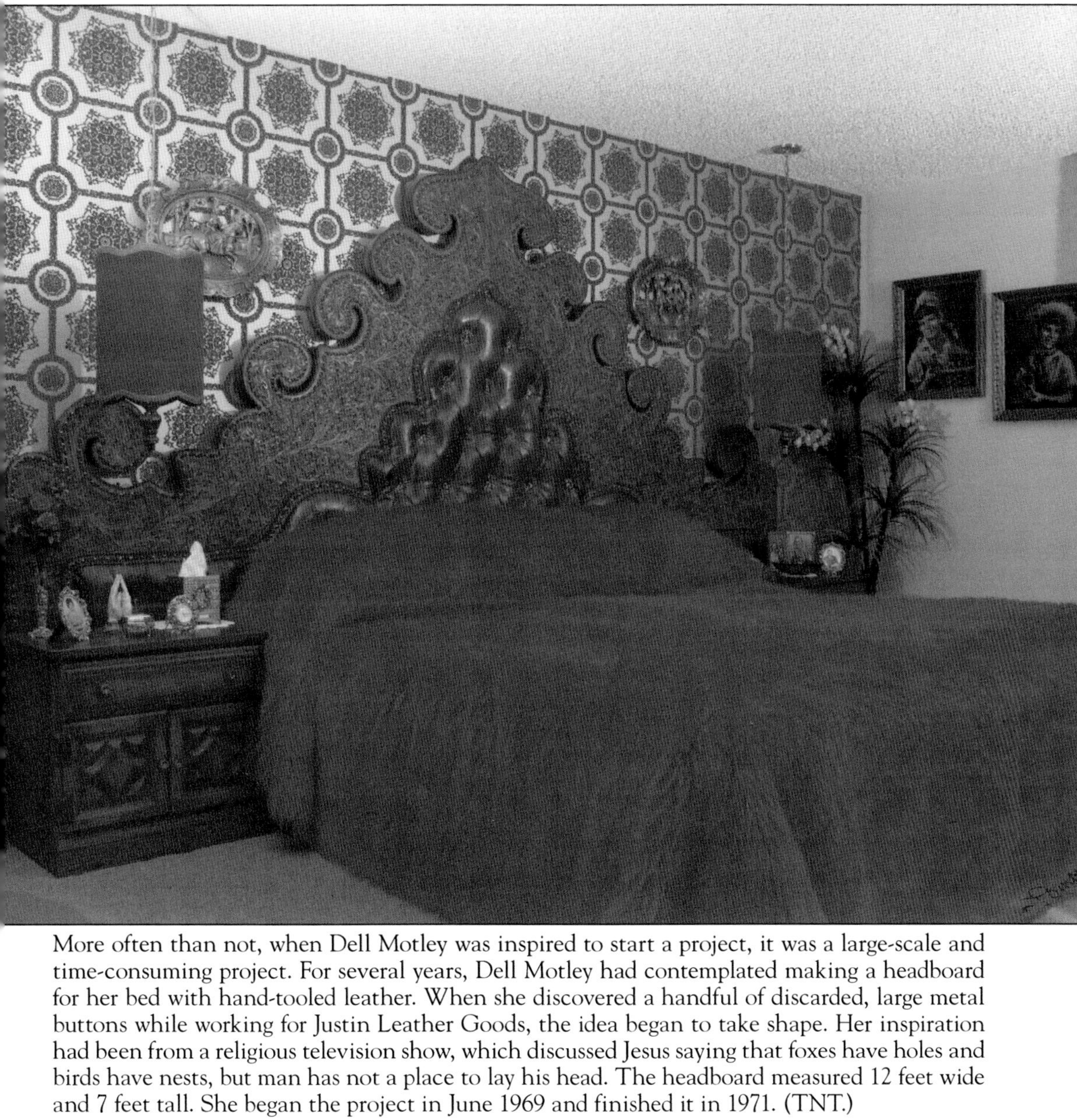

More often than not, when Dell Motley was inspired to start a project, it was a large-scale and time-consuming project. For several years, Dell Motley had contemplated making a headboard for her bed with hand-tooled leather. When she discovered a handful of discarded, large metal buttons while working for Justin Leather Goods, the idea began to take shape. Her inspiration had been from a religious television show, which discussed Jesus saying that foxes have holes and birds have nests, but man has not a place to lay his head. The headboard measured 12 feet wide and 7 feet tall. She began the project in June 1969 and finished it in 1971. (TNT.)

While working for Kirkpatrick in Gainesville, Dell Motley was approached by a mysterious stranger who suggested she tool the Last Supper. Motley believed this was a vision from God and was inspired to complete this project. Motley used an old Last Supper print from above her buffet as her pattern. Her brother made custom tools from nails for her to use to carve the delicate facial features. The stem with no beginning or end contains over 230 calla lilies. Motley began the

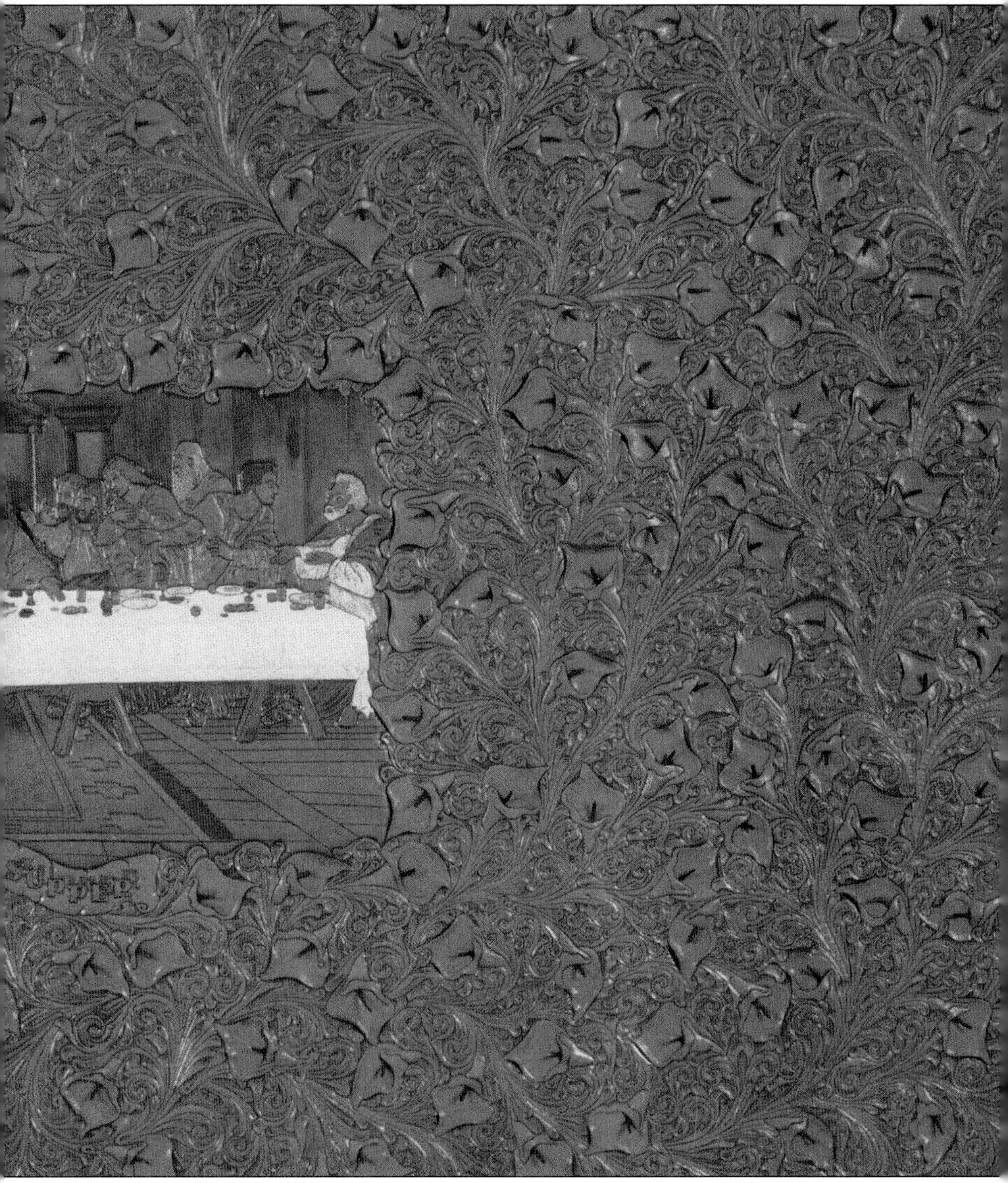

piece in 1963 and completed it in 1965. The project took 2,029 hours to complete. This was the first large Biblically themed piece, measuring approximately eight feet by four feet, which Motley created. She went on to do several more. Motley's beautiful work can be seen today displayed in the Tales 'N' Trails Museum in Nocona. (TNT.)

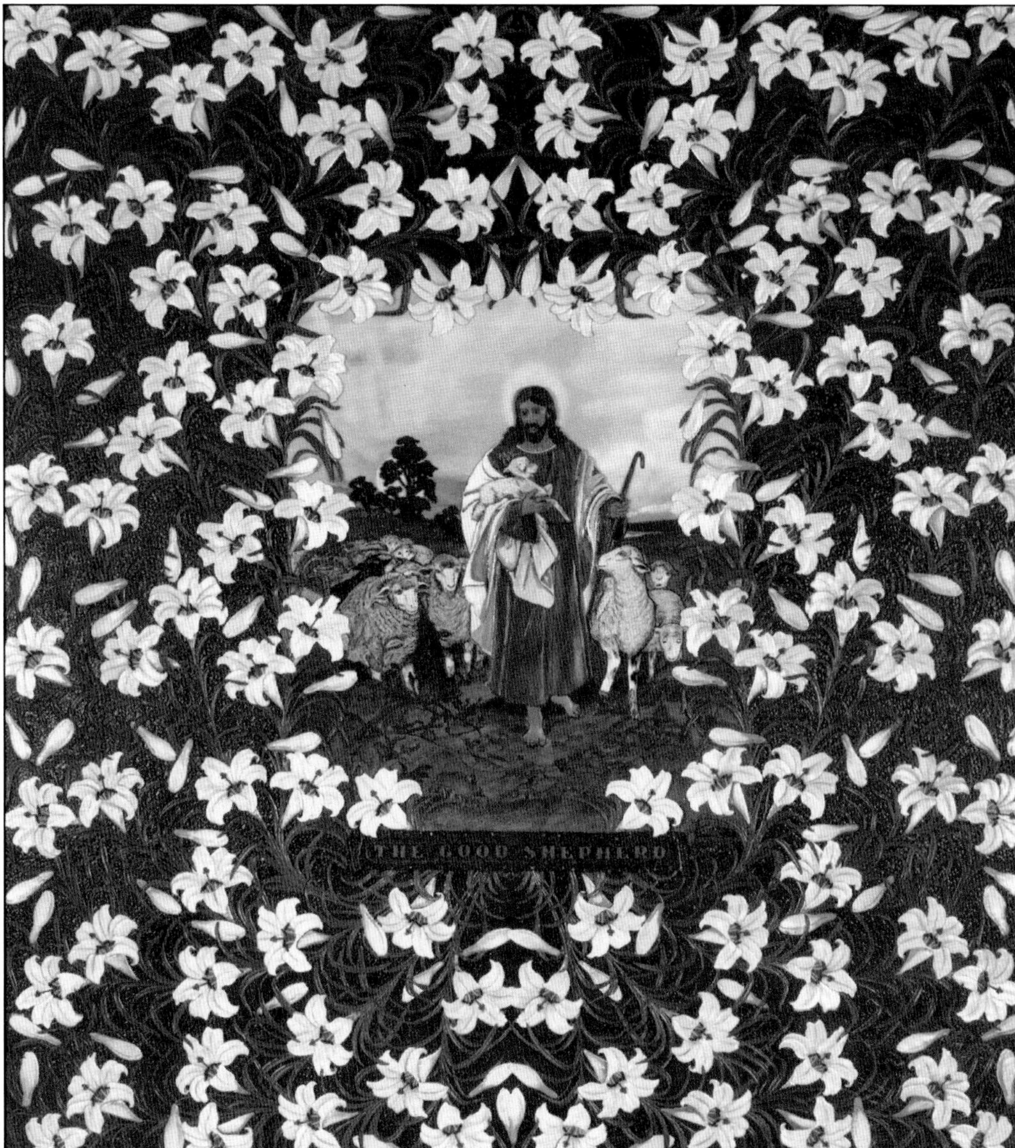

Dell Motley began working on *The Good Shepherd* in 1980. It took over 10 years and 5,014 hours to complete. Motley found divine inspiration and intervention in all of her art work. The halo seen around the head of Jesus in the piece was not intentional. Motley mixed all of her own dyes, developing different shades until she felt she had it right. She applied the dye for the sky portion of this piece one night before going to bed, and upon awaking the next morning, she found the dye had created a perfect halo effect. She believed this was a sign from God. The design is a three-dimensional, hand-cut filigree of 102 lilies and 102 buds. The eyelids appear to open and close, depending on the viewer's angle of sight. (TNT.)

The Nocona Belt Company was established in 1968 by Mel Chapman and his brothers-in-law Chester Taylor and C.W. Leach. During the first couple of years of operation, Chapman was employed by Nocona Boot Company and ran his business on the side. In 1970, he quit the boot company to run the belt company. By 1974, Chapman was the sole stockholder. (Mel Chapman.)

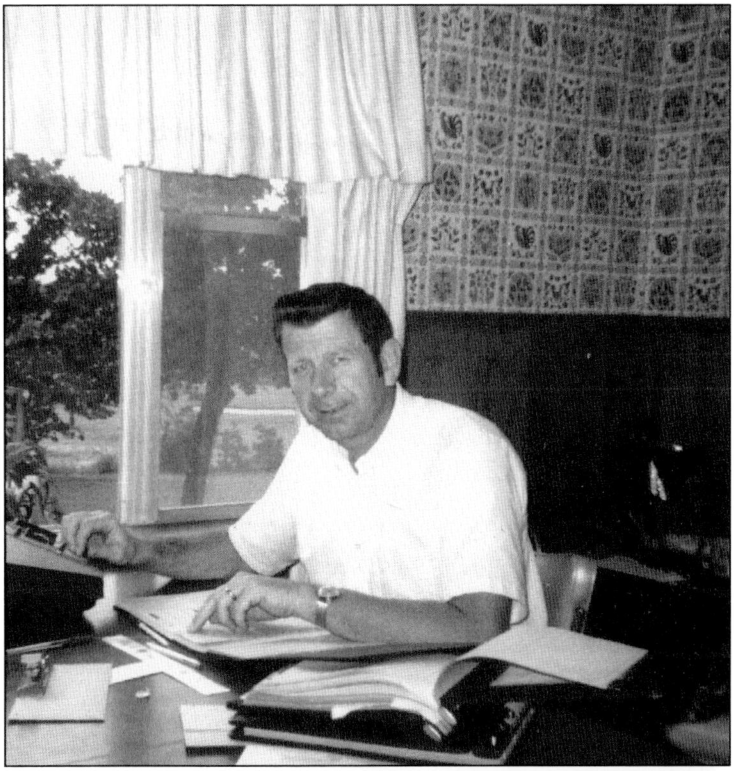

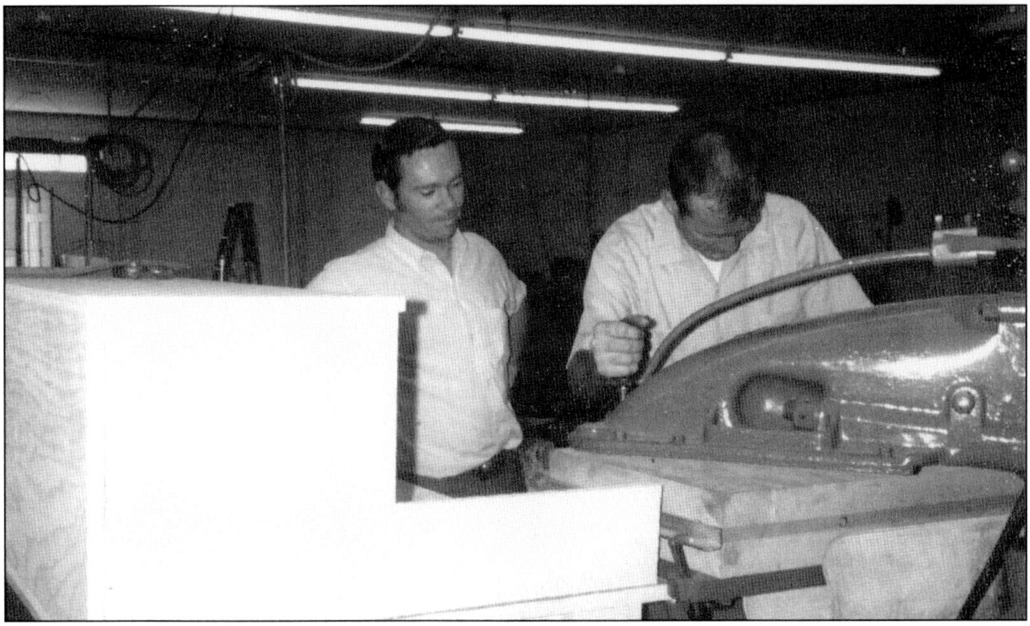

On October 21, 1970, the first belts were cut at the Nocona Belt Company. Shown here are Mike Henry (left) and Emil McEwin beginning the first step in the production process. Henry went on to become the vice president and general manager of the company. At the company's peak, it employed approximately 170 people to manufacture Western belts, buckles, and other small leather goods. (Mel Chapman.)

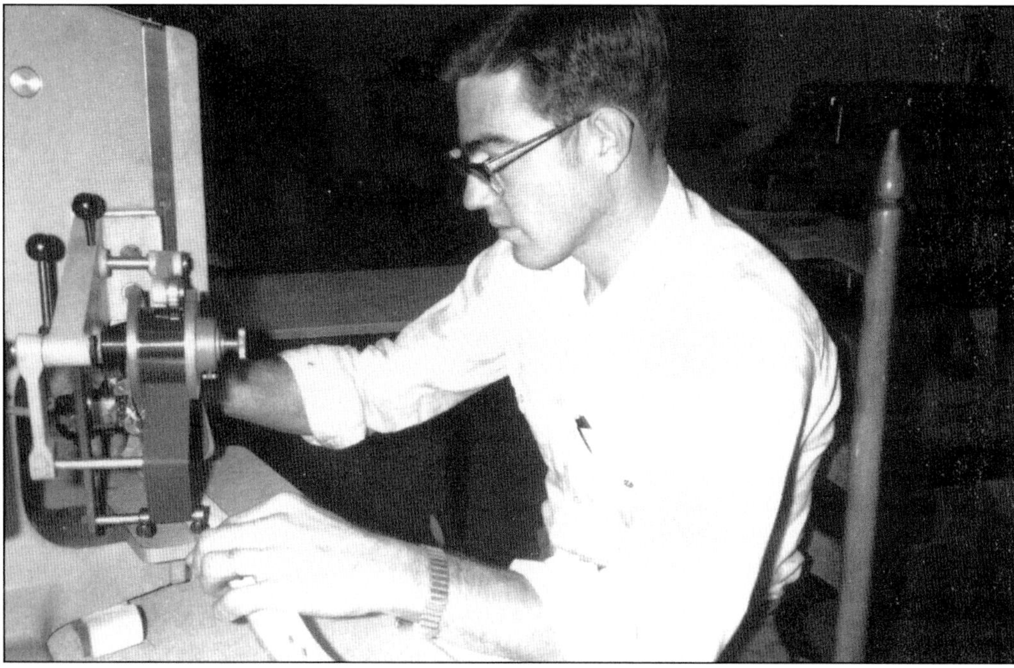

Gary Don King was hired in 1970 by the Nocona Belt Company as a plant manager. He was in charge of setting up the factory as well as handling the purchasing for the company. In this photograph, King is using a hot stamp machine to emboss the logo on the inside of a belt. (Mel Chapman.)

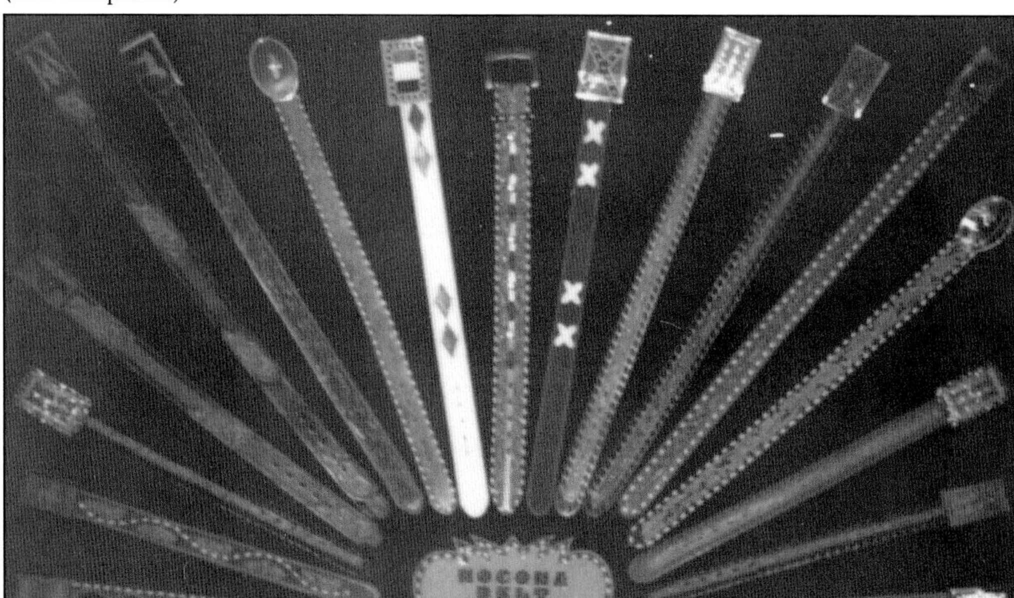

Shown here are several designs manufactured by the Nocona Belt Company. The company also patented a technique to enable a dealer to filigree its name to the back of a belt. It was called the Kona Kut. This process was used by several differ dealers for a faster and more economical alternative to hand-tooled belts. (Mel Chapman.)

Five

Who's Who of Nocona

The list of the who's who of Nocona is very eclectic, ranging from oil tycoons to cowgirls. Many notable persons hail from Nocona. There are several not included in this work due to the lack of corresponding photographs.

Montague County claimed four women who belong to the Cowgirl Hall of Fame, and three of them called Nocona home at some point. Businessmen gained recognition through the oil business and politics. Others were well known due to their athletic ability or their philanthropic deeds.

Enid Justin was a woman ahead of her time; she started her own business in 1925, when women were not in the habit of running companies, much less being in the top of their field nationwide. Ruth Roach Salmon and Hilda Workman both made lasting impressions in the daredevil stunts they performed in Wild West shows across the county. Jack Crain's recognition came from his prowess on the football field. Tony Fenoglio was a hometown boy who went on to became a Texas state representative. Joe Benton was wildly successful in the oil business and also had a lasting effect on the cattle industry in Nocona. He also gained notoriety through his passion for history and his vast collection of Native American artifacts.

Aside from gaining respect from their neighbors because of their accomplishments, most of Nocona's who's who habitually supported their home town, often behind the scenes. As is true with Nocona's distinguished citizens, it is not only what one accomplishes, it is the grace and style with which they advance.

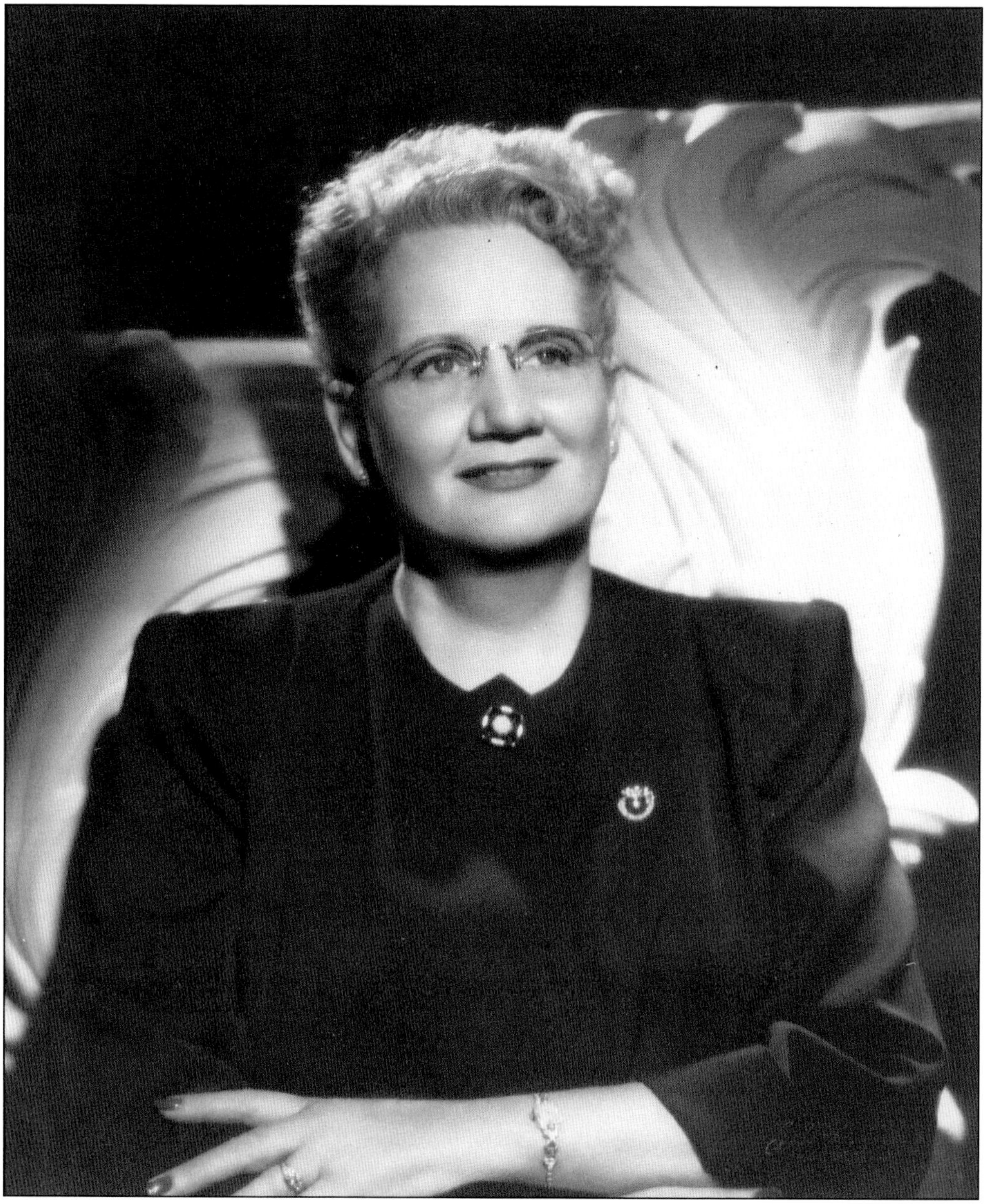

Enid Justin, known worldwide simply as Miss Enid, was born on April 18, 1894, to Herman Joseph and Annie Allen Justin. She began working at her father's boot company at the age of 12 and designed her first pair of boots at the age of 14. In 1925, when it was almost unheard of for a woman to own a company, Miss Enid started the Nocona Boot Company. She survived two divorces and the death of her young daughter. Her business was successful; she sold boots to cowboys, oilfield workers, kings, presidents, and celebrities. She supported the local 4-H, Future Farmers of America (FFA), and Little League. She was very involved in the Nocona Rodeo Association, the Chisholm Trail Riding Club, and the Nocona Chamber of Commerce. She was instrumental in funding the tennis courts at the city park that were named in her honor. Miss Enid was inducted into the National Cowgirl Hall of Fame in 1978. She died on October 14, 1990, at the age of 96. (TNT.)

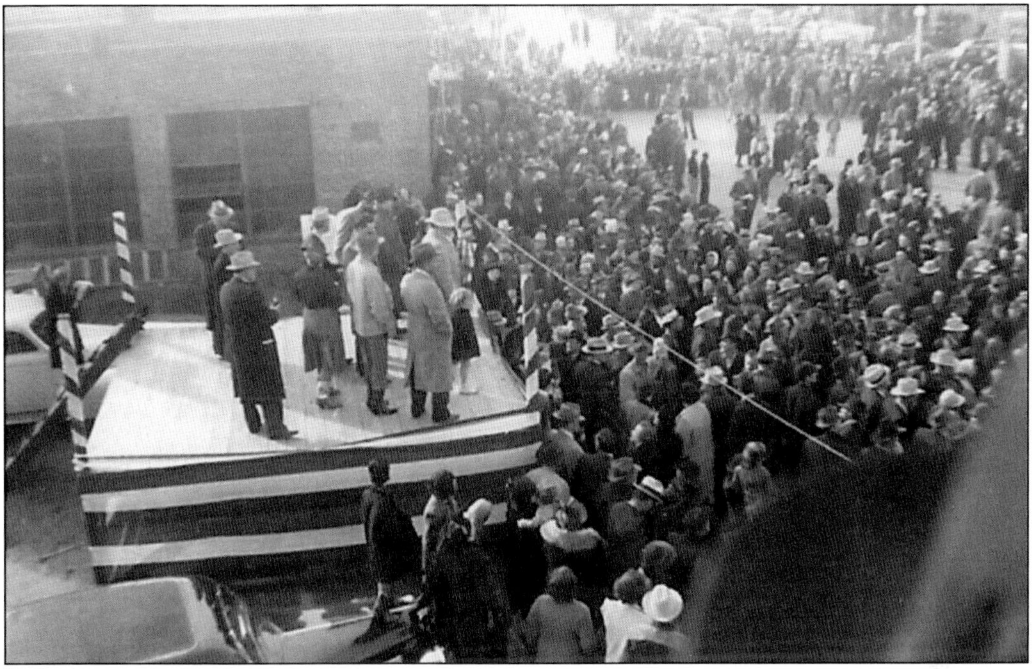

In February 1939, Miss Enid sponsored a Pony Express Race from Nocona to the Golden Gate Exposition in San Francisco. A ceremony was held at a grandstand downtown. Amon G. Carter of Fort Worth gave the official start signal with a gun furnished by Montague County sheriff Dick Lawrence. Miss Enid can be seen standing in the center of the platform in a skirt and cowboy boots. (TNT.)

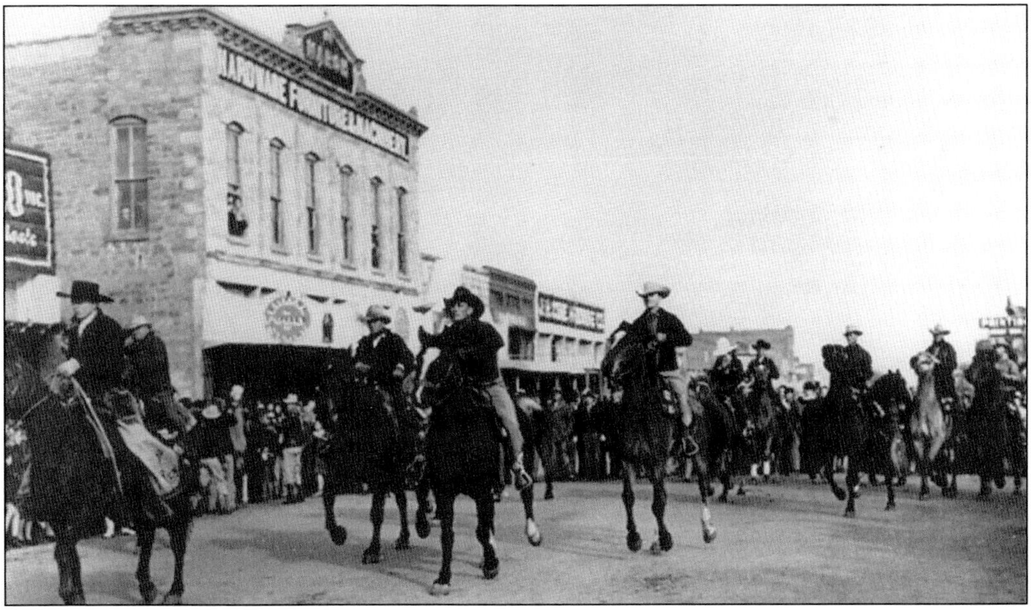

An estimated 2,500 people turned out to see the start of the Pony Express Race. Each contestant provided two horses for the journey. They were followed by a crew in a car and trailer. The horses were switched every 25 miles. Nocona businessman A. Billings led the convoy as head judge to make sure all regulations were followed. (Wanda Billings.)

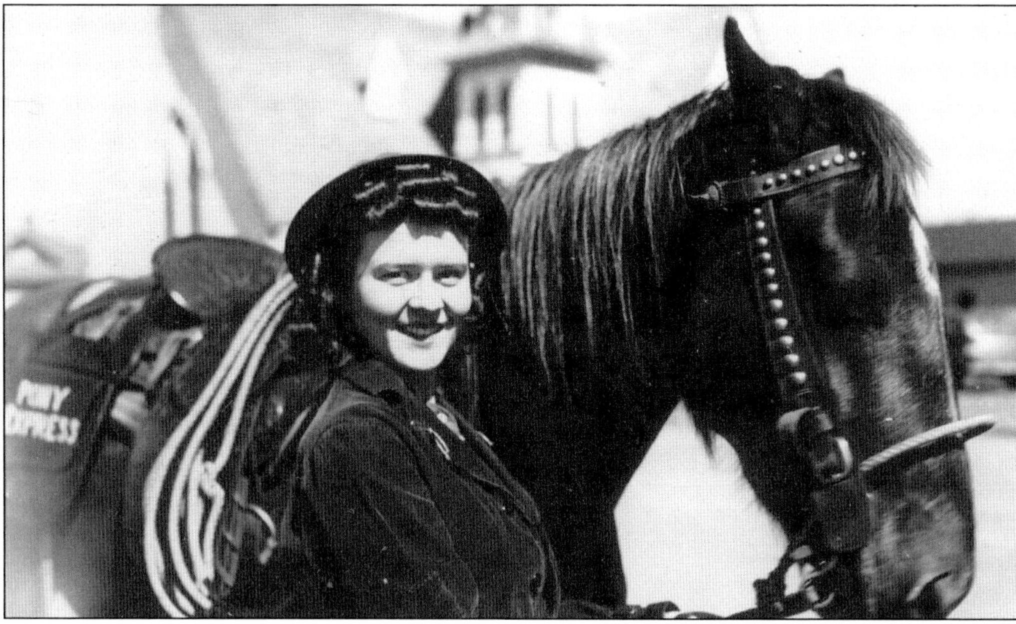

Sixteen contestants participated in the race. The only girl was 15-year-old Vennie Greenwood, who dropped out on the second day. The other contestants were Chris Uselton, the only other Nocona entrant; Lige Reid; Tex Frazier; Taylor Tuck; Jack Clifton; Shorty Hudson; King Kerley; Slim Mathis; V.H. Henderson; Shannon Davidson; L.E. Speers; George Cates; R.L. Scott; T.J. Sykes; and Hudie Helm. (Wanda Billings.)

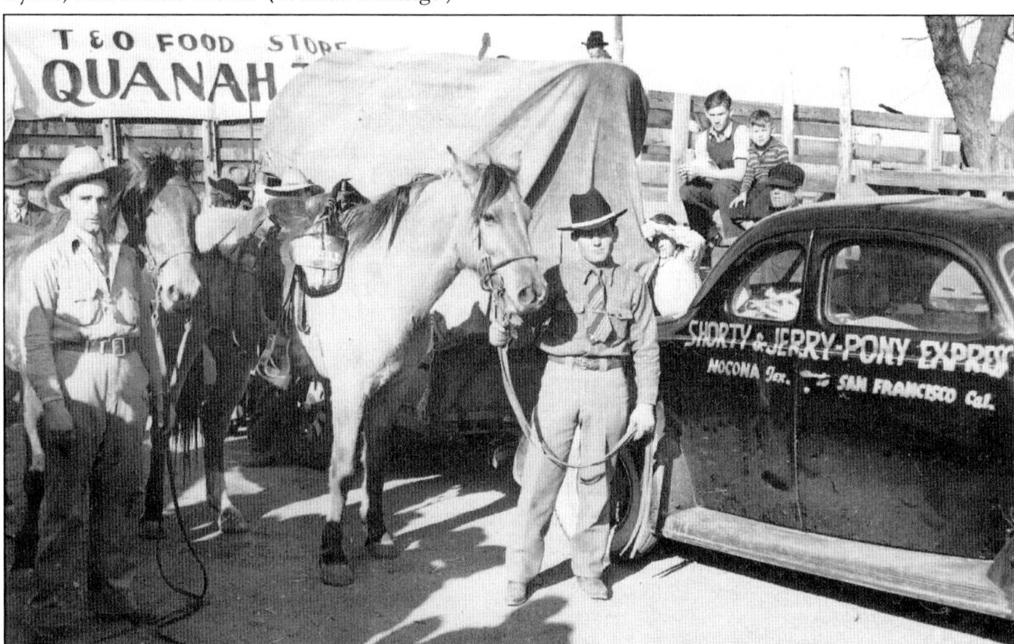

The race route was from Nocona to Wichita Falls, Olney, Throckmorton, Albany, and Abilene. From Abilene, they followed the Bankhead Highway to Los Angeles and then to Oakland, where they were ferried to their Treasure Island destination. Residents of each town on the route cheered them on as they passed through. (Tom Uselton.)

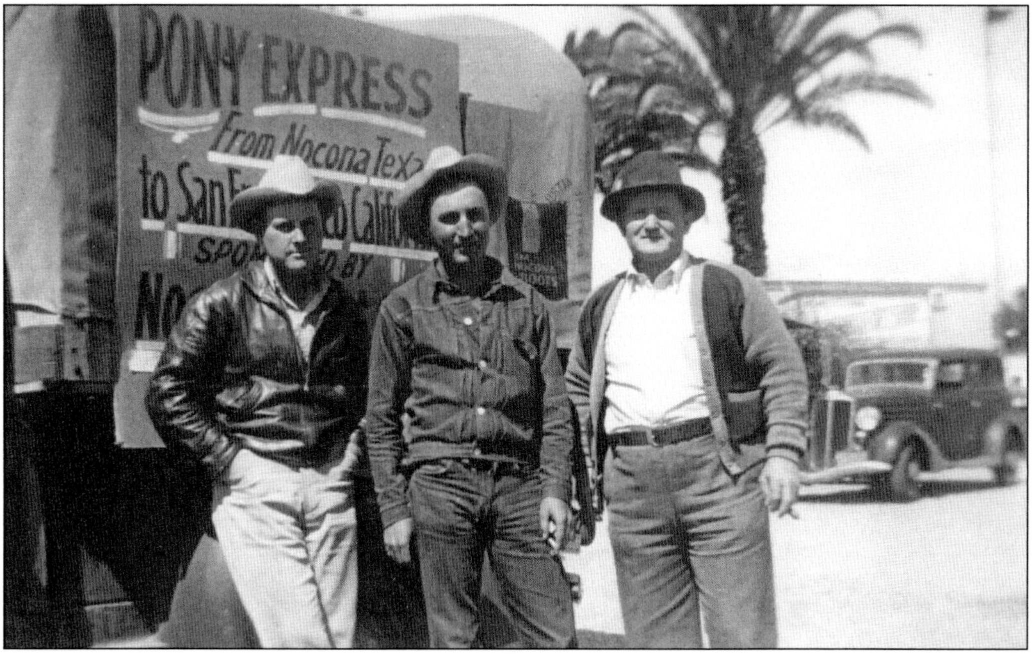

The contestants in the race carried over 10,000 letters to be delivered upon their arrival in California. They also picked letters up en route. These were then stamped with a commemorative postmark and mailed to the original sender as a souvenir. Shown here are, from left to right, Lee Crenshaw, Jack Crenshaw, and Andy Jennings. (Tom Uselton.)

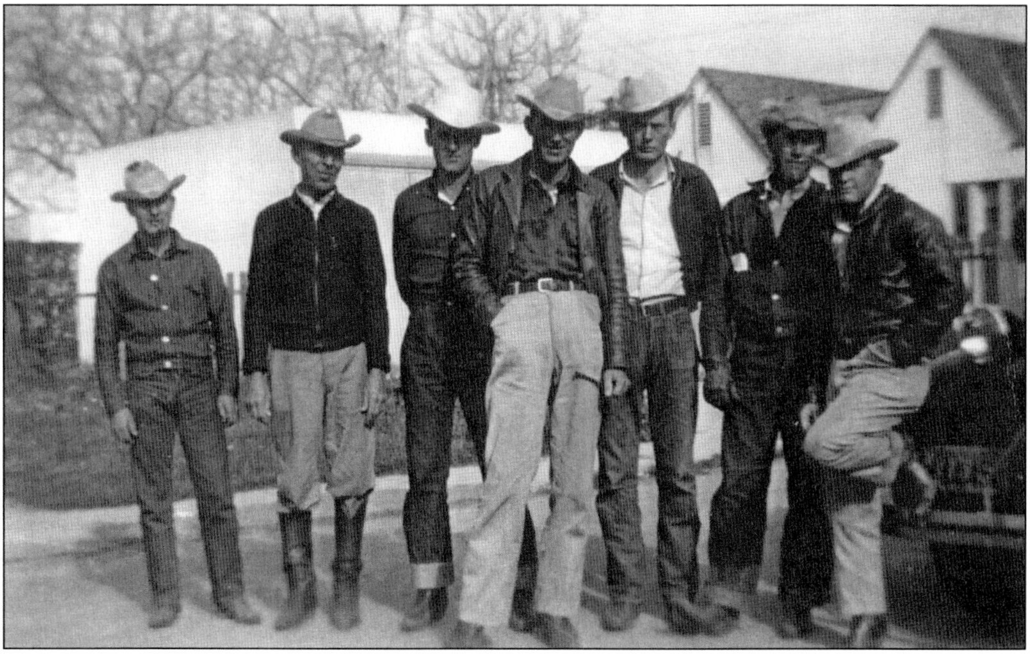

The winner of the race, Shannon Davidson, was presented with 750 silver dollars by Miss Enid. Nocona's entrant was in contention for the win until a vehicle hit him and his horse, forcing him to withdraw. Shown here are, from left to right, Jack Crenshaw, Elmer Brooks, unidentified, Chris Uselton, unidentified, Hop Stout, and Lee Crenshaw. (Tom Uselton.)

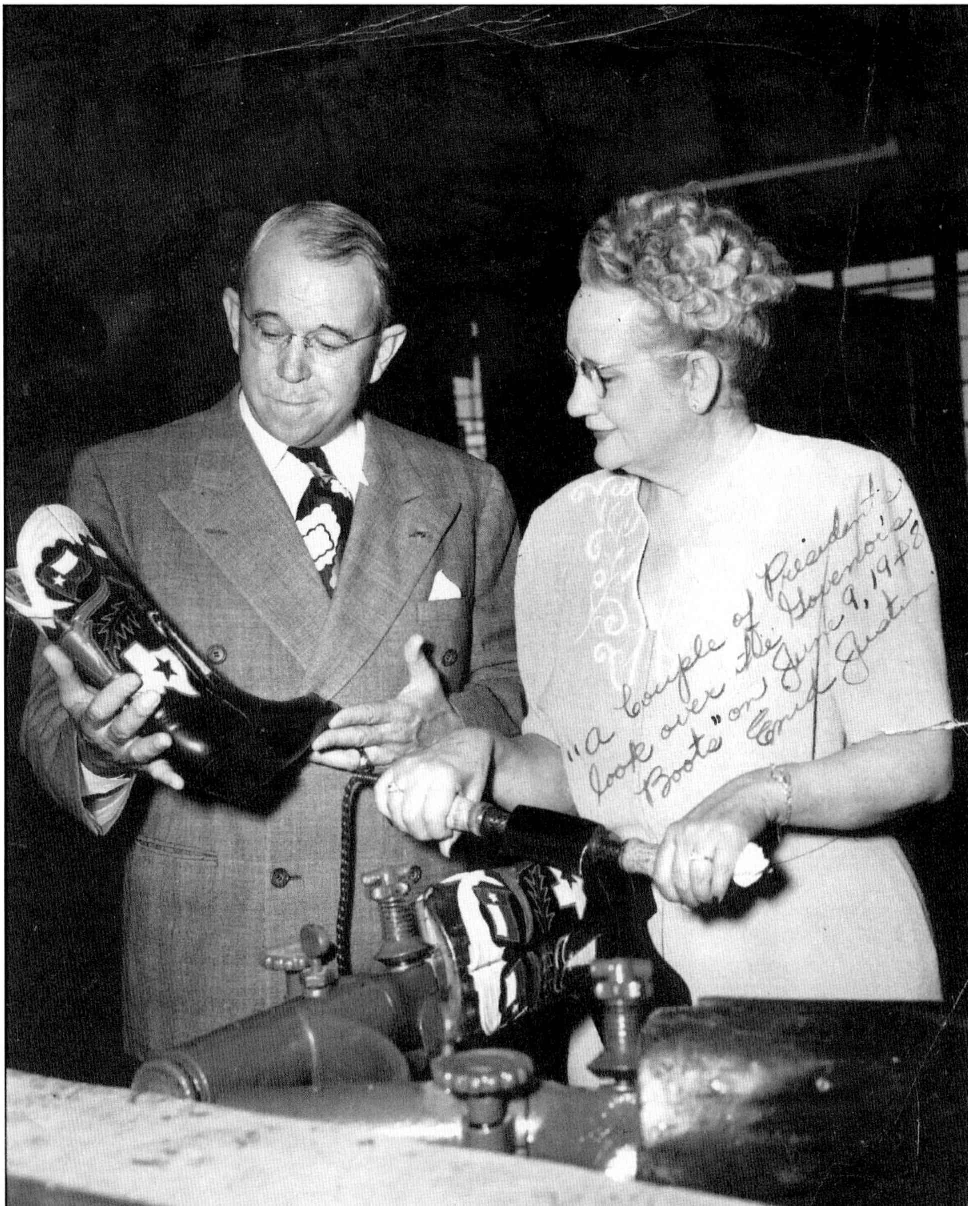

Miss Enid and Calvin Phillips Dodson are admiring the governor's boots in 1948. Dodson was the president of Texas Chambers of Commerce. Nocona Boots was chosen over all of the nation's boot makers to design a pair of boots that were to be presented to each of the 54 governors of the states and territories at their annual convention each year. After the presentation each year, Nocona Boots would offer the "Governor-style" boot in their catalog. Miss Enid and the Nocona Boot Company were known for making special-order boots for different occasions. They made boots with company or organization logos inlaid into the design. They made the Chisholm Trail Riding Club members' matching green and yellow boots with the club's name and longhorn. The boot company made several designs with oil derricks for various oil company executives. Miss Enid presented a special pair of boots each year to the 4-H Gold Star Award winners from Nocona High School. (TNT.)

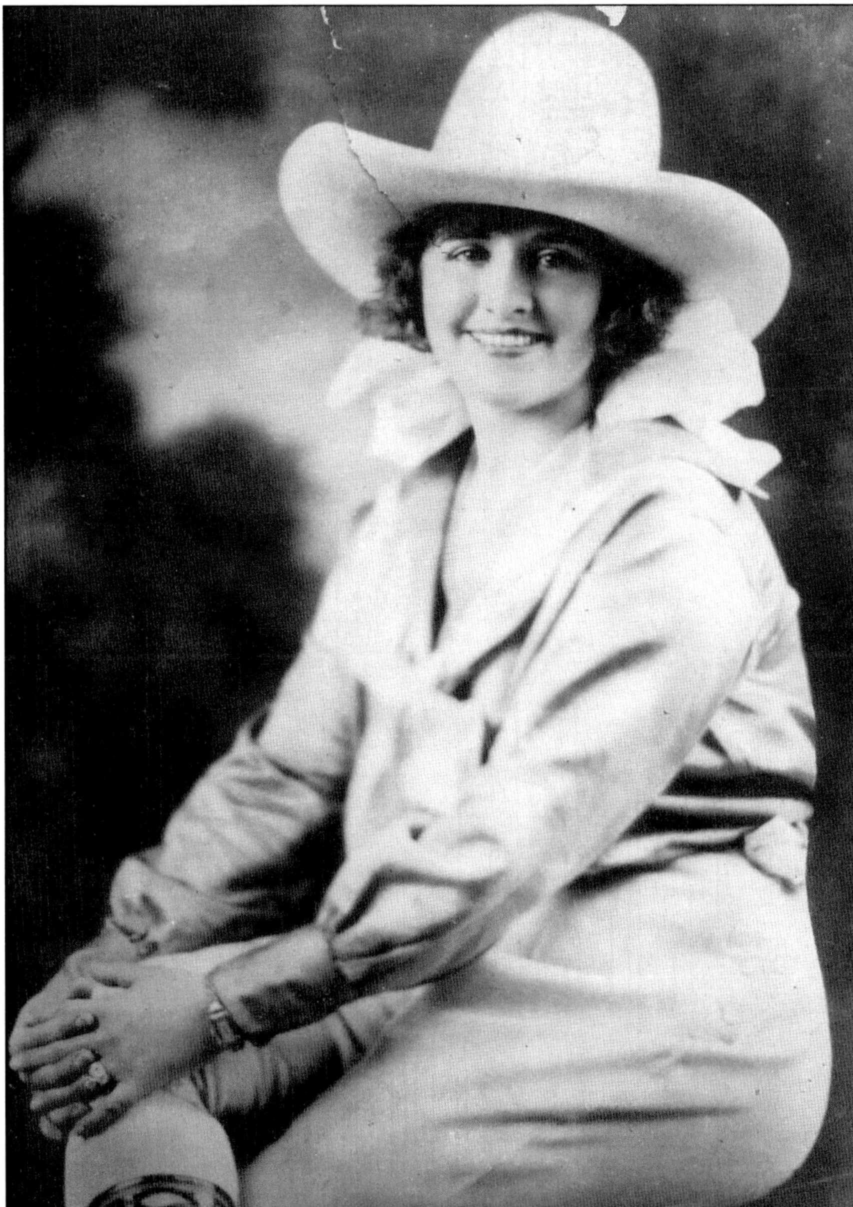

Ruth Scantlin Roach Salmon was a very well-known rodeo personality. She was born in Missouri in 1896. She ran away from home to join the Miller's 101 Ranch Rodeo in 1914 as a trick rider. She performed all over the world in different Wild West shows, including the Buffalo Bill Wild West Show. She met and married Bryan Roach, a bronc rider, in 1915. The couple traveled the world performing but later divorced. She met Nocona rancher Fred "Dick" Salmon while she was performing at the Texas State Fair in 1936, and they married in 1938. They moved to Nocona, where together they ran a successful ranching operation. During her rodeo career, Salmon won several titles, including the World's Champion All Around Cowgirl, World's Champion Trick Rider, and the World's Champion Girl Bronc Rider. She was inducted into the National Cowgirl Hall of Fame and the National Cowboy Hall of Fame in 1989. Salmon died in 1986 at the age of 90. (R. Storey.)

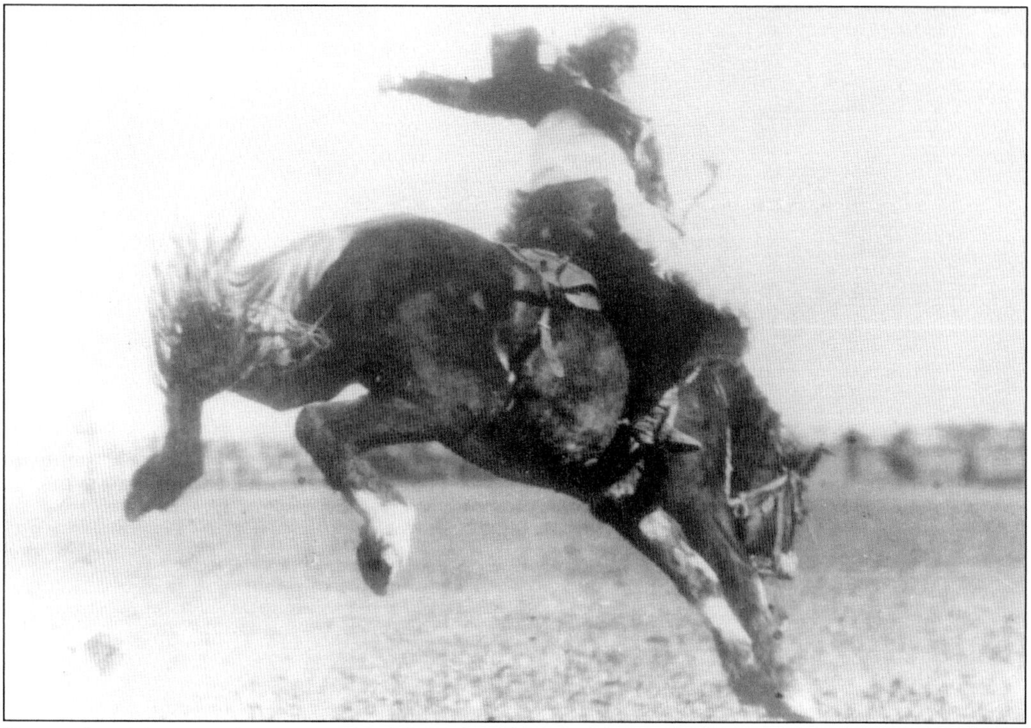

During her 24-year rodeo career, Ruth Roach Salmon's favorite event was bronc riding. She made her bronc riding debut in 1917 at the Fort Worth Rodeo. This was the first indoor rodeo held in the world. She continued performing in rodeo events until she retired in 1938. (R. Storey.)

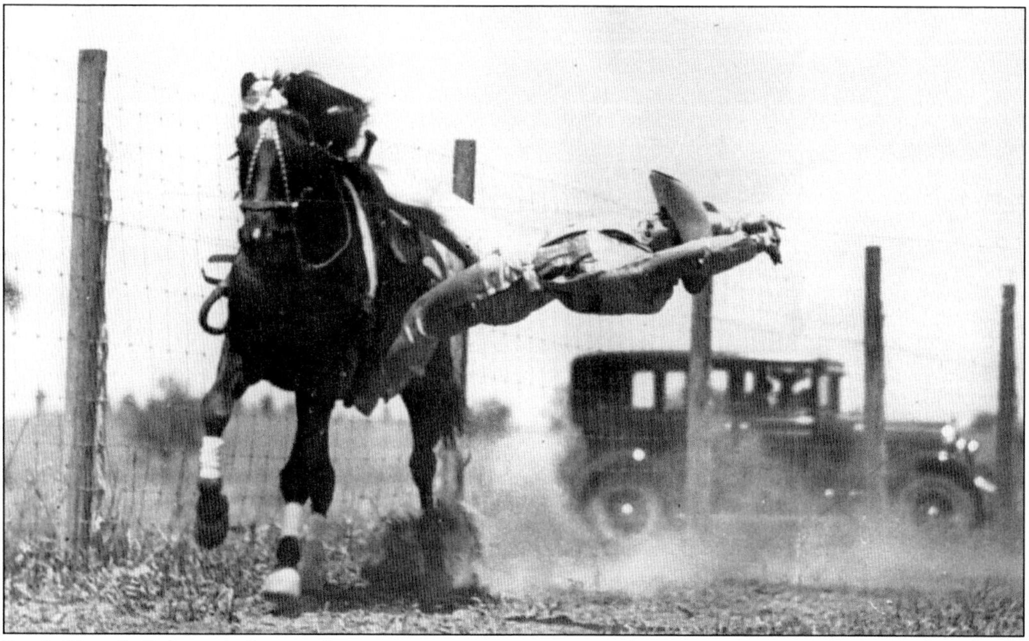

Ruth Roach Salmon's first rodeo experience was as a trick rider with the Miller's 101 Ranch, which was from Oklahoma. She was only 18 years old when she joined the traveling show. She was known as the "soft spoken, rough-riding, golden girl of the West." (R. Storey.)

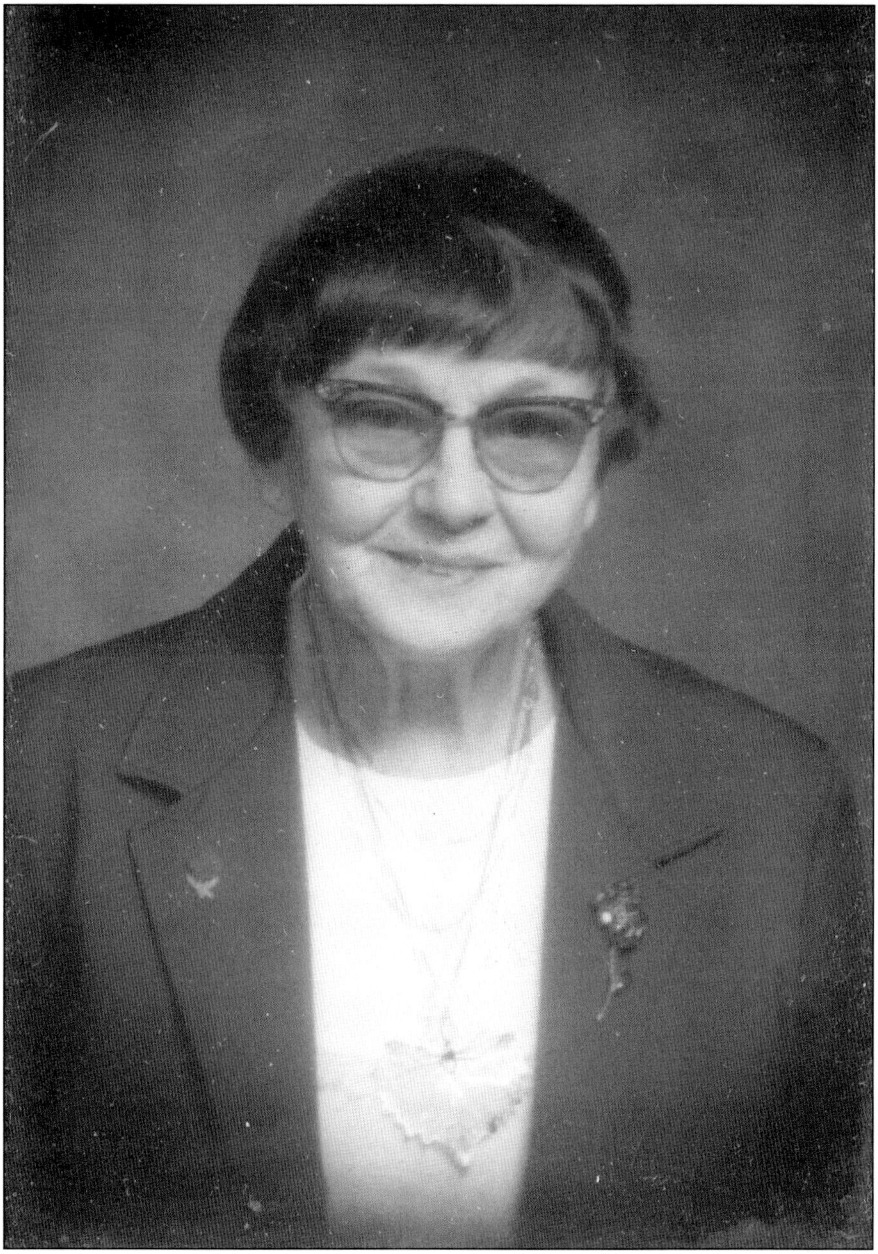

Hilde Engel Workman was born on August 31, 1909, in Long Island, New York. She joined the Miller's 101 Ranch Rodeo and traveled across the country performing in their Wild West shows. She married Peter Workman in 1928. The couple continued to travel and perform in different rodeo and Western events. In the 1930s, the couple moved to Nocona. They both went to work for W.O. Reynolds. Peter worked as a ranch hand. Hilde was given the task of riding herd over 1,800 turkeys. Each morning, she turned the turkeys out on the pasture, riding with them to protect them from coyotes, and rounded them up each evening to return them to the barn. Both Hilde and her husband were involved in creating activities for the teenagers of Nocona. They formed the Nocona Trick Riding Club and the Nocona Quadrille, which is square dancing on horseback. Hilde Workman died in 1992 at the age of 92. (Sam and Robbie Mitchell.)

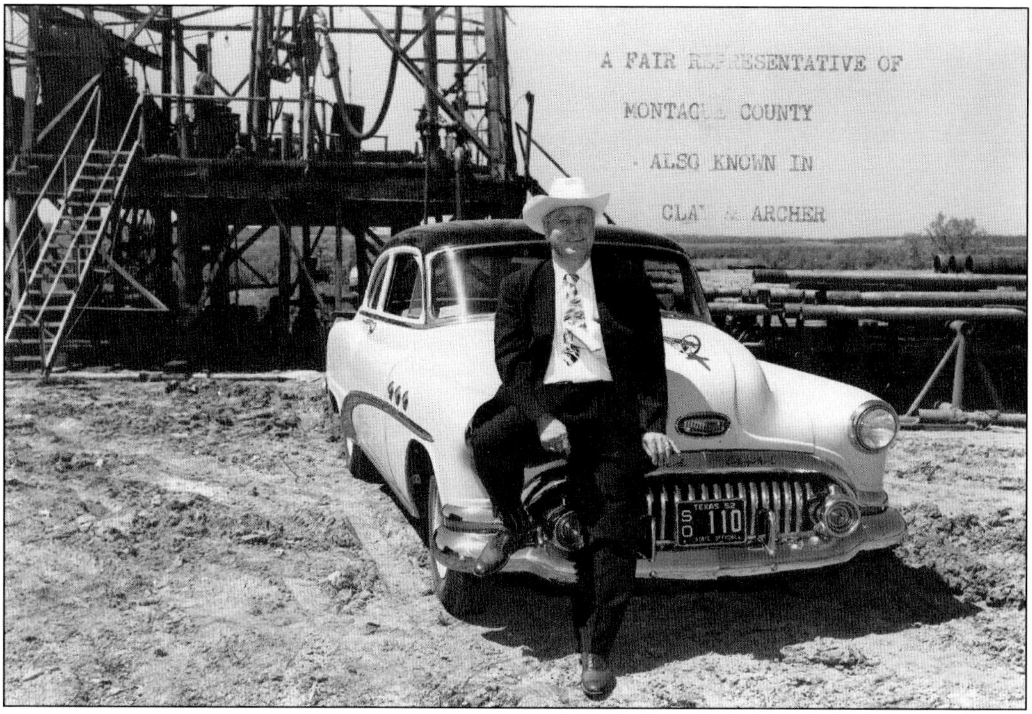

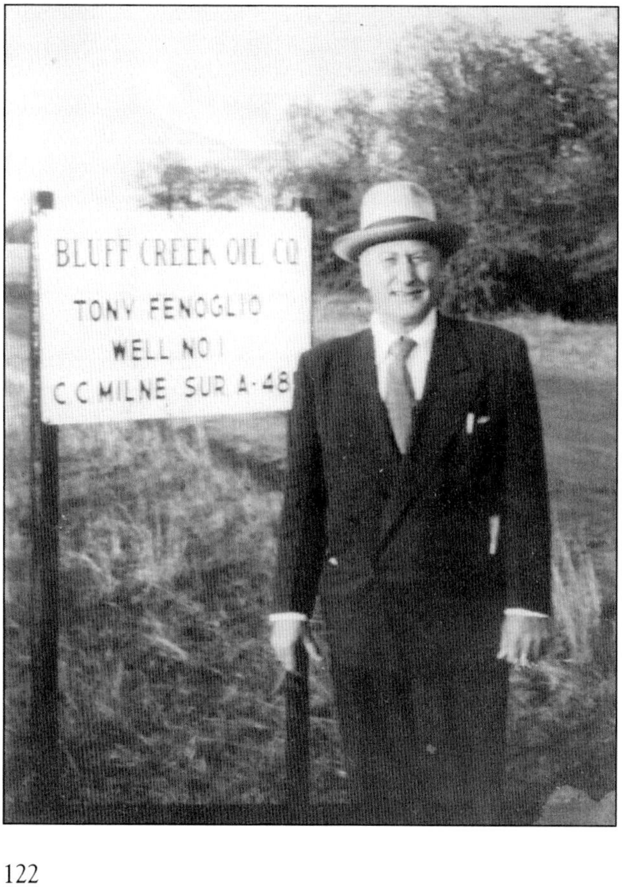

Tony Fenoglio was born in April 1904 and lived his life in the Nocona and Montague County area. He was elected to five two-year terms as a Texas state representative. He was active in several civic organizations, including the Rotary Club. Fenoglio died on June 2, 1980. (TNT.)

Before becoming a Texas state representative, Tony Fenoglio was an oilman. He got his start from Robert H. Rucker, who hired him to put oil leases together for the Bluff Creek Oil Company. Fenoglio often stated that "Montague County's lifeblood is agriculture and oil." He dedicated his political career to these issues. (TNT.)

Jack Crain was born on January 7, 1920, to Laura and Harold Crain. Crain was a legendary football player both on the high school and college fields. While attending Nocona High, his team won the regional championship in 1937. Crain went on to be an instrumental player for the University of Texas. (TNT.)

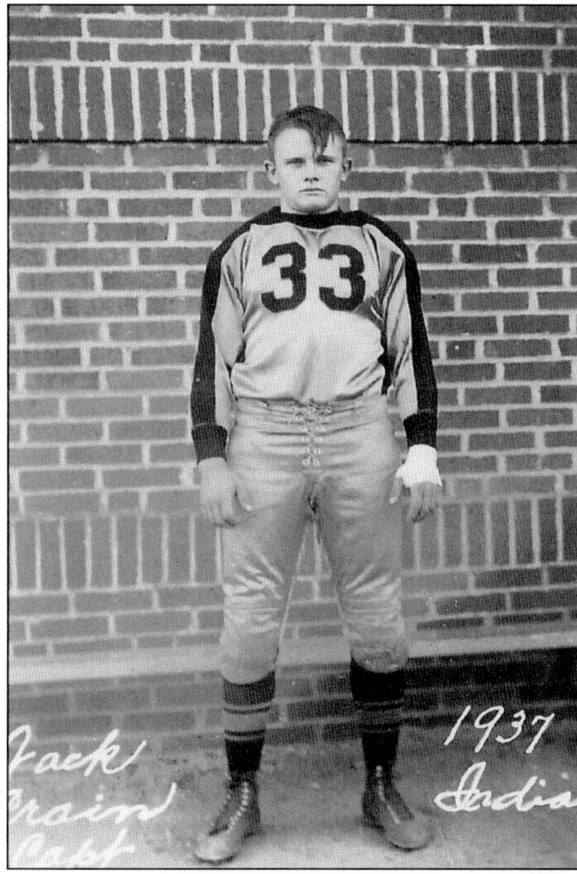

Jack Crain's contribution to history involves more than just his athletic abilities. After college, he joined the navy and served as an officer during World War II. He returned to Nocona after the war and was elected to the Texas House of Representatives for three terms. Crain died on October 22, 1994, at the age of 74. (TNT.)

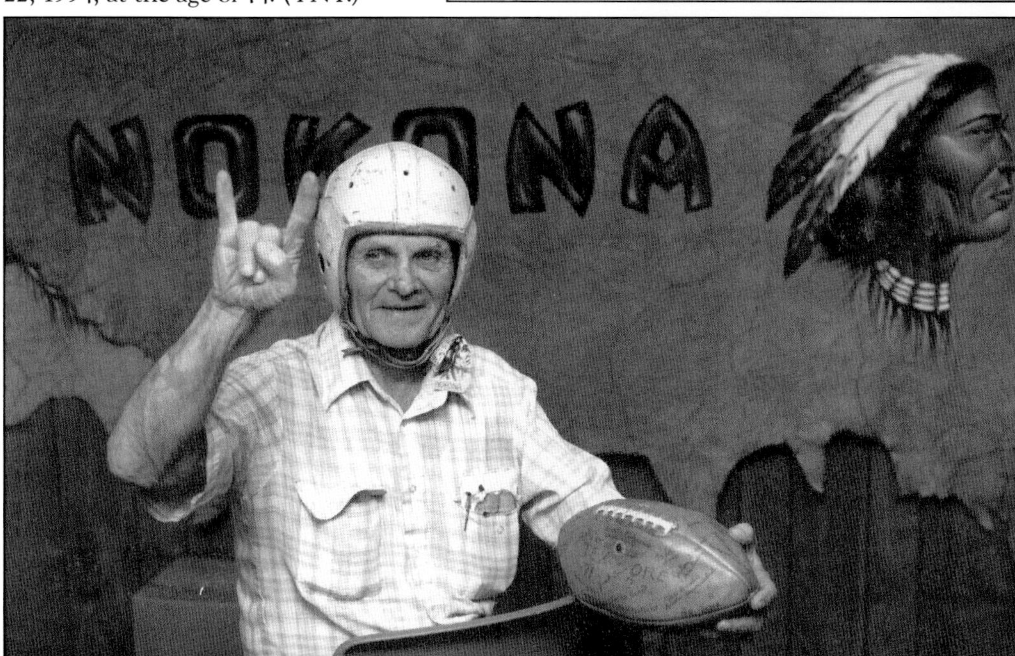

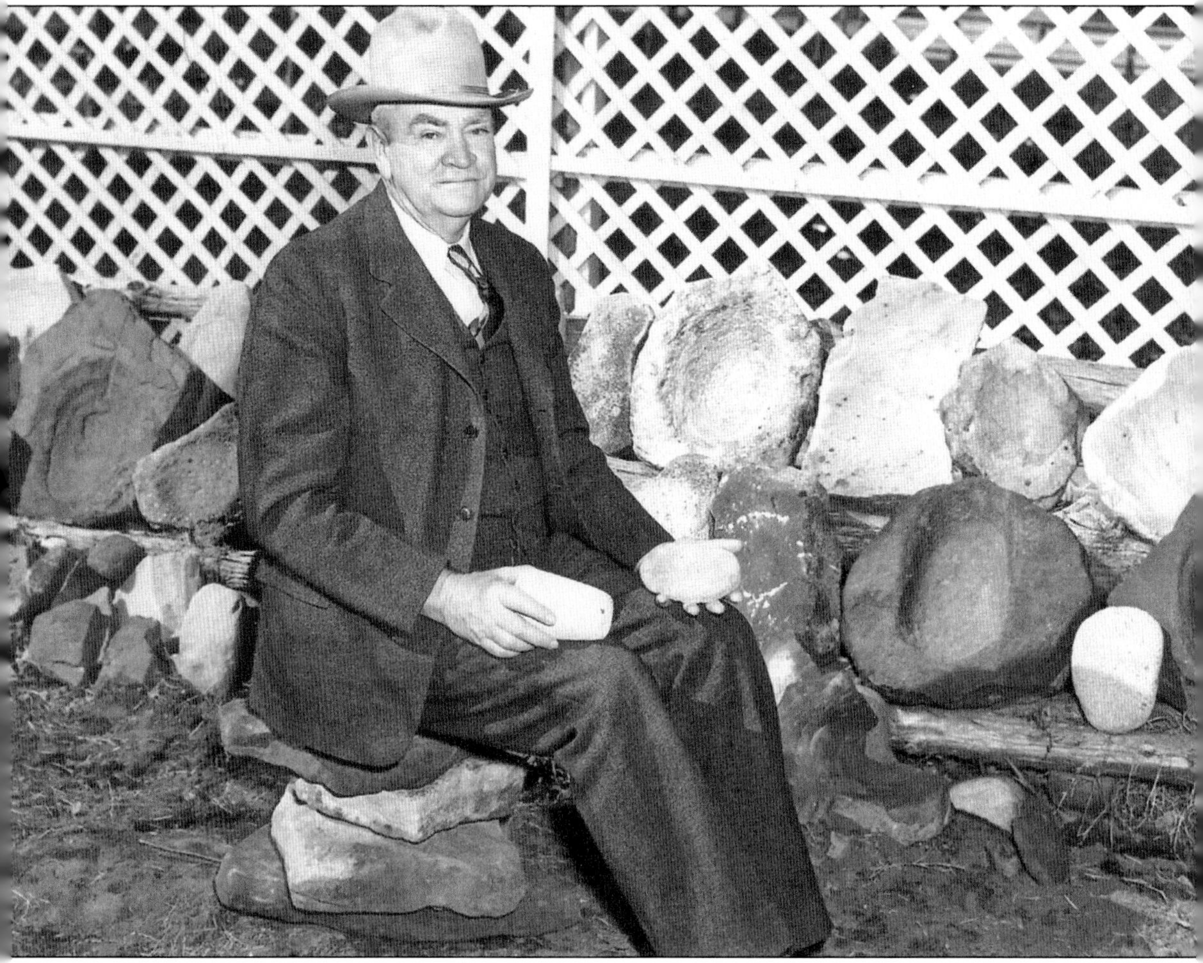

Joe Benton was born in a log cabin in Montague County, near Nocona, on August 3, 1882. His parents were Phillip Jasper and Martha Elizabeth (Miller) Benton. His career focused on cattle and the oil industry, but his love was history. He was especially interested in the Native American history of Montague County. In the hands of a private collector, he amassed the largest collection of Native American artifacts gathered from one single location, the Red River Valley. He would pay area children a nickel for any arrowheads they found and brought him for his collection. Benton was involved in many civic organizations and gave both his time and money to many worthy causes. He was the mayor of Nocona from 1915 to 1917. Benton was instrumental in organizing the county century-mark celebration in 1958, but died just weeks before the event took place. Benton died on June 26, 1958, at the age of 75. (TNT.)

Joe Benton was the first to introduce Aberdeen Angus cattle to the Montague County area. This aerial photograph of the Benton Ranch gives a bird's-eye view of the vast operation. He was also involved in bringing in one of the first successful oil wells in Nocona's North Field. (TNT.)

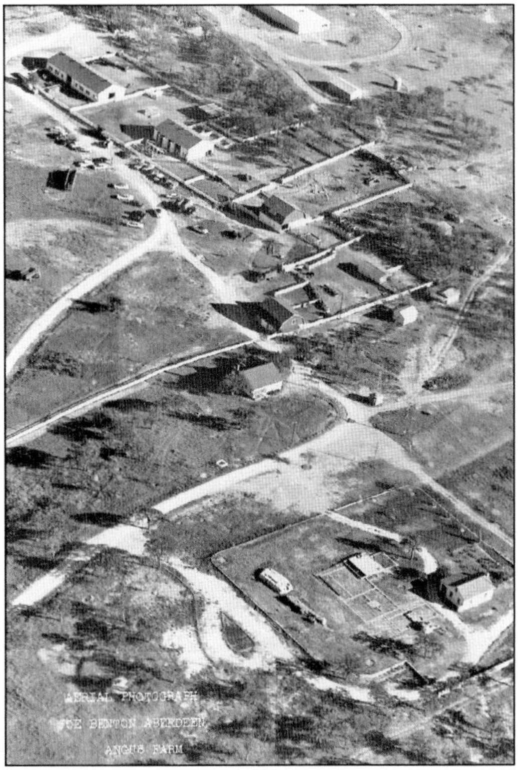

This photograph shows just a small portion of the Native American grinding stone in Joe Benton's collection. Along with these stones, his collection included arrowheads, pottery, beads, and a wide assortment of other artifacts relating to the Native American history in Montague County. (TNT.)

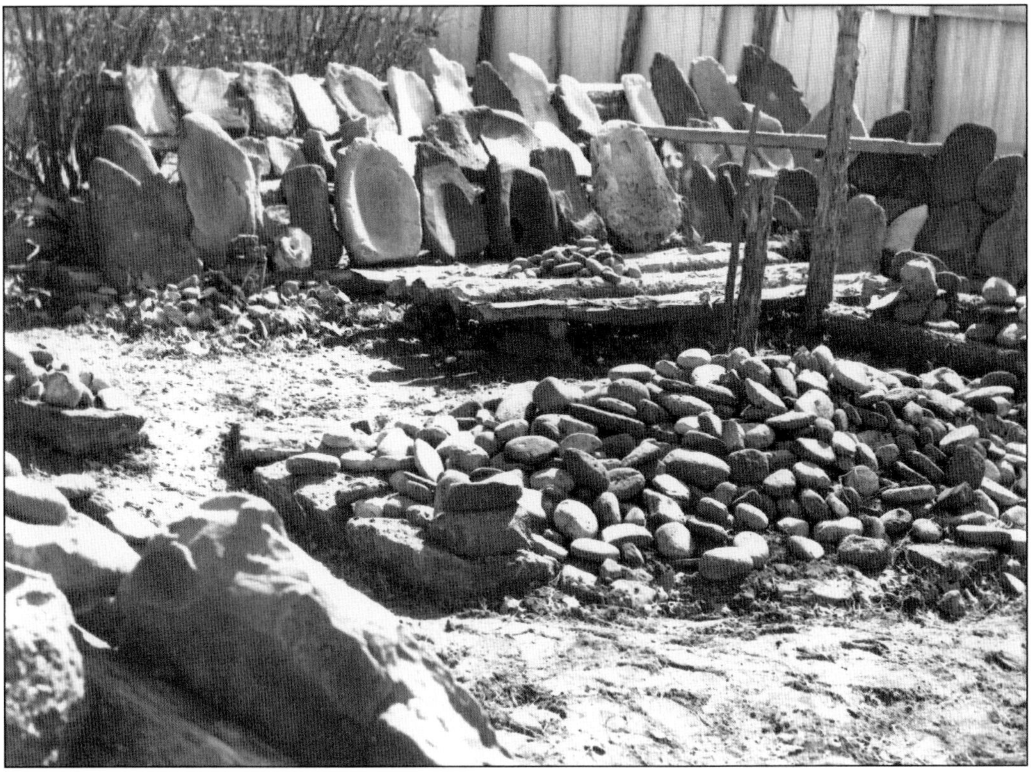

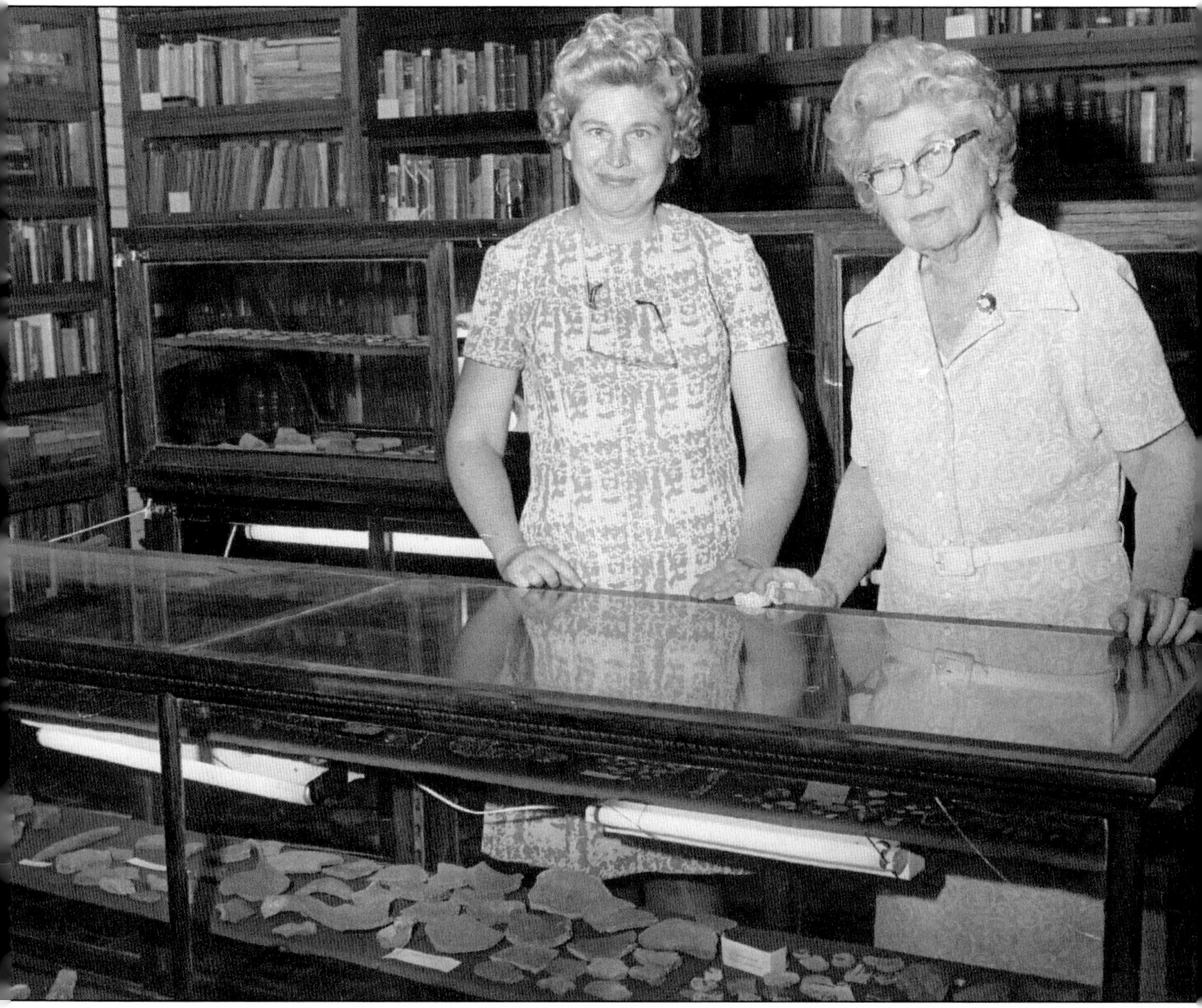

Joe Benton was interested in anything relating to Texas history and especially to Montague County. Other than the Native American artifacts, he collected books, newspaper articles, branding irons of area ranchers, photographs, guns, letters from Chisholm Trail drivers, and even a stuffed longhorn. Benton built a museum to house his collection. The museum was open by appointment, and several academic and professional researchers used the vast collection on their various projects. After his death in 1958, the custodial responsibility for the museum fell to Benton's wife, Geneva (right). When she passed away in 1977, it became the task of his daughter, Clarice Whiteside. Whiteside wanted her father's legacy to remain intact. She donated a portion of the ranch land for a new museum to be built. The contents of Benton's collection were also donated. The Tales 'N' Trails Museum in Nocona is the proud guardian of this amazing collection. (TNT.)

About the Organization

For centuries, people have traveled through what is now known as Montague County. They traveled by foot and horse and wagon. Eventually, they traveled by rail and road. Permanent settlement was slow in coming, but with the establishment of Head of Elm, the county soon began to grow. Every individual who passed through left his or her footprint in time. It has been a longtime dream of the citizens of Montague County to have a place to showcase the mementoes of their history. The Tales 'N' Trails Museum provides the perfect repository for the relics and artifacts of the county's past.

Tales 'N' Trails, much like the county itself, was a long time coming to fruition. In the early 1990s, talk of a museum began. By 1995, the Texas Association of Museums had been contacted to get the ball rolling. Some grants were secured, but the majority of the funding was received from the public and private sector.

With such a vast history, which includes the Chisholm Trail, Nocona's North Field, and Nocona's long leather industry tradition, it soon became apparent that the scope of the museum would need to be fine-tuned. It was decided that the collection focus would feature the following five distinct topics: Native American, Western heritage, oil and gas production, the leather industry, and agriculture. The acquisition of the Benton Collection was a great benefit to Tales 'N' Trails.

The doors to the museum were opened to the public in June 2010. Currently, construction continues on the main gallery. The main gallery will house specific exhibits relating the museum's five focus areas. These exhibits will include permanent and interactive displays along with temporary exhibits with specific themes. In the future, there will be outdoor exhibits, as well. The museum also has a wonderful gift shop with many locally manufactured items.

Tales 'N' Trails Museum is located at 1522 East Highway 82 in Nocona, Texas, The museum is open Monday through Saturday from 10:00 a.m. to 5:00 p.m. and on Sunday from 1:00 p.m. to 5:00 p.m. The phone number is (940) 825-5330. The website is www.talesntrails.org.